The United Nations Convention on the Rights of the Child in Wales

The United Nations Convention on the Rights of the Child in Wales

Edited by

Jane Williams

UNIVERSITY OF WALES PRESS
CARDIFF
2013

www.uwp.co.uk

British Library Cataloguing-in-Publication Data
A catalogue record for this book is available from the British Library.

ISBN 978-0-7083-2562-9
e-ISBN 978-0-7083-2563-6

Typeset by Marie Doherty
Printed in the UK by MPG Books Group Ltd

For Ciarán, Matthew, Megan and Gareth

Contents

Part I: The UNCRC in Wales – and Wales in the UNCRC

Part II: Making it work: realising children's rights in selected policy areas

Part III: Ensuring it works: accountability and participation

Tables and illustrations

About the Contributors

Trudy Aspinwall has worked as an advocate for children's rights in Wales since qualifying as a social worker in 1992. She works directly with children and young people and as a policy, research and participation worker in a variety of roles. She worked with Save the Children to initiate and then support the UNCRC Monitoring Group to influence key children's rights developments in Wales, including the development of the Rights of Children and Young Persons (Wales) Measure 2011. Her policy and consultation work has involved her in working with young Gypsies and Travellers to influence Welsh Government strategy and develop materials and awareness raising on the UNCRC with and for Gypsy and Traveller children and young people during the early stages of the Travelling Ahead project.

Jennie Bibbings has worked in social policy since 2002, joining Shelter Cymru in March 2011. Her background is in consumer policy with a particular interest in public services, rights, redress and regulation. In 2010 and 2011 she conducted in-depth analyses of progress towards implementation of the recommendations of the Pennington Inquiry, which investigated the circumstances leading to the major E. coli O157 outbreak, which hit south Wales schools in 2005. Jennie's role is to manage Shelter Cymru's research and policy work.

Ian Butler is Professor of Social Work at the University of Bath. He is a former special adviser to the First Minister of Wales. Following a career in social work practice, he has held academic posts at the universities of Cardiff and Keele, and is a member of the Academy of Social Sciences. He has published widely on social work with children and families and on welfare policy for children.

Luke Clements is a Professor at Cardiff Law School and a consultant solicitor. He has conducted and advised on many cases before the Commission and Court of Human Rights in Strasbourg involving both Roma and children, including the first Roma case to reach that court (*Buckley v UK* [1996]).

Rhian Croke is the UNCRC Monitoring Officer for Save the Children Wales and is a committed advocate for children's rights. She coordinates the work of the Wales UNCRC Monitoring Group, a national alliance of agencies tasked with monitoring and promoting the implementation of the UNCRC in Wales. She is co-editor of *Righting the Wrongs: The Reality of Children's Rights in Wales* (Cardiff: Save the Children, 2006), and *Stop, Look, Listen: The Road to Realising Children's Rights in Wales* (Cardiff: Save the Children, 2007). She has previously worked as assistant director for Save the Children Wales and at the University of Cape Town Children's Institute as a senior researcher in the HIV/AIDs Programme.

Anne Crowley is a policy and research consultant and obtained her PhD in 2011 from Cardiff University. Anne has undertaken research with children and young people on a range of issues including youth crime, public care, participation, advocacy services and child poverty. She is currently a member of the National Independent Advocacy Board set up by the Welsh Government to provide independent advice on the strategic development of advocacy provision for children and young people, and of the Wales Committee of the Equalities and Human Rights Commission. In 2007 Anne co-edited (with Rhian Croke) the 'alternative' report on progress in implementing the United Nations Convention on the Rights of the Child in Wales, *Stop, Look, Listen: The Road to Realising Children's Rights in Wales* (Cardiff: Save the Children, 2007).

Mark Drakeford has been the Labour Assembly Member for Cardiff West since 2011. He is Professor of Social Policy and Social Work at Cardiff University and has researched and written widely, particularly on social policy and devolution, poverty and social exclusion, and children and young people. He was, during Rhodri Morgan's tenure as First Minister for Wales, Morgan's special adviser and helped to craft many of the iconic policies of Labour in the Assembly.

Funky Dragon is the Children and Young People's Assembly for Wales. It is a peer-led organisation supported by Welsh Government funding and other funding. Funky Dragon gives 0–25-year-olds the opportunity to get their voices heard on issues affecting them.

Kevin Fitzpatrick has thirty-eight years' direct experience of disability and the issues affecting disabled people. He is director of Inclusion21 Ltd, offering training and consultancy promoting equality and diversity. He taught philosophy at Swansea University and is an associate of the Welsh Institute for Health and Social Care at the University of Glamorgan. He is a non-executive director of the Welsh Ambulance Services NHS Trust, a board member of Consumer Focus Wales and chair of the board of trustees of St David's Children Society adoption agency, and of Arts Care/ Gofal Celf. He was the first Disability Rights Commissioner for Wales, carrying out this role from 2000 to 2007. He was awarded the OBE for services to disabled people in Wales in 2011.

Simon Hoffman is a lecturer and researcher at Swansea University where he teaches human rights. His primary research interest is children's rights and socio-economic rights, in particular how to give effect to internationally recognised rights and entitlements in national legal systems and domestic social and fiscal policy. Simon is currently focusing on implementation of children's rights within devolved administrations, and the delivery of rights through duty-creating legal mechanisms linked to programmatic action. With Jane Williams, he is co-director of the Wales Observatory on Human Rights of Children and Young People.

Peter Hosking worked as a teacher and lecturer both in the UK and overseas as well as working as an adviser on special educational needs for a voluntary organisation. From 2001 to 2011, he worked as a policy and service evaluation officer for the Children's Commissioner for Wales. His role was to protect and promote children's rights by influencing policy developments of the Welsh Government.

Helen Mary Jones was educated at the University of Wales, Aberystwyth, has taught in the special education field, and has held various positions in youth, community and social work. She is currently Chair of Plaid Cymru and was Plaid Cymru AM for Llanelli and Mid and West Wales from 1999 to 2011. Her political interests include environmental issues, social justice, equal opportunities, children's rights and employment. She was Shadow Minister for Education and Lifelong Learning, and a member of the Education and Lifelong Learning Committee, the Committee on Equality of Opportunity, the South West Wales Regional Committee and also a member of the Voluntary Sector Partnership during the first term of the National Assembly. She was the Shadow Minister for the Environment, Planning and Countryside in the Second Assembly (2003–7). She was the Deputy Leader of Plaid Cymru in the Assembly between 2007 and 2011, and Chair of the Assembly subject committee on children and young people. Since November 2011 she has been chief executive of Youth Cymru, a voluntary organisation supporting youth work in Wales. She is a member of the Ministerial Advisory Board sent in to Pembrokeshire County Council by the Welsh Government to support and challenge as they improve safeguarding after damaging inspection reports.

Peter Mackie is a lecturer at Cardiff University where he teaches on housing-related policy and theory. A geographer by training, he has a particular research interest in the housing experiences and pathways of vulnerable people, in which he seeks to combine theoretical and practical insights. His recent studies have explored the hidden experiences of prison-leavers in Wales, and the transitions of disabled young people to independent living. A particular focus of his research is on youth housing and homelessness, a field in which he has sought to understand the experiences of young people from their perspectives via participatory research methods, including the peer approach.

Tracey Maegusuku-Hewett previously worked as a social worker and advocacy worker within the voluntary sector with refugee and asylum-seeking children, young people and families, and she currently works as a social work lecturer at Swansea University. Tracey's research interests relate to immigration policy and asylum-seeking children's rights and well-being, for which she has undertaken a number of research projects in Wales.

Osian Rees is a lecturer in law at Bangor University. He was awarded his doctorate from Aberystwyth University in 2007. His thesis examined the role of the Children's Commissioner for Wales, and his current research interests include national human rights institutions for children and the impact of devolution on family and child law in Wales.

Michael Sullivan is professor of policy analysis, and Vice-Chancellor's adviser (external relations) at Swansea University. From 2007 to 2010 he was seconded to the First Minister for Wales as special adviser and then specialist adviser, and was involved in the policy process leading to the Rights of Children and Young Persons (Wales) Measure 2011.

Kathryn Tucker is a member of the Wales Strategic Migration Partnership, graduated from Portsmouth University in 2002 and spent five years working for the Home Office, first as a children's asylum caseworker in the UK Border Agency, and then for some time in criminal casework. In 2008, Kathryn was appointed to the Welsh Government-funded post of refugee children advice and information worker based at the Wales Strategic Migration Partnership, where she continues to be a resource for practitioners working with unaccompanied asylum-seeking children.

Jacky Tyrie is based in the Childhood Studies team at Swansea University, where she works as an academic tutor and researcher. Her focus is on examining issues around gender, children rights and research methods. She specialises in mixed methodology research and has worked on projects funded by UNICEF and the Welsh Government. Jacky's doctorate, completed in 2010, examined gender and access to rights for young people in Wales, with special focus on young people's perspectives.

Jane Williams is a senior lecturer at the School of Law, Swansea University. Formerly a government lawyer in London and Cardiff, she specialises in human rights implementation with a particular focus on the rights of children and young people, and on issues arising in consequence of the growth of multi-level democratic governance with a particular focus on devolution in the UK. With Simon Hoffman, she co-directs the Wales Observatory on Human Rights of Children and Young People, launched in June 2012.

Foreword

Rt Hon. Rhodri Morgan

I am delighted to have been invited to write the foreword to this volume, which offers an account of the ways in which our own Welsh rights-based values have informed the development of policy in relation to children during the dozen or so devolution years in Wales. It also shows the significance of the United Nations Convention on the Rights of the Child (UNCRC) in post-devolution Wales, and the path-breaking nature of the Rights of Children and Young Persons (Wales) Measure 2011. The book describes the negotiation and passage of the new law as well as offering insight into the potential of the new law as force for good in terms of realisation of the human rights of children and young people in Wales.

As First Minister of the One Wales Government at the time, I had both an airline pilot's and worm's view of the process. I was able both to observe and influence its development to some considerable extent from 'above', but, as becomes clear, it was also necessary at times for sleeves to be rolled up and work to be done digging in the dirt of actual policy and law-making. This is a story about consensus and conflict, as is the case with most policy change of any significance.

The headline stories are of agreed Welsh values, of political consensus across the floor of the Senedd in favour of a strong, comprehensive measure that embedded the UNCRC principles within Welsh law, and of the integration of civil society in the development of the Measure, in particular under the umbrella of the Wales UNCRC Monitoring Group for the UNCRC and an ad hoc group of talented Welsh lawyers facilitated by the editor of this volume at the School of Law, Swansea University.

As those familiar with politics and the policy process know, however, consensus is seldom the whole story, and policy and legislative change is most often also about 'change, choice and conflict'.[1] As is also clear in this volume, the headline consensus masked quite fundamental disagreements and a degree of passive resistance to the strong approach to children's rights that eventually emerged – though not usually from those holding elected positions.

The legislative passage was characterised by the high quality of scrutiny by several National Assembly committees: the Children and Young People Committee, chaired by Helen Mary Jones, which made its commitment to UNCRC principles in a robust and clear way; the Legislation

Committee No. 5, whose report was influential in securing vital changes, and the Constitutional Affairs Committee of which I was, following my retirement as First Minister, a back-bench member. All of this, together with some 'full and frank discussions' within the machinery of government led to the Measure in its final form. It is a law which reflects our capacity for innovation and democratic engagement in post-devolution Wales, as well as offering a model of human rights implementation of truly global significance. For all these reasons, this volume is much to be welcomed.

Rt Hon. Rhodri Morgan
First Minister of Wales, 2000–10
Chancellor, Swansea University

Note
1. Hall, P., Land, H., Parker, R. and Webb, A. (1975): *Change, Choice and Conflict in Social Policy* (London: Heinemann).

Preface and acknowledgements

This volume's origin lies in a conference held in September 2008 at Swansea University on the theme of revisiting visions and rethinking implementation of the United Nations Convention on the Rights of the Child (UNCRC). Developed papers and additional contributions featured in the 2011 edited collection published by Ashgate, *The Human Rights of Children, From Visions to Implementation*, co-edited by me and Dr Antonella Invernizzi. That volume includes some examinations of approaches to children's rights in Wales. But soon after the conference, which coincided with the State Party hearings on the UK's third and fourth periodic reports to the United Nations Committee on the Rights of the Child (UN Committee), it became clear that implementation in Wales had acquired prominence and depth which called for consideration in a distinct collection.

At the end of 2008 we could not have imagined the extent of progress in implementation that would occur in Wales, culminating in the enactment in March 2011 of the Rights of Children and Young Persons (Wales) Measure 2011 – the UK's first general legislative measure of implementation of the UNCRC. Publication of the present volume coincides with the first phase of coming into force of the Measure. The book sets out to 'tell the story' of the Measure, to demonstrate the impact of the UNCRC in Welsh public policy post-devolution, and to indicate how the Measure's provisions hold potential for progressive implementation of the UNCRC for the benefit of children and young people in Wales, their families and communities.

Thanks are due to many people for their contribution to these developments and this volume: Dr Antonella Invernizzi; my husband, Professor Michael Sullivan; all members and observers on the Wales UNCRC Monitoring Group for the UNCRC; those Assembly Members, Ministers and advisers who refused to drop or dilute the vision of a law for the UNCRC in Wales; the University of Wales Press for catching the vision and backing the book; and Swansea University for facilitation of workshops and meetings that proved to be significant in developing the case for the new law. Special thanks of course are due to all the contributors, each of whom brings a special and unique perspective to the analysis of the UNCRC in Wales.

Jane Williams
Swansea University
September 2012

Abbreviations and terms

AM	Assembly Member
AWYOS	*All-Wales Youth Offending Strategy*
CEAS	Common European Asylum System
DCELLS	Department for Children, Education and Lifelong Learning (Welsh Government)
ECHR	European Convention on Human Rights
ECtHR	European Court of Human Rights
NAW	National Assembly for Wales
NGO	Non-governmental organisation
UASC	Unaccompanied asylum-seeking child
UKBA	United Kingdom Border Agency
UN Committee	United Nations Committee on the Rights of the Child
UNCRC	United Nations Convention on the Rights of the Child
WG	Welsh Government (formerly Welsh Assembly Government; the name adopted to distinguish the Assembly Cabinet under the Government of Wales Act 1998 and the name that continued to describe the Welsh executive following its formal creation under the Government of Wales Act 2006. The term 'Welsh Government' was adopted by the administration elected in 2011. In the interests of readability, references to publications by the Welsh Assembly Government have been transformed in this text to 'Welsh Government'.)

'Children' is used to refer to persons under eighteen and 'children and young people' to persons under twenty-five, unless the context otherwise requires.

The UN Committee's *General Comments* (1 to 12) and *Concluding Observations* are indicated in the text by initial and year – for example, UN Committee *GC*, 2003. All can be found at *http://www.unhcr.org*.

Editor's Introduction

Jane Williams

The contributions to this collection, which recount and reflect on efforts to secure the rights of children and young people in Wales, engage with or illustrate many issues of global application in UNCRC implementation. Several such issues were explored in an earlier collection (Invernizzi and Williams, 2011) with which this volume shares a provenance. In the following discussion, links are made between the contributions to the two volumes which would, ideally, be read together. As several contributors in this volume note, children's rights have become emblematic of devolved government in Wales, and efforts to make the realities of children's lives match this emblem (as well as the many barriers encountered) provide a valuable case study for those interested in human rights implementation anywhere.

First, there is the abiding issue of how we view children in society and in law. The normative framework of the UNCRC involves a paradigm shift in thinking about the status of children (Freeman, 2011). It presents the 'citizen child' (Doek, 2008) who is entitled to consideration in his or her own right despite lack of formal capacity and political influence. The 'citizen child' demands equal treatment under the law, thus requiring objective justification of different treatment, which justification must itself be rooted in protection and respect for the human rights of the child and others concerned. Scepticism and resistance to the concept of children as rights-holders remain strong. One need only point to the ongoing debate about reasonable chastisement, a defence that is available to perpetrators of common assault against children but not to perpetrators of the same offence against adults.

In Wales, the case for children as rights holders appeared to have been substantially accepted by key political actors in the years following devolution, as explained by Butler and Drakeford in this collection. Yet, as recounted by Sullivan and Jones, the road from high level political commitment to enactment of the Rights of Children and Young Persons (Wales) Measure 2011 ('the Measure') was characterised by strenuous conflict as well as the much-hailed cross-party collaboration. While other reasons no doubt influenced those resisting a general duty on Welsh Ministers to have due regard to the UNCRC, it is hard to believe that the challenge of this shift to acceptance of the 'citizen child' did not figure in it.

Part I of this book assesses from different perspectives the policy background, legislative process and legal effect of the Measure. But, as Fitzpatrick remarks in chapter 5, 'saying does not make it so' (whether in law or high level policy statements): the imposition of legal duties on Welsh Ministers is only a foundation for changes in the culture of administration that may eventually result in widespread acceptance of the new paradigm and, with it, tangible benefits for children and young people. Fitzpatrick argues that for this to happen it is necessary not simply to accept specific obligations flowing from the provisions in the UNCRC as a *legal* text, but to recognise that the rights themselves flow from *moral* obligations which already existed before 'rights' were thought of. The pre-existence of the moral obligation is reflected in the statement of the Office of the High Commission on Human Rights, *Human Rights and Poverty Reduction: A Conceptual Framework* (2004; quoted by Croke and Crowley, chapter 6) in relation to obligations to reduce child poverty: 'Poverty reduction then becomes more than charity, more than a moral obligation – it becomes a *legal* obligation.' Absorption of this message is key to successful implementation of the Measure, because decisions affecting children and young people are made daily by human beings exercising moral judgement as well as seeking to comply with the law. Economic austerity raises the stakes, since it is tempting to scale back on programmes and funding streams impacting on the least powerful sections of society (Croke and Crowley, chapter 6). The case for the human rights of children and young people has continually to be made, perhaps all the more so following legislative acceptance of it, lest anyone should think that 'saying' is enough.

A second issue is interpretation of the legal texts. In the absence of a body of judicial precedent linked to the UNCRC – comparable, for example, to the now sixty-plus years of case law from the European Court of Human Rights on the ECHR – to what sources can we turn for help with its interpretation? There are the *travaux preparatoires*, the various outputs of the treaty monitoring bodies, academic literature and comparative interpretations. In Wales, the Measure itself directs Welsh Ministers to the outputs of the UN Committee as well as to the text of the Convention and protocols. But *authoritative* interpretation is thin on the ground. In this situation Tobin (2011: 84) warns of the danger of subversion of the normative values of the UNCRC to other policy objectives. The character and composition of the 'interpretive communities' which emerge are thus a key factor in implementation. This is discussed by Williams, Hoffman and Williams and Fitzpatrick in this volume – the latter arguing strongly that inclusion in decision-making of those with lived experience of the issues is critical both to legitimacy and to effectiveness of interpretations and action based upon them. This approach to interpretation is challenging, especially to those (like most lawyers) accustomed to consider only what a court would say if asked. Certainly, court rulings should be sought where necessary and accessible, but a lack of judicial precedent should not be allowed to somehow devalue the requirements of the UNCRC as *legal* obligations, nor to leave their interpretation solely to governments and their legal advisers.

This point touches on the third issue: participation. It has been argued that false interpretations have emerged about the nature and scope of the so-called 'participation articles' of the UNCRC, on the one hand over-inflating their demands and on the other suppressing basic due process rights which under-eighteen-year-olds possess by virtue of other human rights provisions (Cantwell, 2011). It has been suggested that the real measure of recognition of the 'citizen child' is to secure for victims of violations of the UNCRC the right to make individual claims to domestic and international bodies (Van Bueren, 2011). A notable success in this regard is the UN General Assembly's adoption on 19 December 2011 of an Optional Protocol to the UNCRC establishing a mechanism enabling children to complain before the UN Committee of an alleged rights violation. The Measure does not deliver remedies for individuals as victims of rights violations, but as discussed by Hoffman and Williams (chapter 12) it demands that Welsh Ministers 'involve' non-governmental groups and children and young people themselves in the creation of a children's scheme. It also requires action to ensure wider awareness and understanding of the UNCRC. These provisions are supportive of the development of a persuasive, participative approach to interpretation, but the effectiveness of the output will depend heavily on the quality and legitimacy of participative processes in practice. The experience of constructive engagement in Wales (Aspinwall and Croke, chapter 3) bodes well in that regard, and Wales can boast fine examples of participatory action by children and young people (Funky Dragon, 2011, and Funky Dragon, chapter 14 in this volume). On the other hand, austerity measures threaten support for many such activities. Perhaps most important is that existing structures, channels and most importantly *habits* of communication should adapt to accommodate the radical notion that those (of any age) external to government are not mere consultees once policy is mainly settled, but are active participants in its development.

Fourthly, there is the question of information – not only about the UNCRC as demanded by Article 42 (and now, in Wales, by the Measure) but also about children and young people. In an example of persuasive interpretation, Ennew (2011) argues convincingly that one can derive from the text of the UNCRC a 'right to be properly researched'. There is still far too little disaggregated data about children and young people in Wales, their living conditions, views and aspirations, their services and the application of resources to meeting their needs (UN Committee *CO*, 2008: 18–19; Croke and Crowley, 2007: 8; 2011, and chapter 6 in this volume). The Welsh Government has made efforts to address this deficit but more is needed. Part of the challenge is to reap full benefit from information already available. Contributions in Part II of this volume, especially chapters 6 to 10, illustrate an active research and policy community in Wales operating independently as well as sometimes with government, generating information and expertise in several difficult, multi-faceted issues. This information and expertise needs to be used effectively to inform government decisions as well as the monitoring and reporting process of the UNCRC itself.

Another part of the challenge is to recognise that 'proper' research in the context of the UNCRC will recognise the part that children and young people themselves should play. Funky Dragon's world-leading research and report, *Our Rights, Our Story* (Funky Dragon, 2011), exemplify the value of child- and young person-led, adult-supported research. Funky Dragon's contribution in chapter 14 of this volume, describing research undertaken by junior school-age children on their local environment and amenities, reinforces the point that 'value' here is not limited to realising participative and developmental rights but includes practical and cost-effective utility for duty-bearers. The research was appreciated by local authorities, housing associations and at national level as an important resource for their own decision-making on the topics covered.

Such research information forms part of the UN Committee's vision of 'resource' for the purpose of compliance with Article 4 of the UNCRC (obligation to implement social and economic rights to the maximum extent of available resources). A small but clever country such as Wales (as it is often referred to) needs to think imaginatively and utilise all reliable evidence from whatever source – certainly including academia, NGOs and children and young people's own organisations.

The last issue this book addresses (though several others, for which space does not permit here, could be explored) is accountability. Contributions to Part III of this volume all address this in some way. Both within the complex structures of governance and service delivery and outside it – for example in professional conduct, ethics and advocacy – there are many mechanisms that can be used for integration of the requirements of the UNCRC and to render accountability. Law reform is but one, albeit crucial, weapon in the armoury. Others include use of the UNCRC as a policy development and/or evaluative tool (Kilkelly, 2011), as a foundation for strategic litigation (Kilkelly, 2011; Van Bueren, 2011), and as a new perspective on established concepts (Webb, 2011 [discrimination]; Goldhagen and Mercer, 2011 [medical ethics]). Hoffman and Williams (chapter 12) offer an overview of how accountability is enhanced by the Measure. Rees (chapter 13) examines how the role of the Children's Commissioner can be developed. Funky Dragon (chapter 14) illustrates the contribution that children and young people can make. Crowley (chapter 15) explores the as yet tentative theoretical underpinning for children's participation, explains some of the essential features of effective participation, and analyses the steps taken pre-Measure in Wales and the potential of the Measure to develop structures enabling effective participation to take place.

This volume thus offers a picture of aspects of progression in implementation of the human rights of children and young people as a dominant discourse in law and policy in Wales post-devolution. It represents neither a beginning nor an end to the story of the UNCRC in Wales, but it is hoped it will contribute to further thinking, stimulate further case studies and enrich debate about implementation in Wales and elsewhere in the world.

References

Cantwell, N. (2011): 'Are children's rights still human?', in A. Invernizzi and J. Williams (eds), *The Human Rights of Children: From Visions to Implementation* (Farnham: Ashgate), pp. 37–60.

Croke, A. and Crowley, R. (eds) (2007): *Stop, Look, Listen: The Road to Realising Children's Rights in Wales* (Cardiff: Save the Children).

Doek, J. (2008): 'Foreword', in A. Invernizzi and J. Williams (eds), *Children and Citizenship* (London: Sage), pp. xii–xvii.

Ennew, J. (2011): 'Has research improved the human rights of children? Or have the information needs of the CRC improved data about children?', in A. Invernizzi and J. Williams (eds), *The Human Rights of Children: From Visions to Implementation* (Farnham: Ashgate), pp. 33–58.

Freeman (2011): 'The value and values of children's rights', in A. Invernizzi and J. Williams (eds), *The Human Rights of Children: From Visions to Implementation* (Farnham: Ashgate), pp. 21–36.

Funky Dragon (2011): 'Our Rights, Our Story: Funky Dragon's report to the UN Committee on the Rights of the Child', in A. Invernizzi and J. Williams (eds), *The Human Rights of Children: From Visions to Implementation* (Farnham: Ashgate), pp. 327–48.

Goldhagen, J. and Mercer, R. (2011): 'Child health equity: from theory to reality', in A. Invernizzi and J. Williams (eds), *The Human Rights of Children: From Visions to Implementation* (Farnham: Ashgate), pp. 307–26.

Invernizzi, A. and J. Williams (eds) (2011): *The Human Rights of Children: From Visions to Implementation* (Farnham: Ashgate).

Kilkelly, U. (2011): 'Using the Convention on the Rights of the Child in law and policy: two ways to improve compliance', in A. Invernizzi and J. Williams (eds), *The Human Rights of Children: From Visions to Implementation* (Farnham: Ashgate), pp. 179–98.

Office of the High Commission on Human Rights (2004): *Human Rights and Poverty Reduction: A Conceptual Framework* (New York: United Nations).

Tobin, J. (2011): 'Understanding a human rights based approach to matters involving children: conceptual foundations and strategic considerations', in A. Invernizzi and J. Williams (eds), *The Human Rights of Children: From Visions to Implementation* (Farnham: Ashgate), pp. 61–98.

Van Bueren, G. (2011): 'Acknowledging children as international citizens – a child-sensitive mechanism for the Convention on the Rights of the Child', in A. Invernizzi and J. Williams (eds), *The Human Rights of Children: From Visions to Implementation* (Farnham: Ashgate), pp. 117–32.

Webb, E. (2011): 'An exploration of the discrimination-rights dynamic in relation to children', in A. Invernizzi and J. Williams (eds), *The Human Rights of Children: From Visions to Implementation* (Farnham: Ashgate), pp. 207–306.

PART I

The UNCRC in Wales –
and Wales in the UNCRC

CHAPTER 1

Children's rights as a policy framework in Wales

Ian Butler and Mark Drakeford

Introduction

To anyone familiar with the origins, and early days, of devolution in Wales the combined focus on 'devolution' and 'rights' will come as no surprise. In this scene-setting chapter our aim is to set out some of the precipitating factors which, in our view, have made this such a powerful strand in the brief history of the National Assembly for Wales and, in particular, in the approach to policy making for children. We then identify a number of key initiatives in the journey which, in some important ways, culminated in the Rights of Children and Young Persons (Wales) Measure 2011.

Early Days

In order to understand the context in which the UNCRC came to be a cornerstone of responding to children's issues in Wales, it is important to identify some early, influential strands in the emerging institutions. Here we focus on three ps – policy, politics and people.

As far as *policy* is concerned, the National Assembly, which emerged from the smoking ruins of the lost referendum in 1979, and the many debates and compromises that followed over the next quarter of a century, was, more than anything else, a social policy body. While the Assembly lacked some very important levers (gaps in its competence and the absence of full legislative capacity, for example), it did possess very many of the powers in the field of children's policy. Health, education and social services were among the most complete transfers of responsibility from Whitehall to Wales in the original devolution settlement. As a group, children and young people were one of the strands that most clearly allowed policy-making to take place across the range of these possibilities and, as such, helps to explain the early focus on this area.

In terms of *politics* it is important to recall the faltering start of devolution in Wales, and the impact that this produced on the political imperatives of those early years. The wafer-thin referendum victory in September 1997, the failure of Labour to win a majority in the 1999 election, and the Lady Bracknell-like carelessness with which party leaders at the Assembly were lost during the first year of devolution (one retired, one defeated, one arrested) combined to produce a set of powerful, and potentially contradictory, political impulses. In order to recover and rebuild its reputation, the nascent Assembly Cabinet (forerunner of the Welsh Government) needed to be both radical, so as to demonstrate a capacity for effective, relevant action, and also to be conciliatory, so as to reach out beyond its Labour base and to command a level of cross-party support.

It is hard to recall now, even at the distance of only a dozen years, the enthusiasm that existed in 1999 for the soon-to-be-abandoned 'corporate body' which formed the constitutional basis of the first National Assembly. Wales had never succeeded in bringing together a cross-party, cross-sectoral Convention on the pre-devolution Scottish model. The corporate body structure was intended to entrench a new post-sectarian form of politics in Wales in which every Assembly Member had an equal stake in the organisation, operation and success of the institution. The rather high-minded hopes, in which the importance of party politics would be diminished in favour of a uniting determination to 'do the best for Wales', soon evaporated under the pressures of the everyday tussles more characteristic of the political process. The welfare of children and young people, however, provided a relatively rare topic in which the non-partisan form of politics had some purchase.

Finally, we draw attention to the impact of *people* as well as policy and politics in this formative period. Indeed, it could be argued that people were especially important in an institution where all politicians were completely new, and the conventions of day-to-day procedure were yet to be established. An interest in and experience of working with children and young people was a theme that connected a series of key players in the 1999 Assembly. Within the Labour Group, First Secretary Alun Michael drew regularly on his experience as a youth worker in some of the most challenging parts of Cardiff. The first Health and Social Services Minister, Jane Hutt, came to the Assembly from a background in which she had chaired the Children's Committee of the South Glamorgan County Council and worked as head of the child care organisation Chwarae Teg. Among representatives of the second-largest party in 1999, Plaid Cymru, the Llanelli AM, Helen Mary Jones, elected while a leader of the Barnardo's youth justice project, was already emerging as a formidable voice for children's issues.

The earliest example of this combination of policy, people and politics in action can be seen in the establishment of an office of Children's Commissioner for Wales. Its immediate context is usually traced to a specific recommendation of the Waterhouse inquiry (2000) into child abuse in north Wales, but the idea of a commissioner for children had been gathering momentum since the Staffordshire 'pindown' inquiry almost ten years earlier (Levy and Kahan, 1991). Rather than provide the case for a commissioner, 'Waterhouse' provided the opportunity for the Assembly to establish the UK's first independent human rights institution specifically for children. It was an appointment that might easily have been deferred, as it was in England, for several more years. The political consensus that existed across parties in this area was mobilised, however, to establish the post in the Care Standards Act 2000 and to extend it further by the Children's Commissioner for Wales Act 2001.

From the perspective of this text it is important to note that, in law, the commissioner's primary duties are to safeguard and promote the rights and welfare of children in Wales, and, in so doing, to have regard to the UNCRC. In practice, it is generally agreed that the record demonstrates the Welsh Government's commitment to establishing an effective, independent champion of children's rights who is well-resourced to carry out his functions, including holding the government to account. This very early example of policy-making in the field of child welfare suggests that, from the earliest days, not only were children's issues always likely to be near the top of the Assembly agenda, but that the underlying approach to such questions was likely to be rooted in a concern with *rights*. It is to the genesis of that concern that this chapter now turns.

Rights

The foundation document of post-devolution policy-making for children in Wales was published in 2000 under the title of *Extending Entitlement* (NAW, 2000a). It sets out a series of rights to support services and opportunities that are, as far as possible, free at point of use, universal and unconditional. While in England the emphasis has been firmly on making individual young people responsible for exploiting opportunities that may be available to them, in Wales the emphasis has been on ensuring that providers discharge their responsibilities to make new opportunities available, especially to those who need them the most (see Davies and Williams, 2009, for an account of this policy approach across different areas of devolved responsibility in Wales). Specifically in the field of children's policy, the first statement made by the Welsh Government was published as early as

November 2000 as *Children and Young People: A Framework for Partnership* (NAW, 2000b). Intended primarily to bring coherence and focus to the planning and funding of services for children at local level, the framework established, early in the devolution period, the Government's commitment to children's rights and, in particular, its endorsement of the UNCRC:

> Over the past ten years [the UNCRC] has helped to establish an internationally accepted framework for the treatment of all children, encouraged a positive and optimistic image of children and young people as active holders of rights and stimulated a greater global commitment to safeguarding those rights. The Assembly believes that the Convention should provide a foundation of principle for dealings with children. (NAW, 2000b: 10)

It is important to be clear that this approach was, from early on, located in a wider context in which the Welsh Government had set out on a distinctive policy pathway. Perhaps the most rounded and memorable articulation of wider Welsh devolved policy-making was given in the 'clear red water' lecture given by First Minister Rhodri Morgan, in the run up to the 2003 Assembly election (Morgan, 2002). Here Morgan attempted to set out a defining set of principles that characterised Labour policy-making in Wales. While intended primarily to distinguish Labour from other parties in the Assembly elections, it was also capable of being read as opening up conceptual space between Labour in London and in Cardiff. In that context, the lecture firmly rejected an understanding of the relationship between the individual and public services as one based on consumerism. Rather, Morgan argued, Wales had opted for a model in which a reinforced set of unconditional and universal rights, rooted only in citizenship, allowed for a set of relationships based on equality, reciprocity and mutuality. The detail of this approach has been set out at greater length elsewhere (see, for example, Chaney and Drakeford, 2004; Drakeford, 2007; Davies and Williams, 2009). In the same way as the Welsh Government's rights-perspective has deep roots in an established collectivist and nonconformist political tradition, so, as far as children are concerned, there is an inseparable relationship between welfare and rights, with rights being the guarantor of welfare, and participation the key to good governance (see Crowley and Vulliamy, 2002, and Butler, 2007, for an elaboration of these points).

Against that background, the commitment to basing children's policy on the UNCRC was given real substance when, on 14 January 2004, the

National Assembly unanimously reaffirmed 'the priority which it attaches to safeguarding and promoting the rights and welfare of children and young people in Wales, particularly those who are vulnerable', and formally adopted 'the United Nations Convention on the Rights of the Child as the basis of policy making in this area' (NAW, 2004).

From this point onwards, almost every major policy initiative taken by successive Welsh Governments in the children's field has drawn directly on the UNCRC framework. In 2003, for example, an independently chaired task group was established to map out the contribution that might be made, at the Assembly, to tackling child poverty in Wales. Its report, published in February 2005, and titled *A Fair Future for Our Children*, was unambiguously 'built on a set of core values in line with the Convention of the Rights of the Child' (WG, 2005: 9). When the report was debated on the floor of the Assembly, an opposition amendment was tabled to 'commend the Welsh Assembly Government on basing its strategy on the core principles of the UNCRC' (NAW, 2005). Agreed unanimously by all those present, the vote is an example of the cross-party consensus which children's issues have most often attracted in post-devolution Wales, as discussed earlier in this chapter.

By the time the *A Fair Future* report was debated, progress had been made in giving the UNCRC a distinctively Welsh cast. Having formally adopted the convention, the Welsh Government published its statement of *Rights to Action* (WG, 2004a). It translated the Convention into seven core aims which were to underpin policies and programmes for children and young people in Wales. The core aims were designed to ensure that all children and young people:

- have a flying start in life;
- have a comprehensive range of education and learning opportunities;
- enjoy the best possible health and are free from abuse, victimisation and exploitation;
- have access to play, leisure, sporting and cultural activities;
- are listened to, treated with respect and have their race and cultural identity recognised;
- have a safe home and a community which supports physical and emotional well-being;
- are not disadvantaged by poverty.

Rights to Action helped to cement an approach to children's policy in Wales that continued to enjoy cross-party support. The radicalism of the rights-based agenda ought not to be under-estimated. The mid-2000s were characterised, more generally, by high levels of anxiety about the treatment of children in public policy. Events in Wales had contributed to this climate, with the Waterhouse inquiry (2000) continuing to cast a long shadow. The death of Victoria Climbié, and the publication of the *Victoria Climbié Inquiry Report* (Laming, 2003) provided the momentum for the Every Child Matters programme (2003) in England, and the Children Act 2004. Yet, when a debate took place at the Assembly on the consequences of Lord Laming's recommendations for Wales, it was most remarkable for an amendment proposed by Liberal Democrat AM, Kirsty Williams that:

> regrets that the UK Government continues to retain the defence of reasonable chastisement and has taken no significant action towards prohibiting the physical punishment of children in the family. (NAW, 2004)

The Assembly had already established its opposition to corporal punishment during a short debate introduced by Labour AM Christine Chapman, some two years previously. Now the debate was located firmly as a rights issue in the post-Climbié context. Even Welsh Conservative AMs who voted against the amendment itself, voted in favour of the amended substantive motion. It provided a further indication, not only of the Welsh Government's preparedness to put 'clear red water' between itself and Westminster, but also of a progressive, largely consensual approach to policy-making on behalf of children and young people.

If *Rights to Action* was a key policy statement, then *Rights in Action* (WG, 2007) provided a practical programme for its implementation. In many ways *Rights in Action* was a landmark document in that its publication had to be negotiated between the Welsh Government and the UK Government as Wales's contribution to the periodic reporting required of States Parties to the UNCRC. After some determined negotiations, often with rather reluctant Whitehall officials, Ministers in all four UK nations agreed that each would publish what would be, in effect, a separate 'country report'. In the Welsh case, the Government's own report was to be only one strand in the evidence presented to the UN Committee. A UNCRC Monitoring Group, comprised of an alliance of non-governmental agencies, academics and others, submitted a report, *Righting the Wrongs: The Reality of Children's Rights in Wales* (Croke and Crowley, 2006). The Children's Commissioner for Wales, along with representatives of young people's organisations also provided submissions to the process. It is beyond the scope of this chapter to trace the development of children's participation in policy-making in Wales, other than to note the fact that this is, in itself, an integral part of the Convention, certainly at the level of the individual young person. Article 12 states that:

> States Parties shall assure to the child who is capable of forming his or her own views the right to express those views freely in all matters affecting the child, the views of the child being given due weight in accordance with the age and maturity of the child.

The Convention does not define the scope of a young person's right to the kind of participation described in Article 12 and there is no reason to think that the rights of the individual do not equally operate collectively. As such, Article 12 can, quite reasonably, be understood to extend to the kind of political participation that is extended to adults through their general enfranchisement. By this reading of the Convention, it is not surprising to record that Funky Dragon, the collective voice of children and young people in Wales, submitted two reports to the 2008 periodic reporting process, describing the experience of young people living in Wales, in order to determine how well they are able to access their rights under the UNCRC (Funky Dragon 2007a; 2007b). The reports do not make the most reassuring reading, especially in relation to young people's awareness of the provisions of the Convention. Yet not only were these views reported directly to the UN Committee at its meeting in Geneva, they were also relayed to First Minister Rhodri Morgan as part of a presentation at the Welsh Government's Cabinet committee on children and young people.

The periodic review process culminated in an oral hearing of the UN Committee on the Rights of the Child in September 2008. From a Welsh perspective, it proved a positive experience, as reflected in the Committee's *Concluding Observations*, published in the following month (UN Committee *CO*, 2008). This was further reinforced, in 2011, when a Save the Children report, assessing how far the general measures of implementation of the UNCRC have been realised across five European countries and EU institutions, concluded that, within the UK, 'great progress has been made by the Welsh Government', in ensuring the incorporation of the Convention into Welsh law (STC, 2011: 9). In addition, Wales was singled out for the steps being taken to raise the general awareness of the UNCRC (STC, 2011: 70) and for the 'extremely positive progress' made in making funding for children visible in the Welsh Government's budget (STC, 2011: 51).

Three policy areas

Other chapters in this book trace the developing influence of the UNCRC on Welsh policy-making in more detail, and in specific instances of rights-based legislation for children. Here, looking at three specific policy areas, we aim to provide an introductory account of the way in which these general principles have been applied in policies that impact primarily on children and young people, but which have not previously been located primarily within context of the Convention.

Free swimming in local authority leisure centres

One of the direct ways in which a Welsh preference for universal services has been manifested is to be found in the policy of providing free swimming, in school holidays and at weekends, for children aged sixteen and under. The policy has a combination of different aims. It makes a contribution to public health strategies, in encouraging exercise. It has the potential to make an impact on anti-social behaviour (or the fear of it), where young people lack opportunities for constructive occupation. It certainly makes a difference to the least well off families. The Ely estate in Cardiff, for example, forms the single largest Communities First area in Wales. Thanks to the deliberate decision-making of a Labour-controlled city council during the 1970s, the area benefited from the first of a new generation of leisure centres to be built in the city. Yet for many families, struggling to manage on breadline benefits or low-wage employment, these facilities remained out of reach. Now, as part of the 'social wage' strategy pursued by the Welsh Government, the cost of using the swimming pool has been removed, making it accessible, as a right, to a new range of potential users.

Free breakfasts in primary schools

The policy of providing free breakfasts in primary schools draws on much the same basic set of beliefs about social welfare services as a fundamental tool in binding together complex, contemporary societies. Free breakfasts also contribute to a range of different policy purposes.

The programmes' emphasis on healthy breakfasts – brown toast, sugar-free cereals, fruit and milk – helps to lay down nutritional habits at a formative stage; by ensuring that children do not go into the classroom hungry, they aid concentration and promote sociability and make children more receptive to learning; by extending the school day, they assist those working families for whom child care can be both difficult to find and expensive to secure, and for workless families they provide a further social wage contribution to hard-pressed budgets. Taken together, these purposes demonstrate, again, a sense of social welfare services as an invest-ment, rather than a drain on public resources, and as a means not only of providing a more equal start in life, but also securing more successful futures for children whose needs are greatest.

Youth justice

Youth justice services stand at the margin of the devolution settlement. Formally, responsibility remains at Westminster. Practically, activity on the ground depends very largely on devolved services. That gap has been bridged through a Youth Justice Committee for Wales, and its major prod-uct, an *All-Wales Youth Offending Strategy* (*AWYOS*). The *AWYOS* (WG, 2004b), was agreed between the Youth Justice Board (YJB) and the Welsh Government, and jointly signed by the then-responsible Welsh Minister, Edwina Hart, and the then-Chair of the YJB, Professor Rod Morgan.

The *AWYOS* document sets out a key principle that 'young people should be treated as children first and offenders second', in a man-ner underpinned by the UNCRC (WG, 2004b: 3). The 'children first' approach denotes an attitude of mind in which offending is understood as only one element in a much wider and more complex identity. When things go wrong in the lives of children and young people, the Welsh focus has been on trying to put right flaws in the systems on which they depend. The rights-perspective set out earlier in this chapter focuses on what chil-dren and young people can do for themselves, for each other and for the communities in which they live. It focuses on their strengths and not their weaknesses and/or deficits. It takes on board the problems that adults cause for children as well as the problems that young people may cause for the wider community. It adopts a language of justice, equality and participa-tion rather than a language of competition, business and consumerism. The model of children and young people it deploys is confident, posi-tive, imaginative and optimistic. As such, it stands at a considerable, and deliberate, distance from the dominant approach taken in England, where 'all "offenders" are, by definition, "undeserving"' (Goldson, 2002: 690), and 'the humane logic of progressive anti-poverty responses is eclipsed by disciplinary measures encoded within an increasingly repressive and responsibilizing correctionalism' (Goldson, 2002: 685).

Against this general background, the *AWYOS* contains a set of prin-ciples that are derived from the distinctive post-devolution policy agenda. These include the direct identification of the UNCRC as the cornerstone of the strategy; the explicit extension of the rights set out in *Extending Entitlement* to young people in trouble with the law; a commitment to work with the Children's Commissioner for Wales; a commitment to mainstream and embed consultation with, and the participation of, children and young people in the youth justice system; a determination that young people should be treated as children first and offenders second, and an emphasis that custody for children really should be deployed only as a last resort.

These principles have, more recently, been further endorsed by the responsible Minister in a position paper which makes it clear that, as far as youth justice policy is concerned, the work of the *AWYOS* remains 'under-pinned by the [UNCRC] and its requirement for consideration of the rights of children and young people' (WG, 2009: 3).

Conclusion

This chapter has attempted to set out the distinctive space in which the Welsh 'policy child' emerged in the dozen years of devolution. We hope that we have established the contention that children and young people's policy in Wales has been founded on the assumption that children are rights holders with an entitlement to participate in decisions on matters which affect them. Such an assumption has its roots in Welsh radicalism and in the progressive ideals and democratic socialism of the Welsh Labour Party as well as in the emancipatory rhetoric of the specific children's rights 'movement'. Specifically, it has been given shape and substance by placing the UNCRC at the heart of its policy-making, giving reasonable grounds for continuing optimism that future policy-making will continue to be shaped by an enduring recognition that 'the inherent dignity and . . . the equal and inalienable rights of all members of the human family is the foundation of freedom, justice and peace in the world' (Preamble to the UNCRC).

References

Butler, I. (2007): 'Children's policy in Wales', in C. Williams (ed.), *Social Policy for Social Welfare Practice in a Devolved Wales* (Birmingham: Venture Press), pp. 159–84.

Chaney, P. and Drakeford, M. (2004): 'The primacy of ideology: social policy and the first term of the National Assembly for Wales', *Social Policy Review*, 16, 121–42.

Crowley, A. and Vulliamy, C. (2002): *Listen Up! Children and Young People Talk About Poverty* (Cardiff: Save The Children).

Croke, R. and Crowley, A. (eds)/UNCRC Monitoring Group (2006): *Righting the Wrongs: The Reality of Children's Rights in Wales* (Cardiff: Save the Children).

Davies, N, and Williams, D. (2009): *Clear Red Water: Welsh Devolution and Socialist Politics* (London: Francis Boutle).

Drakeford, M. (2007): 'Devolution and social justice in the Welsh context', *Benefits*, 19/2, 173–80.

Every Child Matters (2003): Cm. 5860 (London: HMSO).

Funky Dragon (2007a): *Our Rights, Our Story* (Swansea: Funky Dragon).

—— (2007b): *Why Do People's Ages Go Up Not Down?* (Swansea: Funky Dragon).

Goldson, B. (2002): 'New Labour, social justice and children: political calculation and the deserving-undeserving schism', *British Journal of Social Work*, 32, 683–95.

Laming Report (2003): *The Victoria Climbié Inquiry: Report of an Inquiry by Lord Laming*, Cm. 5730 (London: HMSO).

Levy, A. and Kahan, B. (1991): *The Pindown Experience and the Protection of Children* (Stafford: Staffordshire County Council).

Morgan, R. (2002): National Centre for Public Policy Annual Lecture, Swansea, University of Wales, 11 December.

NAW (National Assembly for Wales) (2000a): *Extending Entitlement: Supporting Young People in Wales* (Cardiff: Policy Unit, National Assembly for Wales).

—— (2000b): *Children and Young People: A Framework for Partnership* (Cardiff: National Assembly for Wales).

—— (2004): Record of Proceedings, 14 January (Cardiff: National Assembly for Wales).

—— (2005): Record of Proceedings, 9 February (Cardiff: National Assembly for Wales).

STC (Save the Children) (2011): *Governance fit for children: To what extent have the general measures of implementation of the CRC been implemented in the UK?* (London: Save the Children UK). Available at *http://www.savethechildren.org.uk/resources/online-library/governance-fit-children* (accessed 27 June, 2012).

Waterhouse, R. (2000): *Lost in Care: Report of the Tribunal of Inquiry into the Abuse of Children in Care in the Former County Council Areas of Gwynedd and Clwyd since 1974* (London: The Stationery Office).

WG (Welsh Government) (2004a): *Children and Young People: Rights to Action* (Cardiff: Welsh Assembly Government).

—— (2004b): *All-Wales Youth Offending Strategy* (Cardiff: Welsh Assembly Government/Youth Justice Board).

—— (2005): *A Fair Future for Our Children: The Strategy of the Welsh Assembly Government for Tackling Child Poverty* (Cardiff: Welsh Assembly Government).

—— (2007): *Rights in Action: Implementing Children and Young People's Rights in Wales* (Cardiff: Welsh Assembly Government).
WG (Welsh Government)/Youth Justice Board (2009): *All-Wales Youth Offending Strategy: Delivery Plan 2009–11* (Cardiff: Welsh Assembly Government).

CHAPTER 2

Made to Measure: cooperation and conflict in the making of a policy

Michael Sullivan and Helen Mary Jones

Introduction

This chapter, which needs to be read in conjunction with the chapters between which it is sandwiched, is about the extent to which the children's rights Measure (the Rights of Children and Young Persons (Wales) Measure 2011) was born of the political consensus claimed by Butler and Drakeford (chapter 1 of this volume) and to what extent it emerged from a policy-making process characterised by political and intellectual street fighting. It argues that both the intention to see such a Measure on the Welsh statute book and the eventual passage of the Measure through pre-legislative scrutiny and the Senedd reflected the high water marks of the third Assembly, with AMs from all parties pressing for its passage as a pervasive piece of legislation. Against this background of political consensus, it documents, however, the resistance of some interests – particularly the senior civil service and, for a time, relevant departmental Ministers – to a pervasive Measure that would effectively extend the rights of children in Wales in ways consistent with the UNCRC. Instead, following the retirement of Rhodri Morgan as First Minister, the original proposal for such a pervasive piece of legislation changed to a proposal from government that suggested that Ministers should have 'due regard' only to 'relevant functions' (which were undefined), or, later in the process, to 'relevant decisions'. The conversion of Ministers in the leading portfolio to the sort of strong Measure that has eventually emerged occurred very late in the policy-making process, and appears to have been forced by the robustness of evidence from a surprisingly well-informed NGO community, the advice of an ad-hoc group of prominent academic and practising lawyers, and the uncompromising scrutiny of three of the Assembly's committees: the Legislation Committee, the Children and Young People Committee, and the Constitutional Affairs Committee.

Political contexts

As Butler and Drakeford argue in this volume, the political context in which the then First Minister, Rhodri Morgan, announced in 2009 the intention to introduce a children's rights Measure was one characterised by the presence in Cabinet and outside it of politicians with a strong and long record of support for the UNCRC as a guide to children's policy. The First Minister himself, Jane Hutt (who in various portfolios carried responsibility as 'Minister for Children'), Gwenda Thomas, latterly Deputy Minister for Children and Social Services and Helen Mary Jones (Plaid Cymru AM between 1999 and 2011, and Chair of the Children and Young People Committee between 2007 and 2011), were among the major Welsh politicians at the forefront of support for a simple, stand-alone, pervasive children's Measure. But this support was equally a feature of the views of back-bench AMs in the Labour-Plaid coalition of 2007–11 and of the leadership and members of the two opposition parties. In late November 2010, by which time the principle of pervasiveness had been won (against the initial resistance of the then Deputy Minister for Children, Huw Lewis, and his officials), Jenny Randerson AM for the Liberals was able to say in the Legislation Committee, which was scrutinising the proposed Measure, that 'the legislation, in principle and in most of its details, has the support of the Welsh Liberal Democrats. We welcome the fact that Wales has seized the opportunity to lead in this regard' (Legislation Committee No. 5, 2010). Darren Millar AM for the Conservatives had, in the same committee, proved to be a consistent thorn in the side of the Deputy Minister until he conceded, late in the day, on the principle of pervasiveness.

Devolved government policy in Wales has seen children as rights bearers:

> Children and young people should be seen as young citizens, with rights and opinions to be taken into account now. They are not a species apart, to be alternately demonised and sentimentalised, nor trainee adults who do not yet have a full place in society. (WG, 2004: 4)

As noted in chapters 1 and 3, as early as 2002, the UN Committee had welcomed the Welsh Government's adoption of the UNCRC as the framework for its strategy for children and young people, and had welcomed the Assembly's support of that policy. In 2004, the emphasis on the importance of children's rights could most clearly be seen when the Assembly, within the limits of its powers, adopted the UNCRC as the basis of all its policy-making for children and young people, positioning its overarching strategy for children within a rights-based framework linked to UNCRC implementation.

Also in 2004, the Welsh Government issued *Rights to Action*, a policy document adopting seven core aims which are presented as a direct translation of the UNCRC's articles into the policy objectives that are listed in chapter 1 of this volume. This strategy received the support of other parties in the Assembly at plenary level and in the Children and Young People Committee.

The national policy initiatives which followed – such as the National Service Framework for Children, Young People and Maternity Services in Wales (NSF), the *All-Wales Youth Offending Strategy*, and the Sexual Health and Well-being Strategy – all embedded the seven core principles. Both the first Child Poverty Strategy for Wales and the new strategy are seen as contributing to the UN's goals in relation to children's rights, and the Welsh Government has developed the Children and Young People Well-being monitor with statistics that are linked to the UNCRC and can be seen as measures to implement the seven core aims.

In 2009, the Welsh Government published *Getting it Right*, an action plan for Wales developed in line with the principles as set out in the UN Committee's *Concluding Observations* (2008). This action plan is subject to regular review and updating to ensure that it keeps abreast of new developments in policy and strategy and remains relevant and timely. This will enable the Government to add any new priority areas if and when they emerge during the five-year period of the action plan, and remove from priority status any areas where the Welsh Government and partners may consider sufficient progress has been made during the course of the five-year period.

By the time of reporting to the UN Committee in 2014, the Welsh Government aims to demonstrate significant progress across all of the priority domains for which Wales has legislative competence and devolved powers, in supporting all children and young people across Wales to know about, exercise and access their UNCRC and human rights.

These initiatives, rooted in UNCRC principles and values, are consistent with the underpinning philosophy of Labour in the Assembly – the lead or sole party in all four post-devolution governments – and expressed most clearly in Morgan's 'clear red water' lecture at Swansea in 2002. In his words, then as First Minister: 'the actions of the Welsh Assembly Government clearly owe more to the traditions of Titmuss, Tawney, Beveridge and Bevan than those of Hayek and Friedman' (Morgan, 2002). The creation of a new set of citizenship rights has been a key theme in the first twelve years of the Assembly – a set of rights, which are, as far as possible, 'free at the point of use; universal, and unconditional' (Morgan, 2002). Here is a conception of social policy as a legitimate response to the social needs of a population rather than the consumer preferences or demands of individual customers. In Wales, policy emerging from the Welsh Government between 1999 and 2007 indicated the retention, within Welsh Labourism, of a strong commitment to collective solutions to collective and individual problems: the individualised, consumerist approach to planning, provision and participation in social policy. In relation to social policy in general and children's policy in particular the emphasis is on the attribution of citizen rights. These were, in part, rooted in the Morgan Administration's commitment to 'classic Labour' nostrums developed initially in the post-war years in the work of Tony Crosland (1952a, 1952b, 1956, 1975). Crosland was a firm advocate of developing rights-based public services. He was such a firm advocate because he took the view that part of getting more equality, or, as he was to describe it later, 'equality of opportunity', was aided by public services.

Crosland's social democracy saw the state exercising a duty to correct, supplement and, if necessary, displace the market system of exchange. Governments should do so to promote and develop greater equality, democracy and welfare, and 'to guide the private (and public) sector to forms of collective action to achieve collective goals which individuals cannot achieve with the same measure of success, by their isolated efforts' (1956: 61). Crosland's views on the role and nature of a mixed-economy welfare state represented a social democratic manifesto and rationale for welfarism: a justification for maintaining a centrally funded universalist welfare state; a rationale for the extension of that welfare state to provide more equality through consumption-orientated social policies rather than production-orientated economic policies; a refutation of right-wing prescriptions for less welfare; and a prospectus for equality of opportunity.

If Crosland was the architect of a post-war social democracy which continued to influence the Labour party in Wales, and indeed Plaid Cymru and the Liberal Democrats, then the citizenship theorist T. H. Marshall was the foundation-layer. In relation to social policy and social democracy, Crosland's views were rooted in and built on Marshall's views about the rights of citizens. Indeed Marshall had made explicit Crosland's implicit assumption that social democratic politics were inextricably linked with developments in citizen rights.

Welfare states, according to Marshall, mitigate the tendency of markets to create inequality by giving equal social rights to all. Social rights confer citizenship on their recipients. The right to welfare (one of Marshall's social rights) is connected with full membership of the community for the individual. The objective and outcome of state welfare is a sort of equality that comes, in Marshall's words 'from full membership of the societal community' (1963: 80). The right to welfare confers on the citizen rights to be treated like all other citizens in relation to welfare, and therefore bestows a sort of equality of regard. If all citizens are to be treated alike as far as their right to welfare is concerned, then the welfare state, within a capitalist society, must be based on a framework of universal social policies (Marshall, 1972). For Marshall, the social democratic settlement was an agreement on a package of rights, 'from the right to a modicum of economic welfare and security to the right to share to the full in the social heritage and to live the life of a civilised being according to the standards prevailing in the society' (1963: 74).

The Welsh Assembly's programmes in relation to children's rights draw on this rich vein of thinking, which emphasises the importance of both welfare provision and rights-based policies in creating equal citizenship for all. They also owe much to a notion of active and collective citizenship that stands within and goes beyond Marshall's notion of citizenship (Sullivan, 2004; Drakeford, 2005). This has meant an emphasis on policy priorities being shaped by the views of those most likely to benefit from them – citizens and communities in Wales. This much is clear, for instance, in the participation of children and young people in the development of relevant policy, particularly – though not exclusively – through Funky Dragon, the youth parliament. The emerging and progressive adherence to UNCRC principles on children's rights will require the Welsh Government to involve children and young people in developing policy.

But these values and principles, at least in relation to children, while the property of Labour in the Assembly, do not confer sole ownership on Labour. Other political parties, as we see in Elis-Thomas's argument below, hold these views no less strongly and would see them as expressions of 'Welsh' rather than 'Labour' ideals.

It is these shared values in relation to children that has fed a cross-party consensus which has been the hallmark of Assembly consideration of children since the inception of devolved government in Wales. It has most recently been expressed by Dafydd Elis-Thomas, the senior Plaid Cymru AM and former Presiding Officer of the National Assembly, as a commitment to regarding children as full citizens with the rights attributed to other citizens. Speaking in an individual member debate urging the Welsh Government to bring forward legislation to end the defence of lawful chastisement for an offence of assaulting a child, he couched his support for the motion in the language of rights and citizenship:

> what is happening here today is entirely consistent with the way in which Welsh legislation is developing in terms of its treatment of children. This is the clear argument for me: children are not children, but citizens of Wales. They receive public services that have been provided by the Welsh Government and Welsh Ministers, and they go through educational systems that have been put in place for them. They also receive, in difficult family circumstances, the support of social services. Therefore, they are full citizens. Children are not citizens in the making, some sub-species of citizen, or citizens that are to be treated differently, either ethically or legally, to other citizens. (NAW, 2011)

The dark arts

Another salient part of the policy-making process, less formal but widely practised, is that provided by the civil service. In constitutional theory the implementation arm of government, carrying out the will of the elected government, the civil service appears consistently to have thwarted the wishes of the proposed Measure's original sponsors and to have sought to reopen the debate about the wisdom of such a Measure with incoming Ministers following Rhodri Morgan's retirement. One is reminded of the late Barbara Castle who advised that if a Minister is minded to take on the departmental civil service she had better be 'bloody, bold and resolute' (Castle, 1984), or of Richard Crossman's lament about the 'companionable embrace of the departmental civil service' (Crossman, 1975). In relation to the proposed Children's Rights Measure, the activity of this group of political actors was *Yes Minister* without the funny bits.

For reasons that may remain the subject of debate and conjecture, the idea of a strong and pervasive Measure on children's rights engendered opposition from ranking officials from the day that then First Minister Morgan announced the intention to introduce such legislation. Indeed, there is evidence of fairly entrenched hostility to the idea even before his announcement. According to evidence seen by one of the authors of this chapter, officials in the civil service departments that were likely to be responsible for the development of children's rights legislation were seeking to build a case against the introduction of such legislation – an enterprise in which they were aided by the Welsh Government's own legal service – two months ahead of Morgan's announcement. This hostility may have been borne out of a view that there was no obvious 'mischief' to be remedied by the introduction of such a law. It may have been rooted in a belief that a law which obliged Welsh Ministers to have regard to the UNCRC in the exercise of all their functions would risk significant additional expenditure on administration, training and implementation. Perhaps officials were nervous of a perceived additional burden of work. Or perhaps there were deeper-seated objections to the notion of children as rights-bearers.

Whatever is the case, opposition to the idea of developing and introducing a children's rights Measure was already forming part of the informal political context, even before it became part of an intended legislative programme. At the formal level, however, the Measure's sponsors – the Minister for Social Justice and Local Government, the Minister for Children, Education, Lifelong Learning and Skills and the Deputy Minister for Social Services – remained committed to the proposal to introduce a Measure and were supported by the One Wales Cabinet in general and the First Minister in particular. The latter announced in July 2009 the intention to legislate, and for the Measure to be a straightforward, stand-alone law that pervaded all Ministerial functions. The announcement was welcomed by all political parties in the Assembly. Notwithstanding this very clear statement of intent by the politicians, officials – having apparently moved from a position of open hostility – presented in September 2009 a proposal that was little more than a local restatement of the obligations of the UK as a UNCRC State Party, which removed the notion of Ministerial responsibility to have regard, and replaced it with an obligation to establish a 'scheme' which would describe how Ministers would decide which of their functions should be the object of synchronicity with UNCRC principles. Part of the apparent justification for this approach was the (in the event, non-existent) spectre of the UK Foreign and Commonwealth Office objecting to the Assembly trespassing into international affairs, the province of the FCO, by developing a Measure which related to an international convention.

This drew a clear and sharp response from the sponsoring Ministers, through their political advisers, to the effect that they had no wish to move from their original proposal. What followed were attempts to square the circle, with officials presenting drafts that restricted the areas in which the proposed Measure would bite, and Ministers, through their advisers, restating the importance of a pervasiveness principle. At around this time, the then First Minister became directly involved once more and commissioned an academic lawyer who had formerly been a government lawyer to work with those officials developing the Measure to ensure that the eventual proposal met the objectives set by Ministers – an offer that officials found easy to refuse in substance if not in form.

The issue came to a head in November 2009, when officials presented to the Cabinet's Legislation Committee a proposal that restricted the duty to have regard to what were termed 'relevant functions' within a Minister's responsibilities, but placed a secondary duty on Ministers to do something less than having regard in relation to other functions. At this point, the First Minister intervened robustly and by early December it appeared that the politicians had prevailed, and a proposal emerged from officials which reflected the aspirations of sponsoring Ministers, Cabinet and the First Minister. Elation, if there was any among proponents of a pervasive Measure, was short-lived. Morgan retired as First Minister on 8 December 2009 to be replaced by Carwyn Jones AM, and the new First Minister chose a new Cabinet and clutch of Deputy Ministers. The new Ministerial team saw children's issues placed in the hands of a Deputy Minister for Children (in DCELLS) and also saw a new Minister for Education at the head of the department.

Within a month, officials were to reopen discussions with the Minister and the Deputy Minister about whether a pervasive Measure was wise, affordable or necessary. They were largely successful, and a pause for thought was ordered by the Minister for Education. Following reflection, the more restrictive proposal referred to above was reintroduced. That it did not ultimately form the basis of the Measure was the result of resolute and informed opposition by the NGO community, the ad hoc group of lawyers referred to above, the scrutiny carried out by the Legislation Committee, the Children and Young People Committee and the Constitutional Affairs Committee. The abandonment by the government of a restrictive approach, and the last-gasp acceptance of a pervasive model provided by the ad hoc group of lawyers, among others, was also influenced by the clear warning, from the then Deputy First Minister and Leader of Plaid Cymru, and from the Deputy Leader of Plaid Cymru, that they would not ensure a government majority in plenary for the weaker proposal.

The NGO community
Aspinwall and Croke, in chapter 3 of this volume, document clearly and in detail the activity of the NGO community – here taken to include the Wales UNCRC Monitoring Group, the lawyers' group, and individual children's organisations including the charities and the office of the Children's Commissioner for Wales. It is not intended to rehearse details related by Aspinwall and Croke but to indicate salient issues.

Throughout the process described in the preceding pages, the community maintained a clear preference for a pervasive Measure. It variously monitored developments, lobbied Ministers and AMs, provided critiques and analyses – from policy and legal perspectives – of restrictive, non-pervasive approaches, presented evidence to Assembly scrutiny committees and, as part of this process, provided amendments to the government's proposed Measure which, while rejected as late as early October 2010, were conceded by the end of November 2010.

Essentially, the NGO community transformed itself during this period into an effective and cohesive coalition. Notable was the almost unanimous stance of individual NGOs in favour of a strong and pervasive law in consultations on the legislative proposal. The community was peculiarly well-informed, which appears to have been the result of several factors. First, the UNCRC Monitoring Group and the individual children's organisations were blessed with memberships with significant expertise and experience in both the development and analysis of children's policy, and many had played roles previously in the crafting of policy with and for the Welsh Government and the Assembly. Secondly, the effectiveness of the NGO community in this particular episode was heightened by the legal and policy expertise of the ad hoc group of lawyers and the seminars hosted by Swansea University School of Law. Thirdly, there had no doubt been informal interaction between various members of the NGO community and the government's political advisers, based on long shared histories and joint working: it is hard to believe that the speed and agility with which the community responded to issues was not, in some small part, facilitated by insider knowledge.

A cold-light-of-day analysis will, in our opinion, indicate the central importance of the community in ensuring that the government remained honest and true to its original intentions. In the face, for instance, of indications from officials that the community should accept the less pervasive model because it was 'that or nothing' – advice which appears to have convinced the Children's Commissioner to reluctantly support the government stance until it was clear that change was afoot – the community as a whole remained solidly behind arguments for the pervasive principle.

Assembly scrutiny committees
Into this policy mix we must add the formal and informal scrutiny of Assembly committees which considered the draft proposals for the Measure through the summer and autumn of 2010. That is to say that the committees considered a proposal indicating the government's preferred direction:

a non-pervasive Measure wherein the duty of due regard was restricted to decisions Welsh Ministers determined to be 'of a strategic nature'.

As early as its third meeting (in July 2010), when it took evidence from representatives of the NGO community including the UNCRC Monitoring Group, it was clear that the Legislation Committee was sympathetic to arguments that the Measure proposed by the Minister and the government would not strengthen children's rights and might well be a retrograde step. During the proceedings of this committee, the Minister was, on three occasions, challenged by its members as to how the proposed Measure enhanced children's rights and to what extent it embedded the UNCRC in the policy-making process. It was clear that the committee already took the view that the Measure, as proposed, was deficient. This view, and a suspicion that the Deputy Minister for Children – no doubt influenced by officials – was intransigently attached to this weak approach, seemed to be reinforced when the Children's Commissioner, while he was giving evidence to the committee, indicated in response to a question that he had supported the government's proposal because he had been told that it was that proposal or nothing. By late September 2010, the committee appeared convinced by the arguments of those who favoured a pervasive approach, and by early November, bolstered by the near-unanimous support in the consultation exercise for a pervasive Measure, the committee had reported that it was, itself, unanimously in favour of amendments that would rectify deficiencies in the Measure. Those amendments, crafted by the ad hoc group of lawyers, were pressed on the Minister with sufficient vigour that, along with the consultation results and the within-government discussions, it proved sufficient to effect a conversion of the Deputy Minister that was of Pauline dimensions. By late November, the Deputy Minister had conceded the principle of pervasiveness and had agreed to consider how this would change the proposal. By the plenary debate on the proposal in January 2011, the government had adopted in substance the key recommendations of the ad hoc group of lawyers and the UNCRC Monitoring Group.

Though much of the 'heavy lifting' during the scrutiny process was done by the Legislation Committee, both the Constitutional Affairs Committee and the Children and Young People Committee also played a part. The Constitutional Affairs Committee questioned in particular the notion of 'decisions of a strategic nature'. The Children and Young People Committee, consistent with earlier positions, supported the Measure being pervasive – support which its Chair, Helen Mary Jones, was able to point to in discussions with the Deputy First Minister and which reinforced opinion within Plaid Cymru that its AMs should not be expected to support the Measure in a plenary vote unless the government's proposal was changed fundamentally. This committee had also had a very significant, if less than formal, influence on the final outcome even before the government had published its proposed Measure on 17 March, 2010. The committee, having received intelligence that the proposed Measure might be far from pervasive and comprehensive, undertook a short piece of pre-legislative scrutiny of the government's intentions, particularly asking the Children's Commissioner and NGOs what they thought the Measure should look like (Children and Young People Committee, 2010). The clear support for a strong, pervasive Measure was transmitted by the committee to Ministers along with advice that a less than pervasive Measure was likely to run into trouble. This shot across the policy bows was unprecedented, and procedurally novel. In other circumstances it might have been seen as cutting across the legitimate role of the Legislation Committee. The Children and Young People Committee took the risk of running into procedural controversy but was not challenged, no doubt because most AMs in all parties supported the strong Measure the committee was seeking to achieve. This clearly led to a softening of the Deputy Minister's position, and the proposed Measure, while still deficient as far as most policy actors were concerned, marked the beginning of a process by which the government aligned its views with those of the majority of AMs, its scrutiny committees and the NGO community. As we have seen, in the event, the Deputy Minister performed a complete and dignified U-turn and the proposal, as amended, that was placed before plenary on 18 January 2011 matched up to the hopes of the proponents of a pervasive Measure. It received Royal Approval on 16 March 2011 and is now being regarded as a possible model by the Scottish Government.

Policy lessons to be learnt

As we consider the passage of this Measure – the last to be introduced via a process which required the agreement of Westminster as laid down in the Government of Wales Act 2006 – two questions present themselves: how do we explain the eventual success in securing a simple, stand-alone and pervasive Measure against the preferences of the civil service and the apparent hostility of the Ministers who replaced the original Ministerial sponsors when the administration changed in 2010, and what lessons are thus learnt for future policy-making?

In considering the making of this particular policy, we are reminded that the process of policy-making, even in the apparently consensual political context of children's (and much other social) policy in Wales is, in fact, characterised by change, choice and conflict (Hall et al., 1975). In this case the need for policy change was perceived by politicians of all hues within the National Assembly for Wales. This was given expression by the preference of sponsoring Ministers and the then First Minister to introduce legislation further to develop Wales's adherence to UNCRC principles. However, notwithstanding consensus among political parties and significant segments of civil society, conflict was an important characteristic of the policy process and passage of this Measure. That conflict was first between the preferences (for no change) of the civil service in Wales and the choice for change of the politicians, and then, when Ministerial positions changed, the conflict was between civil service and DCELLS Ministers on the one hand, and a well-informed, coordinated coalition of forces (the NGO community, Assembly backbenchers, the scrutiny committees and academic and practising lawyers) on the other. In this case it proved to be a creative conflict of ideas in which the overwhelming preference of politicians, professionals, children's organisations and children themselves won out over the conservative inclinations of the civil servants, who had managed to embrace and persuade departmental Ministers of the need for caution.

We need to note that this policy victory was, nonetheless, hard-won. Until the very last moment, it appeared that government would resist the pressure for change despite the fact that the evidence for change seemed clear and the pressure seemed overwhelming from within the Assembly as well as from outside it. Without coordination and knowledge-sharing at formal and informal levels, effecting change might have been even more difficult than it was.

We should draw from this process, however, the lesson that evidence and expertise are powerful weapons, especially when presented cogently, bravely and by well-placed members of civil society outside the Assembly. A refusal by some policy actors within and outside the Assembly to be restricted by threats or blandishments might also have been a contributory factor.

And, finally, a caution against optimism. In this particular case, the original intentions of politicians were carried through to enactment of a Measure that reflected their views. That should not be remarkable, but it is. Here, as in many other areas, the civil service acted as a brake on change, at times in direct opposition to the prevailing political view and at times through seeking to delay and or minimise change. In relation to the Rights of Children and Young Persons (Wales) Measure, this conservative impulse was, in the end, washed away by pressure for change from a coalition of policy forces described above. That coalition of forces emerged from both within the Assembly and from wider civil society. It was made up of backbench AMs, powerful organisations and important individuals. It came to be supported by the Assembly's own committees. It was supported by Ministerial advisers. And it still nearly failed because of the coalition of civil service and departmental Ministers unenthusiastic about change. What is now lauded as path-breaking very nearly did not happen.

For us, it is clear that facilitating change in the future is dependent, in part, on changing the nature of the civil service in Wales. In turn that means addressing a situation in which that civil service, despite deepening and widening devolution, is answerable to Whitehall rather than to politicians in Cardiff Bay. One model would, as Rhodri Morgan has suggested, be the creation of a public service in Wales serving both local and national government and answerable to the Assembly. There may be other models, but whatever form it takes, change here is vital.

References

Castle, B. (1984): *The Castle Diaries* (London: Weidenfeld).

Children and Young People Committee, National Assembly for Wales (2010): Papers 2 and 3, 27 April (Cardiff: National Assembly for Wales).

Crosland, C. A. R. (1952a): *The Conservative Enemy* (London: Cape).

—— (1952b): 'The transition from capitalism', in R. H. Crossman (ed.), *New Fabian Essays* (London: Turnstile Press), pp. 33–68.

—— (1956): *The Future of Socialism* (London: Cape).

—— (1975): *Socialism Now* (London: Cape).

Crossman, R. H. (1975): *Diaries of a Cabinet Minister* (London: Cape).

Drakeford, M. (2005): 'Wales and a third term of New Labour: devolution and the development of difference', *Critical Social Policy*, 25, 497–506.

Hall, P., Land, H., Parker, R. and Webb, A. (1975): *Change, Choice and Conflict in Social Policy* (London: Heinemann).

Legislation Committee No. 5 (2010): Record of Proceedings, 25 November (Cardiff: National Assembly for Wales).

Marshall, T. H. (1963): 'Citizenship and social class', in *Sociology at the Crossroads* (London: Allen and Unwin).

—— (1972): *The Right to Welfare and Other Essays* (New York: Free Press).

Morgan, R. (2002): National Centre for Public Policy Annual Lecture, Swansea, University of Wales, 11 December.

NAW (National Assembly for Wales) (2011): Record of Proceedings, 19 October (Cardiff: National Assembly for Wales).

Sullivan, M. (2004): 'Wales, devolution and health policy: policy experimentation and differentiation to improve health', *Contemporary Wales*, 17/1, 44–65.

WG (Welsh Government) (2004): *Children and Young People: Rights to Action* (Cardiff: Welsh Assembly Government).

CHAPTER 3

Policy advocacy communities: the collective voice of children's NGOs in Wales

Trudy Aspinwall and Rhian Croke

Introduction and Background to the Wales UNCRC Monitoring Group

This chapter explores the role of alliances of non-governmental organisations (NGOs) in using and supporting the monitoring process of the UNCRC, engaging with government, statutory and treaty bodies and influencing change in national laws and policy. The influence of the Wales UNCRC Monitoring Group ('the Group') on the making of the Rights of Children and Young Persons (Wales) Measure 2011 has been noted in the first two chapters in this volume. The authors of this chapter occupied in succession the key supporting role for the Group since 2000. We offer here reflections on the achievements of and future challenges for NGOs promoting UNCRC implementation in Wales.

Strong links between government and NGOs have supported the historical commitment to children's rights in Wales (Croke and Crowley, 2006). Devolution brought a new compulsion not only to act on this commitment but also to accelerate positive partnership working between government and the NGO sector.

The UNCRC is unusual among international human rights instruments in conferring a formal role on NGOs: Article 45(a) refers to them as 'competent bodies' to which the UN Committee can turn for advice and assistance. This reflects recognition of the expertise residing in these groups and also the unusual extent of NGO involvement in the ten-year drafting process. The UN Committee

welcomes the development of NGO coalitions and alliances committed to promoting, protecting and monitoring children's human rights and urges Governments to give them non-directive support and to develop positive formal as well as informal relationships with them. (UN Committee *GC*, 2003: para. 58)

In 2001, two of the leading children's NGOs in Wales, Save the Children and Children in Wales, recognised that there was a need to develop an alliance of NGOs to support the monitoring and implementation of the UNCRC in Wales. The first meeting was held just prior to the examination of the UK Government's second periodic report to the UN Committee. Membership consisted of Save the Children, Funky Dragon and Children in Wales, with officials from the Welsh Government and the Children's Commissioner for Wales as observers. While Save the Children and Children in Wales had prepared an NGO report for the UN Committee in this round, a strong immediate focus was on ensuring a more broadly based, evidence-rich alternative report in the next and future reporting rounds. Crucially, Save the Children supported this goal not only by providing a chairperson but also by deploying a full-time policy officer to coordinate and facilitate the Group's work. Membership increased to include representatives of Action for Children, Barnardo's Cymru, Children in Wales, Funky Dragon, Nacro Cymru, NSPCC Wales and Save the Children; legal and medical experts from Aberystwyth, Cardiff and Swansea universities; and, as observers, officials representing the Welsh Government, Equalities and Human Rights Commission, Children's Commissioner for Wales and the Welsh Local Government Association.

The UNCRC reporting process 2002–2008

A watershed in the Group's progress was the production of an interim report in 2006 (Croke and Crowley, 2006). *Righting the Wrongs* was the first attempt at a systematic, treaty-based report on the state of children's rights in Wales. It took the UN Committee's 2002 recommendations and charted progress in Wales towards compliance. The report was launched at an oversubscribed conference held in Swansea in January 2006; speakers included the chair of the UN Committee, the Welsh Minister for Children, the Children's Commissioner for Wales and two academics. The conference was an opportunity both to promote the report and to strengthen the policy advocacy community for children's rights in Wales, encouraging more people to become involved in the monitoring and reporting process.

The Righting the Wrongs conference also provided an important opportunity for a closed meeting between the chair of the UN Committee, the Children's Commissioner for Wales, Welsh Government officials,

Funky Dragon, and representatives of the Group to discuss the presentation of alternative reports and effective representation of the views of children. The conference and follow-up effectively launched the next round of periodic reporting to the UN Committee, secured a commitment from the Minister for Children to oversee the Welsh Government submission, influenced the *Rights in Action* strategy (WG, 2007a) and provided a strong base for the Group's next steps towards preparation of the eventual NGO report.

The NGO report, *Stop, Look, Listen: The Road to Realising Children's Rights in Wales*, submitted to the UN Committee in the summer of 2008, was described by Dr Kamel Filali, one of the UN Committee's UK Country Rapporteurs, as having 'a robust academic approach' (Filali, 2008). As noted by Butler and Drakeford in this volume, the 2008 reporting round also saw alternative reports submitted by the four UK children's commissioners (jointly, on the basis of four-way negotiation of the text) and by Funky Dragon (2007) (the latter had taken the opportunity of the Righting the Wrongs conference to secure the UN Committee's agreement to their report being in whatever form they chose, not necessarily adhering to the Committee's guidelines for reporting). While each organisation had its own constituency, there was significant collaboration in the period of preparation, utilising professional networks and contacts with relevant bodies at UK, international, all-Wales and local levels. The Group played a pivotal part in this collaboration, from organising UK-wide meetings to hosting and programming the pre-sessional visit of one of the UK Country Rapporteurs, Norwegian Lucy Smith, and coordinating and chairing the UN Committee's pre-sessional meeting in Geneva in June 2008.

Impact on Welsh Government policy development: the 'dynamic' of the UNCRC

In September 2008, coinciding with the sessional hearings of the UK's third and fourth periodic reports to the UN Committee, a further conference was held in Swansea, this time hosted by Swansea University. This brought the Wales protagonists together with international experts whose involvement spanned the whole period of the UNCRC from the negotiations during the 1980s to the present. Speaking at the conference, Professor Jaap Doek, then recently retired chair of the UN Committee, described how the treaty monitoring system had evolved, increasing its potential to contribute to domestic change (an augmented version was later published – see Doek, 2011). Events in Wales following the second UK reporting round had amply demonstrated this potential. The Group and its partners had engaged with remarkable success with an (admittedly politically largely receptive) Welsh Government. Both *Righting the Wrongs* and *Stop, Look, Listen* set out clear recommendations for government, drawing on a wide pool of external expertise from local to international levels. Further, *Stop, Look, Listen* was one of a number of non-governmental resources to which the UN Committee could turn and which could influence its *Concluding Observations* issued in the joint third and fourth reporting rounds (UN Committee *CO*, 2008).

At the same time, engagement with the UN process helped the Group to develop its collective thinking and grow more confident in its inter-actions with government. Responding to *Rights to Action* in 2004, the Group had urged the Welsh Government to ensure greater prominence for the seven core aims and to make a national plan of action with adequate monitoring processes (Croke and Crowley, 2007). When, in response to the 2008 *Concluding Observations*, the Welsh Government published *Getting it Right* (2009b), its five-year 'rolling action plan', the Group was a natural constituency to be represented on the UNCRC Implementation Support Network, which was set up to oversee and advise on progress in implementing the plan. The Group pressed for early review to embrace important omissions from the initial plan. These omissions included the lack of a budget for the process, lack of an adequate monitoring arrange-ment, and lack of 'buy-in' across government, as well as short time-scales and concentration on actions already in train.

Another point of impact has been in the search for ways to make children visible in budgets, a matter regularly referred to by the UN Committee in *Concluding Observations* on State Party reports, as well as featuring prominently in its *General Comment No. 5* (UN Committee *GC*, 2003: para. 51). A research report commissioned by Save the Children (Sefton, 2003) was presented to the Welsh Minister for Children, Jane Hutt, stimulating discussion about greater transparency of spending on children. The Welsh Government consequently commissioned an ana-lysis of financial provision for children within its budget for 2004/5 (WG, 2007b) which would enable it 'to comply with a responsibility under the [UNCRC] to report on the amount and percentage of national budgets spent on children' (WG, 2008).

While the analysis was described as 'fairly rudimentary' (Croke and Crowley, 2007), it was significant as the first attempt to identify spend-ing on children in Wales. Reporting to the UN Committee in 2007, the Welsh Government included its budgetary analysis (the only UK country to do so) and indicated planned future work to develop more sophisticated analysis. In March 2009 a statistical bulletin was published which presented estimates for the proportion to be spent on children in the period 2007/8 to 2010/11 (WG, 2009a). One of the sixteen priorities in *Getting it Right* is 'improving the transparency of budgeting for children and young people' (WG, 2009b). The National Assembly for Wales's Children and Young People Committee held an inquiry into the issue and reported in October 2009. This led to a Welsh Government task and finish group, including representation from the Group. Save the Children's report, *Children's Budgeting at the Local Level* (STC, 2009), impacted on the discussions and conclusions of the task and finish group. The Group then set about developing an advocacy strategy to hold the Welsh Government to account to deliver on its recommendations.

This and other examples, of which space constraints preclude mention here, illustrate the fact that when the opportunity arose in 2009 to create a general legislative measure of implementation for Wales, it was in a context of established dynamics involving policy advisers, politicians, officials, external activists and NGOs, with the Group playing a significant part variously as coordinator, facilitator, partner, lobbyist and conduit to the UN system itself. The creation of the Rights of Children and Young Persons (Wales) Measure 2011, to which we now turn, owes much to this context, as well as the 'three ps' of policy, politics and people described by Butler and Drakeford in this volume.

The Rights of Children and Young Persons (Wales) Measure 2011

The drafting stage

Following Rhodri Morgan's historic statement of the intention to explore 'the possibility of introducing a Measure to embed the principles of the [UNCRC] into law on behalf of Welsh children', the Group and the Children's Commissioner met with the First Minister to welcome the proposed Measure and emphasise its significance and importance.

The support of the Group and in particular the legal expertise of Jane Williams of the School of Law, Swansea University, was offered to give advice on the development of the legislation. The involvement of the Group in this way was notable for the government's willingness to engage with NGOs in the development of legislation, more usually a closed process in the iterative stages.

The summer and autumn of 2009 saw the initial stages of work on the proposed Measure. In November 2009 the Group was confident that the Measure appeared to be broad and encompassing, giving real hope that it would prove to be a ground-breaking and radical legislative Measure. It was set to be the first piece of children's human rights legislation in the UK, and a model for comprehensive incorporation of the UNCRC across all government functions.

Meanwhile, following Rhodri Morgan's retirement, political changes were occurring in the Welsh Government. A new First Minister, Carwyn Jones, was in office and a new Deputy Minister for Children, Huw Lewis. The Group was concerned that progression of the Measure might be seen as part of the previous incumbents' legacy, and that what was now effectively a 'new' government in Wales might wish to introduce different emphases. With that in mind the Group sought early discussions with Ministers and officials on progress on the Measure. However, the previously open process seemed to have changed course (see also Sullivan in this volume) and no further information was made available to the Group until the Welsh Government published its *Proposals for a Rights of Children and Young Persons (Wales) Measure* (2010) for public consultation on 17 March 2010.

Pre-legislative proposals for the Measure
The proposals that emerged differed significantly from the draft the Group expected to see on the basis of its understanding of the policy on the eve of Rhodri Morgan's retirement as First Minister. The document proposed that the Welsh Ministers and the First Minister must have 'due regard' to the UNCRC and its Optional Protocols only when they are carrying out 'relevant functions'. The proposals went on to explain that:

> The Measure says that a function (a legal power or duty) will only be a 'relevant' function if the Welsh Ministers have put it in the children's scheme which the Welsh Ministers must make (Section 2 of the Measure). Once a function is in the children's scheme, every time the Welsh Ministers do something using that function they will have to have 'due regard' to the UNCRC and its Optional Protocols. (WG, 2010: 10)

The impact of this duty of due regard was described as intending to ensure that Ministers 'think about' the rights and duties in the UNCRC and how they might be able to give further effect to them in carrying out particular functions in those 'areas where the rights and duties in the UNCRC and its Optional Protocols are most likely to make the biggest difference to the lives of children in Wales'. However, the consultation document went on:

This does not mean that we will ignore other areas; it just means that we think that the law should allow the Welsh Ministers to choose where to concentrate their efforts for the best result. Therefore, we think that the 'due regard' duty should apply only to functions which have been put in the children's scheme. (WG, 2010: 11)

The proposals went on to say that the functions to be included in the children's scheme would be subject to public consultation, including children and young people and the Children's Commissioner, and subject to the political scrutiny and agreement of the National Assembly for Wales. The document also included a proposal to look at extending the rights contained within the UNCRC to young adults, those aged between eighteen and twenty-five years. This was to reflect the existing policy framework in Wales, which guaranteed rights and entitlements for young adults up to the age of twenty-five.

Response to the draft proposals
The Group convened a number of meetings and discussions to plan the response to the government consultation. There was agreement that the 'administrative/parliamentary law' approach (see Williams, chapter 4 in this volume) should be supported: this was agreed to be a useful device and appropriate for a 'Wales only' law. However, to be truly effective, the duty must apply across the exercise by Welsh Ministers of *all* their functions. The narrow, 'sectoral' approach taken in the proposals would limit the application of 'due regard' to a few policies and programmes, and, given that the UNCRC was currently used as a basis for policy-making for children and young people in Wales, there was a real risk of the Measure adding nothing to the current position, or even backsliding from it.

Concurrently, the Group was aware that there was a genuine division of opinion within the Labour/Plaid Cymru coalition government about whether this duty should be pervasive or limited; statements to this effect were made in plenary sessions of the National Assembly, and the Deputy Minister was urged to agree to a commitment that the government would keep an open mind to developing a stronger, pervasive Measure (NAW, 2010a).

Outside Wales, the proposed Measure was attracting interest; the disappointment in the non-pervasive nature of the Measure was shared by the wider UK NGO community. The Rights of the Child UK (ROCK) coalition offered support by preparing a consultation response, as did Save the Children UK, and UNICEF planned to submit a response which would support the call for a stronger, pervasive Measure. The Group felt therefore that all the signs pointed toward a real prospect of achieving improvement in the Measure if the collective responses from the children's rights advocacy community were strong and consistent.

Activities undertaken in response to the public consultation
With this in mind the Group prepared a strong consultation response but also encouraged and supported submissions from individual organisations represented on the Group, and supported a wider group of NGOs to do the same. During the public consultation period a number of other activities took place. The Children and Young People Committee, a cross-party committee of the National Assembly, took the unusual step of scrutinising the pre-legislative proposals and invited the Children's Commissioner for Wales and the Group to present evidence on the government proposals. The Group's concerns regarding the non-pervasive nature of the proposed Measure were taken up by the committee and communicated to the Welsh Government (see further Sullivan and Jones, chapter 2 in this volume).

An 'expert' seminar held at the School of Law, Swansea University, brought together Wales, UK and international experts to debate the implications of the proposed Measure. A report from this meeting was submitted as a further response to the public consultation.

The Partnership Support Unit hosted by the Welsh Local Government Association convened two public consultation days on behalf of the government. Over 150 people attended, representing the twenty-two children and young people planning partnerships and statutory and non-statutory bodies. Separate sessions were facilitated on the days by Funky Dragon to support children and young people to contribute to the consultation.

Clear support for a pervasive Measure
Some seventy-five written responses were submitted in response to the consultation. The majority of respondents favoured the 'due regard duty' but over 75 per cent disagreed that this should apply only to 'relevant functions': there was a shared, clear and consistent support for a 'pervasive' Measure.

The legislative process
On 14 June 2010, the proposed Rights of Children and Young Persons (Wales) Measure was laid before the National Assembly, marking the beginning of the legislative process. The government stated it had listened to concerns about the sectoral 'relevant functions' aspect of the early proposals and the Measure would now be applied across governmental

departments. However, the duty on the Ministers was now to have due regard to the UNCRC in making any 'relevant decision'. Section 1(2) of the proposed Measure described a relevant decision as 'a decision of a strategic nature about how to exercise any function exercisable by the Welsh Ministers'. This was greeted with dismay by the Group and many others. The feeling was that the government had exchanged one kind of sectoralism for another, and only increased the confusion about which decisions, actions and government processes were to fall under the term 'strategic'. It was felt that both these formulae were intended to contain the impact of the due regard duty within what officials viewed as 'manageable', and to minimise the perceived burden of change.

Stage 1: committee consideration of general principles
Stage 1 of the legislative process began on 17 June 2010, and it was allotted to the National Assembly's Legislation Committee No. 5 to undertake a consideration of the general principles of the Measure. At their first evidence session with the Deputy Minister, the committee members were particularly exercised with the concept of 'strategic' decisions and questioned the Deputy Minister at length as to his definition of the term and what this would actually mean in practice; what difference the Measure would make to the lives of children and young people, and the accountability and scrutiny of the actions of government. The Deputy Minister and officials at this stage did not demonstrate a very clear understanding of the arguments or appear to convince the committee members that the proposed Measure was the robust and radical measure it was claimed to be.

The Group was invited to the next evidence session. Members of the Group took the opportunity to press the case for a fully pervasive application of the duty to have due regard to the UNCRC, arguing that, as then-drafted, the Measure would not add anything to the current legal and policy position in Wales. Rather, the Measure should have the effect of making the UNCRC a ubiquitous reference point for the exercise of Welsh Ministerial functions – similar in effect to the principles of sustainable development and equality of opportunity to which Welsh Ministers are obliged to pay due regard under sections 77 and 79 of the Government of Wales Act 2006. Then it would be clear to all that the UNCRC was to be considered, without embarking on diversionary debate as to whether any decision was 'strategic'. The Group argued that officials' fears about managing a pervasive duty were in practice misplaced, the concept of 'due' regard being sufficient to prevent trivial assertions of a duty to consider the UNCRC when it clearly had no purchase. The Group also opposed the potential inclusion of eighteen- to twenty-five-year-olds on the grounds that the UNCRC was created to give special protection to those under eighteen and it was inappropriate (if not impossible) to extend rights designed for children to young adults whose needs are different and whose rights are already protected under adult human rights legislation (Legislation Committee No. 5, 2010a).

The Group was able to test its position at a second expert seminar in July 2010, again hosted by Swansea University, this time also attended by Assembly Members and government officials. The majority view was that the Measure in its current form remained problematic. It was agreed that the legal academics present would coordinate preparation of a draft amendment to be offered to the Legislation Committee.

The legislative process continued after the summer break seeing the committee taking evidence from teaching unions, advocacy services and children and young people from Funky Dragon who made it very clear that they considered *all* government decisions at both a national and a local level to have an impact on children's rights.

The ad hoc lawyers group, now comprising academic lawyers from Swansea and Bangor universities and a widely respected private practitioner from a Welsh law firm, attended the penultimate Legislation Committee evidence session. They presented a detailed case which included examples drawn from the second Swansea seminar, and were able to offer amendments that would render the Measure pervasive.[1]

The final committee evidence session saw the Deputy Minister again in front of the committee, whose members, across parties, continued to challenge the government to 'deliver on their principles' and on the initial intentions to give further effect to the UNCRC in law as stated back in July 2009.

Stage 1 report
The committee's report, published in October 2010, endorsed the general principles of the proposed Measure, noting the support both in and outside government for this legislation. However, the committee believed that the proposed Measure required strengthening in order to meet the intended policy objective of improving its rights-based approaches for children and young persons. The committee made a number of recommendations to the government which clearly reflected the evidence submitted by the Group and the associated ad hoc lawyers group. This was a real result for the activities of the Group and the full range of organisations that had worked together to inform, advise and influence the legislative scrutiny process.

However, the political process still needed to find a way to ensure the recommendations would be accepted.

Stage 1 debate in plenary on general principles (November 2010)

The proposed Measure and the committee's report were debated in plenary session on 2 November 2010. The Deputy Minister's speech made clear his willingness to seek resolutions to enable the legislation to be strengthened, acknowledging that more clarity was needed regarding 'strategic decisions'. He stated that there was 'a perception that the duty will not be effective at embedding the consideration of the UNCRC into the Assembly Government's work. I accept that that is a concern.' He also stated his intention to explore further resolution in the next stage of the legislative process (NAW, 2010b).

The debate that followed illustrated the strength of cross-party support for a pervasive and effective Measure. It seemed this support had been maintained and had grown during the legislative process. The views of the Group and its associates were mentioned by a number of Assembly Members and its influence was clear. Following this debate, the question was whether government amendments would be brought forward and if not, which other Assembly Members might be willing to table amendments.

Stage 2 committee consideration of amendments

In the event, government amendments were tabled for consideration at the meeting on 25 November 2010 of the Legislation Committee. The Deputy Minister explained that these amendments removed the phrase 'decisions of a strategic nature' and ensured the 'due regard duty will apply directly to the exercise by the Welsh Ministers and the First Minister of any of their functions' (Legislation Committee No. 5, 2010c). So the proposed Measure was now truly pervasive. The only concession the government requested was a two-year phased introduction to the implementation of the Measure enabling the government to plan, prepare and develop its expertise in the new duty.

Stage 3 and 4 plenary consideration of amendments and passing of the Measure

On 18 January 2011, the National Assembly considered the amendments to the Measure. During the debate Andrew Davies AM stated:

> I will say that I think that this is a historic piece of legislation and I pay tribute to all those involved – the Deputy Minister and those who have

taken part in the scrutiny. I am particularly pleased that the Deputy Minister has listened to the considered points that have been made through the process of scrutiny, particularly by a wide range of organisations. I pay particular tribute to the UNCRC monitoring group, which I think gave high-quality evidence. (NAW, 2011)

The Deputy Minister, Huw Lewis, then moved the motion to 'approve the Proposed Rights of Children and Young Persons (Wales) Measure' and stated:

Today marks a big step forward in realising the rights of children and young people in Wales. As I have said before, I am proud to be able to present to the Assembly what I consider to be a trailblazing piece of law. It will take Wales's commitment to its children and young people further than any other country in the UK has managed to do. (NAW, 2011)

Stage 4

On January 18 2011, the Rights of Children and Young Persons (Wales) Measure was passed by the National Assembly for Wales. The Measure received Royal Approval on 16 March 2011, thereby becoming Welsh law and the first piece of human rights legislation for children in the United Kingdom.

Conclusion

Since 2002 the Wales UNCRC Monitoring Group has increased in size and strength, resulting in an increasing engagement of NGOs and academic institutions in developing understanding of the importance of the UNCRC. Capitalising on the power of the international framework, especially the UNCRC reporting process, the Group has developed a constructive, collaborative yet critical collective voice. This has contributed to significant changes to strategic policy-making for children in Wales, and to Wales becoming the first country within the UK to incorporate the UNCRC (within devolved limitations) into its domestic law.

The Group's strength lies in its strong repository of knowledge and multi-disciplinary expertise as well as its links to wider spheres of knowledge and influence both within Wales, across the UK and internationally. Its ability to publish robust evidence-based reports on the state of children's rights in Wales has contributed to external accountability. As demonstrated by the Group's influence during the legislative passage of the Measure, its credibility and authority has strengthened over time. Having a dedicated Group coordinator (funded by Save the Children) to service and coordinate the work of the Group has been instrumental to ensuring its continuity and momentum and, put simply, in making sure that the Group's collective work plan is delivered effectively. Factors critical to the Group's success have included its decision to retain its strong independent role at the same time as engaging in direct and regular dialogue with Welsh Government and the National Assembly for Wales, its accumulation of knowledge on children's human rights and its ability to advise on how to progress a children's rights perspective across the machinery of government.

The Group will continue to monitor and hold government to account for implementation of the UNCRC. The key priorities for the Group leading up to reporting to the UN Committee in 2014 will be: carrying out a cycle of rolling reporting against the *Concluding Observations 2008* and the Wales national action plan on children's rights; holding seminars and encouraging dialogue with government; producing reports on current children's rights violations, and lobbying duty-bearers to respond to them. The Group will continue its dialogue with government and professionals on the best way to promote knowledge and understanding of the UNCRC across Wales. The Group is also determined to build on the legislative foundation of the Rights of Children and Young Persons (Wales) Measure, continuing to act as critical friend and offering support through capacity building and interpretation on the UNCRC. No-one should underestimate the challenges of promoting human rights within public administration in a time of austerity, and part of the Group's mission must be to demonstrate that human rights based approaches are in fact most needed and most relevant in such times.

References

Croke, R. and Crowley, A. (eds) (2006): *Righting the Wrongs: The Reality of Children's Rights in Wales* (Cardiff: Save the Children).

—— (eds) (2007): *Stop, Look, Listen: The Road to Realising Children's Rights in Wales* (Cardiff: Save the Children).

Doek, E. J. (2011): 'The CRC: dynamics and direction of monitoring its implementation', in A. Invernizzi and J. Williams (eds), *The Human Rights of Children: From Visions to Implementation* (Farnham: Ashgate), pp. 99–116.

Filali, K. (2008): personal communication to the authors.

Funky Dragon (2007): *Our Rights, Our Story* (Swansea: Funky Dragon).

Legislation Committee No. 5 (2010a): Record of Proceedings, 1 July (Cardiff: National Assembly for Wales).

—— (2010b): Record of Proceedings, 7 October (Cardiff: National Assembly for Wales).

—— (2010c): Record of Proceedings, 25 November (Cardiff: National Assembly for Wales).

NAW (National Assembly for Wales) (2010a): Record of Proceedings, 24 March (Cardiff: National Assembly for Wales).

—— (2010b): Record of Proceedings, 2 November (Cardiff: National Assembly for Wales).

—— (2011): Record of Proceedings, 18 January (Cardiff: National Assembly for Wales).

Sefton, T. (2003): *A Child's Portion: Public Spending on Children in Wales* (Wales: Save the Children).

STC (Save the Children) (2009): *Children's Budgeting at the Local Level* (Cardiff: Save the Children).

WG (Welsh Government) (2004): *Children and Young People: Rights to Action* (Cardiff: Welsh Assembly Government).

—— (2007a) *Rights in Action: Implementing Children and Young People's Rights in Wales* (Cardiff: Welsh Assembly Government).

—— (2007b): *Financial Provision for Children within the Assembly Government Budget: A Technical Note*, February 2007 (Cardiff: Welsh Assembly Government).

—— (2008): *Financial Provision for Children within the Assembly Government Budget: A Summary* (Cardiff: Welsh Assembly Government).

—— (2009a): *Financial Provision for Children within the Welsh Assembly Government Budget* (Cardiff: Welsh Assembly Government).

—— (2009b): *Getting it Right 2009: United Nations Convention on the Rights of the Child. A 5-year rolling Action Plan for Wales setting out key priorities and actions to be undertaken by the Welsh Assembly Government in response to the Concluding Observations of the UN Committee on the Rights of the Child 2008* (Cardiff: Welsh Assembly Government).

—— (2010): *Proposals for a Rights of Children and Young Persons (Wales) Measure*, consultation document number 082/2010, 17 March (Cardiff: Welsh Assembly Government).

Note

1. CR 23, response from School of Law, Swansea University, referenced in the Legislation Committee's Stage 1 committee report (2010b: 69).

CHAPTER 4

The Rights of Children and Young Persons (Wales) Measure 2011 in the context of the international obligations of the UK

Jane Williams

Introduction

The Rights of Children and Young Persons (Wales) Measure 2011 is an important enactment. Its importance goes well beyond its territorial application. Within the UK it is the first general legislative measure of implementation of the UNCRC, thereby delivering in Wales a clear, positive response to the recommendations of the UN Committee in successive *Concluding Observations* on UK State Party reports (UN Committee *CO*, 2002; 2008). It is a constitutional enactment: it constrains and directs the exercise of governmental power. As such it demonstrates the maturity of the Assembly as the parliament to which Welsh Government is accountable. Its process was characterised by an unusual degree of engagement between key political actors within the Assembly and external stakeholders. It attracted cross-party support, building on consensus achieved earlier within the Assembly (Butler and Drakeford, chapter 1 in this volume). The Measure gives legal force to the proposition that promotion of and respect for the human rights of children and young people are fundamental principles of devolved governance in Wales. This is consistent with the view that children's rights have become an emblem of Welsh devolution (Rees, 2010).

This chapter explains the law contained in the Measure against the backdrop of the UK's international obligations and the UK's existing equalities and human rights enactments. It considers the implications of the Measure for processes supporting Welsh Ministerial decisions. It situates the new law and its implications in the context of the fused jurisdiction of England and Wales and ventures some speculation on institutional developments that might follow.

Giving 'further effect' to the UNCRC in devolved governance

The long title of the Measure states that it gives 'further effect' in Wales to the UNCRC – the same phrase that was used in the long title of the Human Rights Act 1998, which gave 'further effect' throughout the UK to the European Convention on Human Rights. The phrase acknowledges the pre-existing legal effect of the respective treaties by virtue of the UK's ratification. Ratification attracts the rule of international law that State Party obligations must be performed in good faith in respect of the State Party's entire territory (Articles 26 and 29 of the Vienna Convention on the Law of Treaties 1969). On ratification, the UK as State Party undertook to take 'all appropriate legislative, administrative, and other measures' for implementation (Article 4 UNCRC). The UK as State Party remains accountable for implementation in international law even though many matters critical to UNCRC implementation are devolved within the UK (Williams, 2011, 2012). The UNCRC's mechanism for enforcement is a reporting and monitoring system with the UN Committee as the treaty-monitoring body, extended by a 2011 Optional Protocol to embrace the possibility of individual petition similar to that which exists for the other specialist UN human rights treaties (Van Bueren, 2011). Over the years since the UNCRC entered into force, a large volume of guidance, recommendations and commentary have emerged from the UNCRC system to assist States Parties in identifying the kind of 'legislative, administrative and other measures' required. This body of advice and interpretation has been referred as the 'jurisprudence' of the UNCRC (Doek, 2011). The UN Committee's *General Comment No. 5* on general measures of implementation (2003) recommends, among other things, incorporation of the UNCRC in domestic legal systems, judicial enforcement of all the rights set out in the UNCRC, and mainstreaming in policy and decision-making processes using suitable impact assessment and evaluative tools.

It is a matter for each State Party's internal law how effect is given to the treaty obligations: international law simply requires that effect be given. In the UK the position of the UNCRC, aside from the Measure, is that throughout the UK the courts may use it (like any other treaty by which the UK is bound in international law) as a point of reference in developing the common law and in interpreting statutes. However, the courts will not directly enforce a treaty provision, nor use it as a standard against which to decide on the legality of any UK statute law or government action, unless provision is made in internal or 'domestic' law. Before the Measure, legislation setting up the UK's four Children's Commissioners (at devolved level for Wales, Scotland and Northern Ireland and at UK level for England) required each commissioner to have regard to the UNCRC (Williams, 2005). The Measure is the first enactment within the UK giving broad effect to the UNCRC across governmental functions. It does so by providing, first, a legal requirement to mainstream the requirements of the UNCRC; secondly, a duty to promote awareness of the UNCRC; and thirdly, domestic mechanisms for accountability.

Legislative competence

That such a law could be passed by the National Assembly for Wales is, at first sight, surprising. Not only does State Party accountability rest with the UK Government, but also England and Wales continue, despite devolution, to share a legal system: they are a 'single jurisdiction'. On the other hand the Welsh Ministers and/or Assembly already had powers to implement international obligations including but not limited to the making of regulations under section 2 of the European Communities Act 1972. The case of *R (Horvath) v Secretary of State for Environment, Food and Rural Affairs* ECJ Case C-428/07 had demonstrated that difference in implementation of EU treaty obligations in Wales and England was acceptable, provided it was in accordance with the internal law of the UK, and the methods chosen were proper in terms of the EU obligation concerned. The UK Government's 2009 Green Paper, Rights and Responsibilities, recognised that many of the 'key policy levers' for UNCRC implementation were controlled by devolved institutions (TSO, 2009: para. 3.70). When considering how to construct provisions 'embedding' the UNCRC in law as envisaged in Rhodri Morgan's July 2009 announcement, there was thus no objection in principle to divergence. The key questions were whether the National Assembly for Wales had legislative competence pursuant to the Government of Wales Act 2006 to make an operative law, and if so, what kind of obligations, remedies or other provisions that law should contain.

A basis of legislative competence had to be found in Schedule 5 to the Government of Wales Act 2006, since at that time the broader provisions of Schedule 7 had not come into force. Schedule 5 had been amended by the National Assembly for Wales (Legislative Competence) (Social Welfare and Other Fields) Order 2008 (SI 2008/3132), to empower the National Assembly for Wales to enact Measures concerned (among other things) with 'cooperation and arrangements by and between public authorities' to ensure 'well-being'. Crucially, 'well-being' for this purpose was defined as including 'access to rights'. Although not drafted with a view to enacting the kind of provisions ultimately included in the Measure, this offered scope to adopt a suggestion advocated by the Wales UNCRC Monitoring Group (see Aspinwall and Croke, chapter 3 in this volume). The suggestion was that a duty should be imposed on Welsh Ministers, enforceable in administrative law, aimed at promoting positive action by government to ensure the requirements of the UNCRC would be brought into the Welsh Government's decision-making processes.

Duty to have 'due regard'

The core concept is set out in section 1 of the Measure which states that when exercising 'any of their functions' Welsh Ministers must have due regard to:

a) Part 1 of the UNCRC;
b) Articles 1 to 7 of the Optional Protocol on the involvement of children in armed conflict, except Article 6(2);
c) Articles 1 to 10 of the Optional Protocol on the sale of children, child prostitution and child pornography;
d) the treaty provisions listed are those which set out rights and obligations: provisions of merely procedural effect (such as in Part 2 of the UNCRC on reporting to the UN Committee) are not included.

The 'due regard' formula has the effect that the listed provisions become statutory criteria framing the legality of Welsh Ministers' actions. The listed provisions do not have superior status over any other law, nor are they given priority over other factors that Welsh Ministers must consider. They simply become part of what Welsh Ministers must think about before exercising their functions. An indication of how this works lies in court decisions arising from the UK equalities enactments, now the Equality Act 2010. There, the courts have interpreted 'due regard' to mean that the decision-maker must attend to substance (as opposed to conducting a mere 'tick-box' exercise), and must be properly informed and aware of what must be considered before and at the time of making a decision; that the duty 'must be exercised in substance, with rigour and an open mind'; that it must be 'integrated within the discharge of the public functions' of the decision-maker and that it is a continuing duty, requiring to be kept under review.[1] Such requirements are consistent with the administrative measures recommended by the UN Committee in its *General Comment No. 5* (2003) on general measures of implementation. Review and revision of existing decision-making procedures and investment in training of the civil service are necessary to ensure compliance with this due regard duty.

To accommodate the necessary preparation, the duty is phased in, applying from May 2012 to decisions about policy and legislation, and from May 2014 to the exercise of any function. In fact, the 'due regard' duty requires ongoing review and a practice of progressive realisation: it is not a question of one implementation exercise, but of constructing approaches for continuous implementation.

Interpreting the requirements of the UNCRC

While the equalities precedents help us to anticipate the import of the 'due regard' duty, they do not help us imagine how the UN texts will be interpreted. The public sector equality duty in section 149 of the Equality Act 2010 specifies its own objectives: elimination of discrimination, equality of opportunity and fostering good relations. By contrast the Measure requires due regard to be had to some fifty-eight articles derived from three legal instruments spanning matters as diverse as the right to life, encouragement of mass media to support children's access to their rights, minimum requirements for juvenile justice, the right to play, non-discrimination, support for families bringing up children, sale and exploitation of children and restriction of under-eighteens' involvement in armed conflict. Authoritative interpretation of these provisions can only come from a court. In contrast to the Human Rights Act 1998, the Measure does not provide for an individual legal claim for a rights violation. Thus the only likely legal challenge would be by application for judicial review of a decision or action alleged to have been taken without due regard to one or more of the listed provisions. Because they are set out in the Schedule to the Measure, these provisions become domestic law to be interpreted by the courts as part of the law governing the exercise of devolved Welsh Ministerial functions. The ground is thus laid for the development of a Welsh 'municipal law of children's rights' (Mastermann, 2005).

On the other hand the myriad obstacles to mounting a successful application for judicial review mean that opportunities for judicial interpretation may in practice be few. Interpretation will instead fall substantially to civil servants and other groups and actors within what Tobin (2010) has referred to as an 'interpretive community'. Therein lies both a problem and an opportunity. The problem is the danger of subversion of meaning to other priorities or policies: as Tobin warns, 'advocates can be quick to offer interpretations that reflect personal preferences as to the nature of protection that the advocates think the rights in question *should* accord' (2010: 2). The opportunity is the scope for engagement between governmental and non-governmental actors, civil society and children and young people themselves in the development of an informed and shared understanding of, and commitment to, rights-based approaches to governance.

The Measure itself provides a structure which addresses, at least in part, both the problem and the opportunity. Section 2 requires the Welsh Ministers to make a scheme, to be known as 'the children's scheme', setting out the arrangements they have made or propose to make for the purpose of securing compliance with the duty to have due regard. Section 3 requires Welsh Ministers when making or revising this scheme to have regard to the outputs of the UN Committee (reports, studies, recommendations, etc.). The Welsh Ministers may also have regard to 'any other documents (whether or not issued by the UN Committee) and to any other matters which they consider to be relevant'. In addition the Welsh Ministers are required to 'involve' key external stakeholders, including the Children's Commissioner for Wales and children and young people themselves, in drawing up the children's scheme. These provisions seek to utilise the dynamic of the UNCRC (Doek, 2011) and give statutory compulsion for deliberative engagement. The ideal here is to develop a participative process 'by which the abstract formulations captured in the text of international human rights treaties are transformed into a common understanding of the measures required to secure their effective implementation' (Tobin, 2010: 50). Making this happen – even making it start to happen – is the central challenge in implementation of the Measure.

Accountability

This leads naturally to the question of accountability, discussed further in Part III of this volume. As well as the possibility of judicial review, the Measure makes provision for parliamentary and administrative monitoring. Section 4 requires submission of periodic reports to the National Assembly for Wales to complement the international monitoring process or in response to a request from the Assembly. The Children's Commissioner for Wales is already empowered to make inquiries into and report on the exercise by Welsh Ministers of their functions. Both the Assembly and the Children's Commissioner are thus obvious participants in the 'interpretive community'. Each can also offer opportunities for other stakeholders including children and young people to engage in the process. The depth and quality of engagement ought to be enhanced by action taken under section 5 of the Measure which imposes a specific duty to 'take such steps as are appropriate to promote knowledge and understanding amongst the public (including children) of the Convention and the Protocols' (thereby specifically supporting implementation of Article 42 of the UNCRC). It should be noted, however, that the baseline of knowledge and understanding of the UNCRC among the public at large is low (Aspinwall and Croke, chapter 3 in this volume).

Eighteen- to twenty-five-year-olds

Section 7 of the Measure requires Welsh Ministers to consider application of the duty to have due regard to the age group eighteen to twenty-five. This is a conceptually problematic proposition which compels consideration of whether provisions of the UNCRC are 'relevant' to persons in that age group. The Measure follows Article 1 of the UNCRC in stating that for its purposes 'child' means a person who has not attained the age of eighteen. As a drafting device this has attracted controversy from the time of negotiation onwards. As Cantwell (2011) argues and illustrates, it is inappropriate to refer to adolescents and older teenagers as 'children' and doing so carries a risk of infantilising persons in those older age groups, especially in relation to rights supportive of autonomy. While any age-based demarcation will inevitably produce anomalies, the use of the eleven to twenty-five age range in the Welsh *Extending Entitlement* policy (see Butler and Drakeford, chapter 1 in this volume) reflected both recognition of this problem and also the fact that for most young people in Wales the economic and social vulnerabilities of youth do not disappear on attaining the age of legal majority. Subsequent Welsh Government strategies explicitly linked to the values and principles of the UNCRC covered the whole age range from birth to twenty-five (for example *Rights to Action*: see Butler and Drakeford, chapter 1 in this volume).

When proposing the new law for the UNCRC in Wales, the Welsh Ministers did not want to lose the virtue of this special recognition of the needs of young adults. Yet application to young adults of provisions designed for 'children' seemed to some observers simply wrong-headed (see Aspinwall and Croke, chapter 3 in this volume). Responses to pre-legislative consultation and to evidence submitted in the course of legislative process were divided between those who took a 'legally correct' position about the scope of a Convention on the Rights of the *Child* and those who feared that without application in some form of the Measure to the eighteen to twenty-five age group there would be a risk that hard-won services for vulnerable young adults would be de-prioritised. Section 7 thus represents a compromise in which these issues are left to be teased out and negotiated in the course of public consultation with a view to application of the Measure with modifications if this seems appropriate.

Interface with other equalities and human rights laws in the UK

As stated above, anti-discrimination laws, latterly the Equality Act 2010, supplied a precedent for the 'due regard' formula. Implementation of the 'public sector equality duty' in section 149 of the 2010 Act had already started within the Welsh Government when the proposed Measure was in its legislative process, but little connection appears to have been made between the two streams of work, nor with existing machinery for promotion and enforcement of human rights and equalities generally. Apart from the fact that different teams of officials were responsible within the Welsh Government for the separate streams of work, pressure of time may have accounted in part for this lack of connection. There was also the potential complication that although responsibility for much implementation lies at the devolved level, the Equality Acts 2006 and 2010 and the Human Rights Act 1998 are ultimately the responsibility of the UK Government and UK Parliament. Building something new, specifically for the rights of children and young persons, falling clearly within Welsh devolved competence, would be far easier to handle than an attempt to promote child and young person-focused applications of existing provisions of the Equality Acts 2006 and 2010, which, with the exception of a very few provisions, apply to England, Wales and Scotland, or the Human Rights Act 1998, which is of UK-wide application.

However, these equalities and human rights enactments and the Measure share common underlying values in the notions of social justice, equality and human rights. Enforcement mechanisms in the earlier enactments are relevant to implementation of the Measure. Likewise the Measure will generate processes of potential utility in furthering the objectives of the equalities and human rights enactments. In the interests of efficiency and effectiveness, links should be made between these enactments at the stage of implementation. This was noted but not explored in any depth during legislative scrutiny of the Measure.[2]

Table 4.1 illustrates some common ground or similarity between the enactments in relation to the obligation of non-discrimination. Article 2 of the UNCRC, drawn into the law of Wales via the Measure, requires States Parties to respect and ensure to each child within their jurisdiction the rights set forth in the Convention without discrimination of any kind. The UNCRC's concept of discrimination embraces in substance most if not all the matters treated as 'protected characteristics' in the Equality Act 2010. Several articles of the UNCRC restate human rights already recognised as held by all persons, including children, and drawn into UK law via the

TABLE 4.1 Comparison of equalities provisions

	Section 149 Equality Act 2010 (public sector equality duty)	Rights of Children and Young Persons (Wales) Measure 2011 (UNCRC requirement: Article 2)	Human Rights Act 1998 ('Convention right': Article 14 ECHR)	Section 77 Government of Wales Act 2006 (equality duty)
Protected characteristics	Age, disability, gender reassignment, pregnancy and maternity, race, religion or belief, sex and sexual orientation	Child's or his or her parent's or legal guardian's race, colour, sex, language, religion, political or other opinion, national, ethnic or social origin, property, disability, birth or other status	Any ground such as sex, race, colour, language, religion, political or other opinion, national or social origin, association with a national minority, property, birth or other status	Unspecified: objective is the 'principle that there should be equality of opportunity for all people'
Scope of application	Public authorities must have due regard to the need to: a) eliminate discrimination, harassment, victimisation and other conduct rendered unlawful by the Act; b) advance equality of opportunity; c) foster good relations	Welsh Ministers must have due regard to Article 2 (and all other articles in Part I) UNCRC when exercising any function	Discrimination in access to any of the (ECHR) Convention rights is unlawful if done by a public authority (includes the courts, excludes UK Parliament)	Welsh Ministers must make appropriate arrangements with a view to ensuring their functions are exercised with due regard to the principle

Human Rights Act 1998: for example the rights to freedom of expression, association, religious freedom, life and liberty. Article 14 of the European Convention on Human Rights (ECHR) offers protection from discrimination in access to these and all rights and freedoms stated in the ECHR. To that extent the enforcement mechanisms of the Human Rights Act 1998 may in some cases be available in relation to discrimination in access to a right also stated in the UNCRC.

The requirements these different enactments impose are capable of being mutually supportive. For example, the 'need to advance equality', one of the general objectives stated in section 149 of the Equality Act 2010, expressly includes removing or minimising disadvantage associated with the protected characteristic, and taking steps to meet the needs of and encouraging participation in public life by persons sharing those characteristics. Since the 'relevant protected characteristics' include 'age' this could capture all those under eighteen, or sub-groups such as those above or below the age of criminal responsibility, or the legal age of consent; it could also include the capacity for specific actions, from standing for election to a community or local council, to access to medical treatment or purchasing a box of matches. Thus a public authority reviewing or administering such provisions could be obliged to pay due regard to the need to remove or minimise disadvantage to the younger age groups.

It would be wrong to suggest that this would throw doubt on all age-based restrictions and requirements. First, if the 'relevant protected characteristic' is age, under-eighteens are expressly excluded from the protection of the Equality Act 2010's prohibitions on discrimination, harassment and victimisation. This exclusion would protect many actions and decisions that disadvantage children solely on grounds of age. Secondly, the 2010 Act's general definition of discrimination exempts treatment which can be shown to be a 'proportionate means of achieving a legitimate aim'. Many age-based restrictions and requirements can be justified in this way: in UNCRC-speak, most obviously by reference to the best interests of the child (Article 3) or the right to protection from exploitation or abuse (Article 19). This approach represents an important conceptual step: once inequality of treatment based on age is recognised as engaging the human rights of under-eighteens, justification for unequal treatment must be found in human rights terms, using familiar human rights approaches to balancing conflicting interests. This is wholly supportive of the UNCRC's vision of the 'citizen child' (Doek, 2008; Van Bueren, 2011).

The duty in section 149 of the Equality Act 2010 is supplemented by specific duties prescribed in regulations made by the devolved governments in Wales and Scotland, and by the UK Government for England. For Wales the Equality Act 2010 (Statutory Duties) (Wales) Regulations 2011 (SI 2011/1064 (W. 155)) require public authorities to publish by April 2012 'equality objectives' designed to better perform the general duty, and to establish Strategic Equality Plans to support realisation of those object-ives. Nothing in these first regulations makes particular provision for age discrimination, for children with a relevant protected characteristic or for furtherance of requirements of the UNCRC. However, in future, the 'due regard' duty in the Measure would bite on the exercise of this regulation-making function of Welsh Ministers under the Equality Act 2010 so that arguably such provisions should at least be considered.

Compared with either the Equality Act 2010 or the Measure, the Human Rights Act 1998 provides very little prescription about administra-tive action to support its implementation. Section 6 of that Act makes much stronger provision than the 'due regard' duties, stating that it is unlawful for a public authority to act incompatibly with a (ECHR) Convention right. For Wales there is the additional injunction of the Government of Wales Act 2006, which puts beyond devolved competence any incompatible action. The principal enforcement mechanism is legal action under section 7 of the Human Rights Act 1998. Insofar as certain of the requirements of the UNCRC effectively restate rights already bestowed on European children by the European Convention on Human Rights, this can properly be seen as a domestic enforcement mechanism for the UNCRC. Furthermore, reference is increasingly made to the UNCRC by the European Court of Human Rights in Strasbourg when interpreting the European Convention on Human Rights (Van Bueren, 2008; Kilkelly, 1999). The same applies to interpretation of domestic legislation (Williams, 2007: n.1) and to deci-sions of the European Court of Justice interpreting EU law (Stalford and Drywood, 2011).

Implications for the legal system: institutional development

The Government of Wales Acts 1998 and 2006 provided for a Welsh Government drawn from and accountable to the directly elected National Assembly for Wales. Wider institutional development followed, with Wales-wide bodies exercising functions that were or would have been exer-cised by bodies spanning England and Wales: the Wales Audit Office and Public Services Ombudsman for Wales are but two examples. Some change has also occurred in administration of justice (the law courts, legal profes-sion and tribunals), with the establishment of administrative and mercan-tile courts in Wales and circuit boundary adjustment to create a circuit (a geographical area for administration of justice) comprising Wales alone. Further change can be anticipated on an incremental basis as the implications for the legal system of executive and legislative devolution are worked out.

By providing for judicial interpretation of the UNCRC in a Welsh context and by stimulating development of an 'interpretive community' for the UNCRC in Wales, the Measure adds to the case for increased specialisation within the legal system. Because of the administrative changes that have already occurred, any application for judicial review of Welsh Ministers' actions is likely to take place in Wales and to be heard by judges allocated to the Wales circuit in part for their special knowledge of or connection with Wales. It is too soon yet to anticipate judicial involvement in the 'interpretive community' outside of formal applications to court, but a standing advisory role for the judiciary, or at least senior legal counsel independent of the Welsh Government, would help to avoid some of the problems of dilution or subversion identified by Tobin (2010). There is value in the jurisprudential connections between the UNCRC, the Measure, equalities and human rights enactments, the ECHR and EU law in implementation of each and all of them, but rigorous, *legal* analysis is essential to understand and deploy this interconnectedness.

Conclusion

It is hoped that this chapter has demonstrated the truth of its opening assertion that the Rights of Children and Young Persons (Wales) Measure 2011 is an important enactment. It has been possible only briefly to touch upon its significant implications. Later chapters will examine the Measure's potential to influence Welsh Ministerial decisions impacting on the real lives of children in Wales. At the time of writing, this 'small but clever' (WO, 2009) law of Wales is beginning to attract interest across the globe. While the Measure is rooted in home-grown policy on children and young people, its implementation is inextricably connected with law and governance at all levels, from the local through European regional to global. It has potential to contribute to development of interpretive and advocacy communities engaged in the common purpose of implementation of the rights of children everywhere.

References

Cantwell, N. (2011): 'Are children's rights still human?', in A. Invernizzi and J. Williams (eds), *The Human Rights of Children: From Visions to Implementation* (Farnham: Ashgate), pp. 37–60.

Doek, J. (2008): 'Foreword', in A. Invernizzi and J. Williams (eds), *Children and Citizenship* (London: Sage), pp. xii–xvii.

—— (2011): 'Dynamics and directions of monitoring and implementation', in A. Invernizzi and J. Williams (eds), *The Human Rights of Children: From Visions to Implementation* (Farnham: Ashgate), pp. 99–116.

Funky Dragon (2007): *Our Rights, Our Story* (Swansea: Funky Dragon).

Kilkelly, U. (1999): *The Child and the European Convention on Human Rights* (Dartmouth: Ashgate).

Mastermann, R. (2005): 'Taking the Strasbourg Jurisprudence into account: developing a municipal law of human rights under the Human Rights Act', *International and Comparative Law Quarterly*, 54/4, 907–31.

Rees, O. (2010): 'Dealing with individual cases: an essential role for national human rights institutions for children?', *International Journal of Children's Rights*, 18/3, 417–36.

Stalford, H. and Drywood, E. (2011): 'Using the CRC to inform EU law and policy-making', in A. Invernizzi and J. Williams, *The Human Rights of Children: From Visions to Implementation* (Farnham: Ashgate), pp. 199–218.

Tobin, J. (2010): 'Seeking to persuade: a constructive approach to human rights treaty interpretation', *Harvard Human Rights Review*, 23, 1–50.

TSO (The Stationery Office) (2009): *Rights and Responsibilities: Developing our Constitutional Framework*, Ministry of Justice, Cm. 7577 (London: The Stationery Office).

Van Bueren, G. (2008): *Child Rights in Europe: Convergence and Divergence in Judicial Protection* (Strasbourg: Council of Europe).

—— (2011): 'Acknowledging children as international citizens: a child-sensitive communication mechanism for the Convention on the Rights of the Child', in A. Invernizzi and J. Williams, *The Human Rights of Children: From Visions to Implementation* (Farnham: Ashgate), pp. 117–32.

Wales Office (2009): 'This is Wales'. Available at *http://www.walesoffice.gov.uk/about/wales/* (accessed 25 June 2012).

Williams, J. (2005): 'Effective government structures for children? The UK's four Children's Commissioners', *Child and Family Law Quarterly*, 17, 37–53.

—— (2007): 'Incorporating children's rights: the divergence in law and policy', *Legal Studies*, 27, 261–87.

—— (2011): 'Multi-level governance and the UNCRC', in A. Invernizzi and J. Williams (eds), *The Human Rights of Children: From Visions to Implementation* (Farnham: Ashgate), pp. 239–62.

—— (2012): 'General legislative measures of implementation: individual claims, "public officer's law" and a case study on the UNCRC in Wales', *International Journal of Children's Rights*, 20, 224–40.

Notes

1. *R (Brown) v Secretary of State for Work and Pensions* [2008] EWHC 3158 per Scott Baker LJ.
2. CR 23, response from School of Law, Swansea University, referenced in the Legislation Committee's Stage 1 committee report, October 2010.

PART II

Making it work: realising children's rights in selected policy areas

CHAPTER 5

What is the value of a right if it is never afforded?

Kevin Fitzpatrick

Introduction

The Rights of Children and Young Persons (Wales) Measure 2011 places a duty on Welsh Ministers, when exercising their functions, to have 'due regard' to the requirements of the UNCRC. It is entirely laudable, and those involved in securing this new Measure must be hugely congratulated for securing yet another first for Wales, in their efforts to build on the existing rights-based approach towards policy for children and young people and to strengthen their position in Welsh society. However, what is not clear is how the listed provisions will be interpreted:

> the myriad obstacles to mounting a successful application for judicial review mean that opportunities for *judicial* interpretation may in practice be few. Interpretation will instead fall substantially to civil servants and other groups and actors within what Tobin (2010) has referred to as an 'interpretive community'. Therein lies both a problem and an opportunity. (Williams, chapter 4 in this volume; my emphasis)

A problem *and* an opportunity. Part of the problem lies in what Simone Weil describes as the abstractness of speaking about inalienable rights, and the mediocrity of the very notion of rights (1977: 236). The opportunity lies in understanding why Weil says this, why Rush Rhees (2000: 10) is so clear that we cannot legislate for the removal of injustice, and even less so for the promotion of justice; but the opportunity, most of all, lies in reacting, so that justice for children and young people will actually follow the adoption of the Measure.

The core question here is: if this mediocrity and the poverty of our expression of rights go unnoticed, especially by those who would bring interpretation to them, would it be damaging, possibly fatal to the aspirations of all those looking to the enactment of the Measure for hope and change? This chapter is concerned with the idea of bringing justice to young people through the provision of rights, by giving legal force to fundamental principles, and so will examine some conceptual issues underpinning that idea. I will argue that there are, inter alia, two vitally important points which must be addressed alongside the introduction of the Measure if it is not to fail in its intent. First, fundamental principles inherently involve the notion of obligation which must be understood to be primary, standing above the language of rights. Secondly, in order that those in the 'interpretive community' can have voices of authority to speak about justice (not just about rights) they must have already demonstrated their eligibility by the lives they have led.

The notion of obligation and the poverty of the notion of rights

The introduction of legal instruments, supposedly affording equal rights, is no guarantee of equal outcomes, and can even be used to reinforce existing inequality and discrimination if not used wisely or if perverted wilfully. This is partly why we cannot legislate for the removal of injustice – saying does not make it so, and just because a law appears on the statute books does nothing to guarantee its enforcement, nor does it guarantee access to justice through it.

Specific examples can illustrate the point: in seeking to avoid their duties under the Disability Discrimination Act, some companies decided not to make the necessary adjustments to the fabric of their stores but chose instead to create a 'fighting fund' to counter legal cases, if any were brought against them. In other areas where the law applies, health and safety rules were used as a 'false excuse' to exclude disabled people from events or services. The details are less important than the fact that attempts are made and strategies developed to circumvent anti-discrimination law, thus denying people their rights under that law. The problem will not be resolved by thinking these are just practical exceptions: laws and institutions are important, but enshrining in statute the right to life, to protection from violence, to shelter (warmth), to medical attention, to the meeting of physical needs, but also to liberty, education, a moral and personal life, identity, a name (and all the things which, if denied, can harm a human being without harming them physically) will come to nothing, especially if we fail to notice that something fundamental is being missed in the way we speak about rights.

A confusion of language and ideas can appear and give rise to discrepancies between adopting legal rights, and outcomes based on their recognition. For Weil, one critical element of the continuing confusion lies with the notion of 'obligation' (there are other notions that confuse the issue, but for reasons of space, the focus here is foremost on the notion of obligation).

We immediately recognise that speaking about rights means also speaking of responsibilities, duties, obligations: our discourse about rights would otherwise be empty. This is not to say we have rights on the one hand, and obligations on the other – that is to speak only from different points of view, as Weil (1987) points out; in social relations, from one person's point of view, others have rights. This person in turn, when seen from the point of view of others, has rights when those others recognise that they have obligations towards this person.

For example, we can see that the Measure and the UNCRC reflect the idea that, at some level, everyone should accept the 'rights' that are enumerated there 'belong' to young people just because of who they are – that is young human beings. That sense of, we might say, prior acceptance, gives an indication of how obligations are not a consequence of law, but rather the other way round. Indeed, such laws would be meaningless if, in the first place, no-one at all accepted the fundamental obligation to others just in virtue of being human.

For Weil, this one universal, immutable, unconditional obligation is not based in anything but is recognised by everyone (except when it is attacked out of self-interest or some other reason). The obligation is sufficient of itself: no other condition is needed, not even recognition by the individual to whom the obligation is owed. Even if an individual does not or cannot recognise (whether through poverty of education, severe disability, deep social exclusion, or any other reason) that they are owed a depth of respect simply and solely by being human, this does nothing to diminish the obligation of others towards them. From this one obligation to the human being as a human being, flow others that find expression, however clumsily, in our expression of positive rights.

Thus we can see now that the notion of obligations comes before that of rights; the notion of rights is subordinate and relative to the notion of obligation. Obligations are not based on laws, customs or conventions, all of which may change. Obligations cannot change: they remain independent of conditions. We may feel ready to accept that our discourse on rights must, necessarily, include the notions of duty and obligation. But more than this, we must also be clear that obligations stand above rights, stand outside the domain of rules and regulations, transcending ordinary law.

We can see also that here we engage in necessarily moral discourse: what one ought to do. This is where the personal enters our moral judgements: the question is 'what should *I* do?' or 'how should I act/react/behave?' And we speak of absolute principles involving statements of an absolute kind: '*no-one* should do this/that/behave that way', or, as we saw above, '*everyone* should accept'. It is then an injustice that anyone should be without protection from harm, without shelter, food, water and other basic needs. Universal human rights can be seen as statements of basic needs or interests, statements that invoke the ideals of justice and equality. When a community accepts through political commitment (for example the new Measure) a certain ideal of justice and equality, then that acceptance is an integral part of a social contract which presupposes a minimum standard of life, a threshold below which it is intolerable for any human being to fall in that society or community. But more than any given social contract, which could after all subvert as easily as serve human well-being, it is a statement of what human life should be like: the human right is therefore the out-come of the press for social justice.

The force of fundamental principles

As Weil points out, the relationship between obligations and rights is asymmetrical, and the one precedes the other:

> A right is not effectual by itself, but only in relation to the obligation to which it corresponds, the effective exercise of a right springing not from the individual who possesses it, but from other[s] who consider themselves as being under a certain obligation. (1987: 3)

Likewise, she observes: 'An obligation which goes unrecognised . . . loses none of the full force of its existence. A right which goes unrecognised by anybody is not worth very much' (ibid.).

What is worse is that those rights may be dismissed. For Weil, a crime is committed if the very existence of the obligation here is denied (if, for example, it is demeaned by those who dismiss cultural sensitivity as 'political correctness gone mad', or who dress up and deliver such obligations as 'unrealistic' for reasons of cost, or who view them as merely a form of 'extreme liberalism', or other, similar, objections). But if we put the question in general terms:

> nobody is of the opinion that any man is innocent if, possessing food himself in abundance, and finding someone on his doorstep three parts dead from hunger, he brushes past without giving him anything. (Weil, 1987: 6)

That is an instance of the respect each one deserves in the same measure: the respect solely for being human.

Other people do attack this fundamental right out of self-interest, or dismiss or ignore it. So what is the real force of the promotion of and respect for the human rights of children and young people, if no-one affords them their rights; or if they are brushed past, ignored, disparaged, or trampled on. What good is there then in granting them 'rights', or trying to promote them, even by legal mechanism?

There are physical needs, like hunger, but as the UNCRC recognises, there are others, too, such as the need for liberty, access to the beauty of art or music, and the need for a permanent, loving family life. A child's physical needs can be met but how is a child to thrive without a family life? That is the difficulty: having a right to life, viewed from one perspective as the most fundamental of rights, is meaningless to those experiencing war, famine, or insidious attack. Having the right to vote, for example, comes to nothing for those alienated from society who have no chance to have a home, a living income, to exercise their franchise in any meaningful way. The question then is how to ensure the introduction of the Measure to have 'due regard' for the UNCRC comes to something meaningful?

The force of fundamental principles lies in the absolute nature of such principles: the torture of children is always wrong, for example. We speak of a right of children not to suffer cruelty, but that is to say, anyone who has the power to effect change has an obligation not to stand by and do nothing if a child is being abused or tortured. The nature of the moral judgement that this is always wrong is of the form: 'it is wrong for me or anyone else to do this'. This, as discussed above, is what makes it absolute. It transcends law because even if a law were delivered onto the statute books that made it legal to torture children, it would still violate the moral principle, and could do nothing to change its 'absolute' nature. Taken another way, we can see it is possible that the obligation (not to harm another) exists without a co-relative right being enshrined in any legal system.

In speaking of the new Measure, therefore, we are (or should be) speaking about those obligations that flow from respect due to each solely in virtue of being human (while remembering the role that the state and legal rights play, or not, in offering and attempting to afford rights, and remembering also that the state is not successful often because of the failure to understand obligations as primary). If we say every child has the right to dignity and respect in the same measure as every other human being – the right to have their lives valued, their voices listened to, equally, honouring each human condition with respect due to it – we must ensure they (which is also to say 'we') are not left with what Weil describes as just 'hollow pretence' (Weil, 1987: 18).

The Measure helps create the conditions for this, but the practicalities will be lived out only if those governed by the Measure recognise their obligations and use it as an instrument for living out those obligations. It is all very well having rights, but such rights make not one jot of difference to you if you are a child languishing in the 'looked-after' system. Therefore, in order for the true force of these obligations to be lived out, there has to be effective expression of them in our institutions, and our way of life.

Through adopting the UNCRC, we might be tempted to think that there is no longer any question of whether young people have rights. Nevertheless, discrimination, injury and cruelty continue to be inflicted (which is precisely why this Measure is felt necessary in the first place), so adopting the UNCRC should not be taken as any indication that those who perpetrate such evil are sufficiently biddable that we can make effective law from our understanding of that evil. Without effective law, what difference will there be in the lived experience of children and young people in Wales?

We speak about 'inalienable' rights but we still face the problem of making them real, and we cannot face that problem properly if we do not understand the differences that allow Weil to speak of rights as a mediocre notion, to give the example she does:

> If you say to someone who has ears to hear: 'What you are doing to me is not just' [. . .] it is not the same with words like 'I have the right to . . .' or 'You have the right to . . .' They evoke a latent war and awaken the spirit of contention. To place the notion of rights at the centre of social conflict is to inhibit any impulse of charity on both sides. Relying almost exclusively on this notion it becomes almost impossible to keep one's eye on the real problem. If someone tries to browbeat a farmer to sell his eggs at a moderate price, the farmer can say: 'I have the right to keep my eggs if I don't get a good enough price.' But if a young girl is being forced into a brothel she will not ask about her rights. In such a situation the word would sound ludicrously inadequate. (Weil, 1977: 325, cited in Gaita, 1991)

If only it were as simple as adopting the UNCRC, saying 'now you have these rights'. Rights being thus apparently granted, the question would then become a matter of practicality rather than one of ensuring outcomes (these are not unconnected, of course). But how, in practice, can young people ensure their rights or the rights of others, if, for example, the courts are corrupt, or their opponents are too powerful for them to access their rights, or in the face of systemic failures, or in times of financial crisis? Since young people will depend on this Measure working, how can they access their rights under it? How will they influence, drive, or be assured of its implementation? If adults, 'persuaders' in an 'interpretive community', are left to interpret what the Measure means for government and official agencies, what really changes for children and young people? How do we all ensure their rights are recognised and worth something, rather than being mere rhetoric? This is not simply a matter of practicality: in order for outcomes to flow from rights, we must be clear what obligations accompany those rights, and we must have a clear sight of how to live up to those obligations. This is why the notion of obligation is so critical, and if we do not even begin to explore that relationship, we give up the game before it has even started.

Inalienable rights – who says?

Raimond Gaita (1991) discusses the case of a woman interviewed for the BBC documentary series *The World at War* (1973–4). Since the time when she had witnessed it, she asked herself on a daily basis how a young Nazi officer could over a long period of time have sent trainloads, mostly of children, to the death camps. Her questioning is not based on the idea that he violated their inalienable rights. If she were to ask how he could fail to see the children had natural rights, that would not express her bewilderment: it would be to give way to mediocrity. So, to reiterate: while rights remain inaccessible to a child being 'loaded' onto a train, or, as in the case of the girl in Weil's example, the expression of them in such situations is ludicrously inadequate, what is the point of having them?

There is a further deep difficulty, however. We may be sincerely convinced that all human beings, children and young people included, are unconditionally owed respect. Yet, as Gaita has pointed out, even a sincere profession of this fundamental, unconditional respect can amount to 'mere words', not because it is undermined by what anyone professing such respect does, but because it is 'not informed by anything sufficiently weighty in their lives' to earn the kind of respect given to those of whom we say that they (really) 'know what they're talking about' (Gaita, 1991: 3). It is important to realise that:

> [t]hose who command our respect and provide us with a serious sense that there is something to think about when they either assert or deny

such claims of absolute value, have not arrived either at their assertion or their denial of it by way of argument. (Gaita, 1991: 4)

Having a voice of authority on such a subject is not a matter of force of reason or argument, legal or otherwise. The intentions of some of those bringing forward the Measure will be too easily subverted if the persuaders in the interpretive community do not begin by understanding that the notion of rights is 'too thin' (Gaita), and is too much a 'mediocre concept' (Weil) to deepen our understanding of the evil that is done to children and young people (that is if they have not already shown by how they live their lives that they understand this point). We cannot arrive, nor expect others to arrive, at a deep sense of the obligations standing over the UNCRC by argument: it will be as much a question of what this way of speaking touches in their lives.

This is all the more important when we can have an apparent contradiction between two 'rights' in the UNCRC: the right to live and the consideration of the 'best interests' of the child. In one well-publicised case, a twelve-year-old boy, David Glass, who had complex physical, sensory and learning disabilities, was admitted to a Portsmouth hospital in July 1998 with a respiratory tract infection (Dyer, 2004). David was subject to a 'do not resuscitate' notice without the family's knowledge or consent, due to a judgement on the potential quality of his life; no further intensive therapy unit treatment was to be provided. When doctors decided to actively intervene and administer diamorphine to 'allow' David to 'die with dignity', his family made a dramatic intervention. They took the diamorphine drip out of his arm and administered resuscitation themselves. A near fist-fight broke out on the ward. This case included a challenge by judicial review of the General Medical Council's guidance. After a five-year legal battle, the European Court of Human Rights decided that in imposing the treatment, the hospital had violated David's human right to life.[1]

In recent times, we have indulged more and more in debate and been encouraged to question who in our communities has a life worth living, and who therefore does not, and can be 'helped to die'. (The notion of 'personhood' plays a key role here.) The Glass family's experience and the threat to David's life demonstrate one of the ways in which these 'professional' judgements about the quality of life of another are deeply flawed: it looks as though there is an argument to be made, for example on the grounds of 'the best interests of the child' or from compassion, whereas this is precisely where the 'personal' enters into our moral decision-making. This is not to ignore or dismiss natural, compassionate responses. What goes wrong here is that there is no process of logic, nor force of argument: if there were, most people would be forced to the same conclusion each time. The judgements are first and foremost moral ones, so one question is why it is the case that any 'professional' judgement appears to have more value than the lived experience of the family. Relying on 'consideration of the child's best interests' (as though that were self-evident in all cases), leads to an attitude that it is necessary to take that child's life in his best interest. What is important here is not just the judgement, but who is making it. Here the problem of an 'interpretive community' comes into stark relief. This is why is it important, in most cases, who it is who says 'this life is not worth living', and who says 'here, we grant you your rights'. In many cases it is the medical practitioner who leads in decision-making even about the very life of a child – for example, when a medical team has applied to court to withdraw treatment from a terminally ill baby against the wishes of his or her parents (see *Re C (a minor) (medical treatment)* [1998] 1 FLR 38). There are cases which go against this trend, where the court gives precedence to the parents' wishes over medical advice – for example, *Re T (a minor) (Wardship: Medical Treatment)* [1997] 1 All ER 906, which held that the best interests of the child in withholding treatment is determined in part by the parents' wishes, given the role the parents will play in the child's life). In the case of David Glass, the judgement of the European Court was in favour of the lived experience of the family, and of David as a happy boy.

We cannot ignore the underlying difficulties of trying to assess someone else's quality of life, which is always from the judge's point of view (usually this is a doctor who has none of the lived experience of the one being literally 'argued' to death). There is a pre-eminence of medical, professional opinion over lay judgement, but there is no obligation on someone trained to practise medicine to demonstrate professional competence in making moral judgements. (What might such a 'qualification' look like anyway?) These are not matters of fact, where science and measurement can determine the 'definitive' answer, and so cannot be delivered through laws offering rights.

Anyone engaged in pursuit of such arguments and driven to these conclusions, in the past regarded them as *reductio ad absurdum* – unthinkable consequences, demonstrably false by virtue of the *reductio*. Yet in our time, it has become almost a form of perversity to offer any view against the idea that someone's life should be judged by another as not worth living. The idea that it can and should be, is what allows the debate to degrade: what was previously morally unthinkable becomes now 'thinkable', has become common consideration, wherein the appeal to compassion and human dignity become part of the 'argument' used to urge people to kill those who are affected by 'intolerable suffering' – see, for example, the BBC's screening in 2011 of the 'assisted death' of a man in a Swiss clinic. Hence, also, the doctors' outrage at the Glass family's actions, and a French high court judgement, supposedly based on high-flown legal argument, that a child with Down's syndrome had the 'right not to be have been born'.[2] What this highlights is that the one who says this – the high court judge, the consultant physician – makes a difference to how we hear it (generally speaking). What is not highlighted is the danger of reliance on these opinions about moral matters, where the life lived by the individual making the pronouncements is actually at the heart of the matter.

The subject matter for ethical reflection is primarily action and speech, which have a certain authority, and when it is speech, it is has the weight of some people who 'have something to say': that sense is connected with the right to speak because of an authority which has stemmed from the way they have lived their lives (Gaita, 1991: 4).

The authority of the medical professionals, and their moral judgement, was challenged by the family who made the opposing judgement about the value of David's life. What the doctors missed was that the question of whether someone, David, has a life worth living does not depend on whether he, or they, think it is worthless: this is a distortion. In some cases, the importance and value of a life lies with those who are devoted to him, to whom he is a person. (This does not mean it is therefore alright to put to death someone who has no-one to love them, but it does mean there are more questions to examine, a deeper discussion needed, on that subject.)

The problem and the opportunity: the 'interpretive community' and the 'persuaders'

This kind of debate, arising when two apparently absolute rights come into conflict with each other, demonstrates that deep consideration must be given to the nature of the 'interpretive community', the 'persuaders', to whom fall the task of interpreting the Measure that is intended to bring all the force of the human rights of the UNCRC to children and young people in Wales. As with the earlier example, it would be a mistake to think that the 'persuaders' were somehow 'qualified' merely by dint of position or role to speak with authority on the notion and delivery of inalienable rights, especially if they ignore the role of obligations and do not understand that the idea of rights is such a weak notion. This, according to Weil, is linked with the notion of sharing out, of exchange, of measured quantity. It has a commercial flavour, essentially evocative of legal claims and arguments. Rights are always asserted in a tone of contention; and when this tone is adopted, it must rely upon force in the background, or else it will be laughed at. (1977: 323)

Thanks to the use of the word 'rights', in place of the word 'justice', according to Weil: 'What should have been a cry of protest from the depth of the heart has been turned into a shrill nagging of claims and counter-claims, which is both impure and impractical' (1977: 325–6).

People's everyday experience, even if they cannot always articulate this, proves to them that they do not enjoy an equal position in society, an equal social prestige. This is why some people are afforded an unnatural precedence in judging the lives of others to be 'not worth living'. Calling for equality and equal rights makes it seem as though there is nothing odd about claiming an equal share of privilege for everyone, but this is an absurd claim, since privilege and inequality are the two sides of that particular coin.

No-one can give them any credence if they, the 'interpretive community', the 'persuaders', are generally (though it must be said not exclusively) in

the category of [people] who formulate claims, and everything else, the [ones] who have the monopoly of language, [which] is a category of privileged people ... Many indispensable truths ... go unspoken for reasons of this kind; those who could utter them cannot formulate them and those who can formulate them cannot utter them. If politics were taken seriously, finding a remedy for this would be one of its most urgent problems. (Weil, 1977: 327)

The ones who can formulate them are disempowered, having no real voice, but the ones who do formulate these truths suffer from bad faith, based on the idea that 'I claim for all of you an equal share in the privileges I enjoy'. Not only is that absurd but it drives in the opposite direction from enabling people to be understood precisely because those who would choose words on their behalf know nothing of their lived experience. If, again, it is not the individual who can claim rights but the others who must recognise their obligations to them, how can they achieve real change without having the lived experience that proves such recognition in them?

This is where the real opportunity lies. The interpretive community must be something other than it has hitherto been, and those who replace its members must have both the lived experience and the opportunity to express it in order to develop something other than Weil's 'mediocre' concept of rights. Then justice, in terms of actual outcomes, will provide the evidence that the UNCRC, and the Welsh Government's adoption of this Measure, are not merely so many words.

For Williams, there is 'the danger of subversion of meaning to other priorities or policies'. She cites Tobin's warning that 'advocates can be quick to offer interpretations that reflect personal preferences as to the nature of protection that the advocates think the rights in question *should* accord' (Tobin, 2010: 2). That is an important part of the problem. The opportunity lies in:

> the scope for engagement between governmental and non-governmental actors, civil society and children and young people themselves in the development of an informed and shared understanding of, and commitment to, rights-based approaches to governance. (Williams, chapter 4 in this volume)

The difficulty of the 'subversion of meaning' is readily evident in Weil's challenges about the language and the very notion of rights. So it is that even well-intentioned efforts go awry: some politicians have tried, for example, to approach the notion of 'equality of esteem' but have ended up with a perversion, a caricature, closely akin to 'what people think of you' (but what people think of you is infected by the problem of quantity, how much you have by way of success, power, and income – what Rhees describes as 'sham grandeur' [2000: 33]). Or take the idea that everyone should be treated in the same way and the continuing confusion in understanding this injunction as though it concerned levels of pay, holidays, what school you go to and so forth: here there is no consideration of human beings like these where the imbalance of privilege persists, where there is no real equality of outcome; it entirely misses the point of defeating institutionalised discrimination (for example the lazy fatalism of low expectations of disabled people). The stupidity of this approach is only exacerbated by the pronouncements of those who currently enjoy their place in the privileged 'interpretive community'.

Equality of outcome must be understood as primary to policy, and it depends fundamentally on not treating people in the same way. For equal outcomes to be even possible, there must be a general public recognition which is effective and genuinely expressed in institutions and customs, that the same amount of respect and consideration is due to every human being because this respect is due to the human being as such and is not a matter of degree. (Weil, 1987: 15)

The emphasis here is on effective, not fictitious, expression of the obligations in our institutions, our customs, our ways of life. The effective exercise of a right does not derive from an individual claiming that right, but from the fact that others recognise their obligations to that individual and do not dismiss such claims as 'trouble-making'. Those who recognise their obligations then realise that what flows from this recognition is not a 'matter of degree'. The same amount of respect is due to each – one's station in life does not grant one more (or fewer) rights (although it does bring more responsibility if that is a 'high' station).

Equality of esteem is nothing without action. This has been the theme of this chapter and is reflected in later chapters in this volume. In conclusion, we must: a) be sure that those tasked with implementing the new Measure can speak with the necessary authority from the way they have lived their lives, and from their recognition that it is those fundamental principles, those obligations, that provide the impetus for the very origin of the UNCRC; and b) we must give them the tools by which outcomes can be achieved, where those rights become reality in the lived experience of the individuals covered by our laws and institutions and in our ways of life, so that everyone can participate in the 'life and *language* of [our] society' (Rhees, 2000: 32).

Aneurin Bevan is alleged to have said that the purpose of getting power is to give it away. There is no better sentiment to end here. If outcomes are to be truly delivered, the power to not just deliver them, but to scope them also, must be put in the hands of those with lived experience who can speak with authority, and not be left to an interpretive community that has no such experience. 'Nothing about us without us' has long been the mantra of those in the disability movement. Making decisions about people's lives in their absence, in other words accepting that there will be no real engagement, allows meanings to be subverted as has been the case hitherto. Otherwise the adoption of this Measure will remain just that, mere adoption, which falls into what is, for those for whom it is supposed to be meaningful, so much of the usual meaningless rhetoric.

References

Dyer, C. (2004): 'Doctors violated disabled boy's rights', *Guardian* (10 March). Available at *http://www.guardian.co.uk/society/2004/mar/10/ disability.health* (access date 29 June 2012).

Gaita, R. (1991): *Good and Evil: An Absolute Conception* (London: Macmillan).

Rhees, R. (2000): 'Method and liberty', in D. Z. Phillips (ed.), *Discussions of Simone Weil* (New York: State University of New York Press), pp. 3–15.

Tobin, J. (2010): 'Seeking to persuade: a constructive approach to human rights treaty interpretation', *Harvard Human Rights Review*, 23, 1–50.

Weil, S. (1977): 'Human Personality', in G. A. Panichas (ed.) *The Simone Weil Reader* (New York: David McKay Co. Inc.,) pp. 313–39.

—— (1987): *The Need for Roots: Prelude to a Declaration of Duties Towards Mankind* (1952; Reading: Cox & Wyman).

Notes

1. *Glass v United Kingdom* (61827/00) [2004] 1 FLR 1019 European Court of Human Rights.
2. The French Parliament voted to overturn a controversial legal ruling that established the 'right not to be born' which resulted from three cases in which judges ruled that families whose children were born with birth defects could sue because doctors did not spot the problems during pre-natal scans (BBC News, 10 January 2002).

CHAPTER 6

Child poverty and human rights

Rhian Croke and Anne Crowley

Introduction

Tackling child poverty became one of *the* political issues in the first decade of devolution in Wales. This was at least in part down to the leadership of the Prime Minister, Tony Blair, who in 1999 pledged to end the appalling high rates of child poverty across the UK 'in a generation'. But it was also, as Butler (2011) argues, down to the expressed commitment to children of successive Welsh governments and the National Assembly for Wales as a whole. The fact that in 1999 the UK had one of the worst rates of child poverty in Europe, and that within the four nations of the UK child poverty in Wales was, by all measures, the worst on record, also motivated governments in London and in Cardiff finally to confront this legacy of the 1980s, when the gap between rich and poor had grown faster in the UK than in any other industrialised country (Crowley, 2011).

This chapter reviews the nature and extent of child poverty in Wales and assesses to what extent the approaches taken to tackling child poverty in Wales are based on human rights principles. The chapter concludes with a summary of what more needs to be done, considering the opportunities provided by the Rights of Children and Young Persons (Wales) Measure 2011, to embed a human rights approach in Wales.

The reality of child poverty in Wales

Across the European Union, poverty is primarily understood as a relative concept rather than as an absolute lack of basic necessities. Income is the principal measurement, with children being seen as living in poverty when their household's income is less than 60 per cent of the national median income after deducting housing costs. In Wales, the latest figures (2007/8–2009/10) indicate that 33 per cent of children are living in poverty by this definition (New Policy Institute, 2011).

Recent studies on poverty and social exclusion in Wales show that the proportion of children living in poverty (the child poverty rate) increased in the second half of the last decade, after a fall between 1999 and 2005. The reduction in child poverty in Wales over this earlier period was faster

than that in England or in Scotland, and brought Wales more in line with
the UK average (Kenway, 2010). Variations across the UK and trends over
time are illustrated in Table 6.1.

The New Policy Institute's analysis highlights that all the improvements in child poverty in Wales in the early 2000s were concentrated on
children in workless families. While worklessness is still the single most
important reason for poverty in Wales, and economic inactivity levels and
the incidence of limiting long-term illness in parts of Wales (notably the
south Wales valleys and parts of west Wales) are some of the worst in the
UK, there are also growing concerns about the numbers of children in in-
work poverty (New Policy Institute, 2009). Over half of all children living
in poverty in Wales are living in households where at least one member of
the household is doing some paid work.

Broader definitions of child poverty (which, as we will explain later, can
be seen as reflecting human rights principles) are not solely about household income but also about exclusion and the impact of income poverty on
child well-being. Such definitions include measures of material deprivation
and aspects of all child well-being, including health, education, housing,
participation, financial support and safety. These measures recognise the
different and interrelated ways in which poverty impacts on children and
families. Research confirms the negative outcomes for children associated
with poverty, including poor health, low self-esteem, poor educational
achievement and homelessness (Bradshaw and Mayhew, 2005).

In Wales, despite progress in the early 2000s in reducing the numbers
of children living in relative poverty (see Table 6.1), progress on a range
of child poverty indicators selected by the Welsh Government in 2006
has been mixed (WG, 2010). A major concern is the relatively low level
of basic skills and qualifications of young people from low-income households. With current figures indicating that a quarter of adults in Wales lack

TABLE 6.1   The proportion of children in poverty in the UK

	1996/7–1998/9 (%)	2003/4–2005/6 (%)	2006/7–2008/9 (%)
Wales	36	28	32
Northern Ireland		27	26
Scotland	32	25	25
England	34	29	31
UK	34	29	31

Source: Kenway (2010)

basic skills in literacy, and approximately half lack basic skills in numeracy, this is a serious problem. Yet efforts to reduce the attainment gap in schools between children from low-income households and their more affluent peers have delivered few gains. Using eligibility for free school meals as a proxy indicator of poverty, this gap is apparent by the age of seven when those in receipt of free school meals are already about 21 per cent behind their more privileged peers. By the age of fifteen, whereas 62 per cent of students who are not eligible for free school meals achieve five or more GCSEs at higher grades, the figure for free school meals students is 28 per cent – a gap of 34 per cent (Egan, 2010). Put another way, pupils eligible for free school meals are two and a half times less likely to get A*–C grades in core subjects than their peers (Davies et al., 2011).

The association of poverty with poor child outcomes can perhaps be better understood when comparing the varying range of opportunities available to children from low-income and more affluent households. The Households Below Average Income report in 2007 for the first time pre-sented information on the material deprivation experienced by children living in low-income households. The findings provide a reminder of the stark reality of poverty from a child's perspective. For example, 5 per cent of children in the top quintile are lacking outdoor space or facilities to play safely, compared with a quarter of children in the bottom quintile. Just 3 per cent of children in the top income quintile do not have at least one week's holiday away from home compared with more than half of children in the bottom quintile (Department for Work and Pensions, 2007). Children liv-ing in low-income households have the odds stacked against them.

Approaches to tackling child poverty in Wales – the first decade of devolution

The Welsh Government has power over many of the policy areas asso-ciated with the outcomes of child poverty: education, health, housing and social care, for example. However, the key drivers to reduce income poverty – notably tax and benefits – remain the responsibility of the UK Government. Throughout the New Labour years (1997–2011) a raft of policies and programmes was put in place to boost paid employment as a route out of poverty, notably working and child tax credits, the child trust fund and the national minimum wage, as well as increasing universal child benefit. Welsh governments over this period focused on area-based regen-eration, investments in early years provision, facilitating joint working, encouraging greater financial inclusion and improvements in the uptake of tax and benefits support.

In 2005 the Welsh Government published its first strategy to tackle child poverty in Wales. The strategy stated the Welsh Government's commitment to the UK Government's target of eradicating child poverty by 2020 and its contributions to meeting that target. The strategy included an additional £50 million targeted on early years in the most deprived areas of Wales with at least one integrated children's centre in each local authority area (WG, 2005).

The proposals on the £50 million spend were subsequently developed into the Flying Start programme, a Welsh Government initiative that targets funding on effective early years provision for children from birth to three years old living in the most disadvantaged communities across the country. Provision includes free, part-time quality childcare for two-year-olds and enhanced health visitor support and parenting programmes (WG, 2006). In 2010, the Welsh Government announced the re-aligning of funds to support disadvantaged children and families into a new Families First programme from 2012. Families First aims to support the development of 'family-centred services delivering effective and efficient support to families living in poverty, thus reducing the inequities that they experience' (WG, 2011: 27).

In line with commitments in the 'One Wales Agreement' between Labour and Plaid Cymru in the coalition government of 2007–11, the Children and Families (Wales) Measure 2010 provided a real opportunity for a joined-up approach to tackling child poverty across all key stakeholders and partners (O'Neill, 2010). The Measure places a duty on Welsh Ministers to produce and publish a child poverty strategy and also requires local authorities, local health boards and a range of other public bodies in Wales to include child poverty strategies in their children and young people's plan, which they are required to publish every three years.

The duties imposed on Welsh Ministers in the Children and Families (Wales) Measure 2010 reflect most of the duties placed on UK, Scottish and Northern Irish Ministers in the UK's Child Poverty Act 2010 – that is, to publish a child poverty strategy as well as articulating government pledges to national poverty targets. The Welsh Government issued an ambitious child poverty strategy for consultation in May 2010. The strategy focused on three overarching objectives: to reduce the number of families in workless households; to improve the skill level of parents and young people in low-income families so that they can secure well-paid employment, and to reduce inequalities in health, education and economic outcomes for children living in poverty, by improving the outcomes of the poorest.

The draft strategy and an accompanying delivery plan were warmly welcomed across the children's sector in Wales – not least because of their focus on cross-departmental working, policy integration, strategic coordination and regular monitoring of the impact of policies on child poverty. The lack of a joined-up approach to tackling child poverty by Welsh Ministers and by local government has long been seen as a weakness in the Welsh approach (O'Neill, 2010).

However, a few months is a long time in politics. The final strategy published in February 2011 was much less comprehensive and less ambitious. It devoted just over one page to the task of raising the educational achievement of children from low-income households, with much of this focused on improving the attainment levels of looked-after children. This seems particularly weak when we note that despite the alleged priority given by successive Welsh governments to tackling child poverty, inequalities in educational outcomes have continued to get worse for children aged eleven, fourteen and sixteen and only marginally better in recent years for children aged seven (Egan, 2010).

Much of the draft strategy had been written (or at least conceived) in kinder economic times and with a Labour government at UK level. As unemployment increased in 2009 and 2010 and the new UK Conservative and Liberal Democrat coalition government announced public expenditure cuts to deal with the country's burgeoning deficit, the Welsh Government's ambition appeared to have been scaled back.

The UK Government's measures to tackle the deficit focus on cutting public expenditure rather than increasing taxation. The welfare bill took a particular hit in the new government's emergency budget of June 2010 and the spending review in October of the same year. A whole host of measures took effect in April 2011, falling heavily on those who are already living in poverty. These include: changes to the inflation measure used to calculate benefit increases, which will erode their value over time; reductions to housing benefit; changes to tax credits; freezing of child benefit payments, and reduction in help with childcare costs through the tax credit system. The Educational Maintenance Allowance (EMA) which works to support sixteen- to eighteen-year-olds from low-income households to continue in education was also scrapped (JRF, 2011).

The Welsh Government bravely agreed to continue EMAs for Welsh students – a move that has been widely welcomed – but generally it is powerless to mitigate the worst effects of these welfare reforms on poor children. The block grant to Wales has been reduced (in real terms) and the Welsh Government now has less money at its disposal to do what it planned to tackle child poverty.[1] Despite the UK Government's insistence that its own spending review will have no measurable impact on child poverty in the short term, the welfare cuts (along with cuts to public services) fall disproportionately on children and families, and the Institute of Fiscal Studies forecast a rise in absolute and relative poverty among children and working-age adults (Brewer and Joyce, 2010).

We turn now to consider the key principles underpinning a human rights approach to tackling child poverty, before going on to assess the extent to which these principles have been incorporated into distinctive 'Welsh' policy responses.

A human rights based approach – key principles

A human rights based approach to poverty is based on the concept that the 'poor have rights or entitlements that give rise to legal obligations on the part of others. Poverty reduction then becomes more than charity, more than a moral obligation – it becomes a *legal* obligation' (OHCHR, 2004: 33). The emphasis on universal human needs challenges the 'otherness' of those experiencing poverty (Lister, 2008). It shifts the debate from the personal failures of the 'poor' to the failure of macro-economic structures and policies. The recognition of the existence of legal entitlements of the poor and legal obligations of others towards them is the first step towards empowerment. The empowerment of those living in poverty is an essential precondition for the elimination of poverty and for the upholding of human rights. Human rights can therefore help to equalise the distribution and exercise of power both within and between societies (OHCHR, 2004).

The human rights based approach 'acknowledges the agency of people living in poverty – that they are not just passive victims but also agents in their own lives, capable of making choices and of contributing the expertise borne of experience to policy-making' (Lister, 2008: 13). Seeing poverty 'through the eyes of a child' powerfully reinforces the importance of the human rights perspective (Croke and Crowley, 2011). To understand the lived experience of child poverty we need to bring a child's perspective to the analysis of child poverty and social exclusion and not just focus on income (Ridge, 2009). The evidence from children reveals that experiencing poverty in childhood can be highly damaging, and the effects of poverty long-standing on a child's development.

Children understand that poverty is a multi-dimensional problem and raise broad-ranging issues from education, health, crime, drugs and participation, to access to leisure, safe places to play, social activities and transport. They talk about going without basic necessities such as clothing, heating and food on the table because of a lack of money in the household. Children are concerned that parents (in low-income households) go without so that they can have what they need and to prevent their children from being singled out for being poor. A strong cross-cutting theme in research from across the UK is that children talk of the profound effects of stigma and shame and the lack of respect their 'differentness' evokes. They talk of feeling excluded and being made to feel different to other children and young people (Ridge, 2009; Horgan, 2007; Crowley and Vulliamy, 2002; Middleton et al., 1994).

The impact on children and young people's sense of worth and self-esteem should not be underestimated. These key messages from children and young people present a window into the social and human costs of child poverty and the need for a human rights based approach to challenge 'povertyism' and the discrimination that children experience because of poverty (Kileen, 2008). A human rights perspective recognises that children living in poverty are not just passive victims but agents in their own lives as well as experts on their own lives. They have a right to be listened to and have their expertise brought to bear on policy-making, as well as being active participants in claiming their own rights.

Traditionally across the UK child poverty has been seen as a consequence of family poverty resulting from a lack of economic resources. The key measure of child poverty used in the UK and across the European Union, as we have previously noted, is a relative measure based on the household's income. A human rights perspective, on the other hand, sees children as units of observation in their own right, and focuses the analysis on a broader concept of resources to explain the well-being of children (Eurochild, 2007: 1). Conceptualising child poverty from a human rights point of view privileges this broader perspective, incorporating economic, social and cultural rights (such as a right to health care) as well as civil and political rights (such as the right to be heard). Understanding child poverty as a denial of children's fundamental human rights resulting from a lack of resources emphasises the interrelated and interdependent dimensions of deprivation. For example, access to decent housing, health care, and a balanced and adequate diet will contribute to children's success in school. By contrast, overcrowded accommodation located in a deprived neighbourhood may contribute to poor health, low educational attainment and disaffection from school (Eurochild, 2007).

The international human rights instruments and supporting texts (UN Guidelines, *General Comments* and related publications) provide a framework for developing a human rights based approach to child poverty.

The United Nations has identified key principles of a human rights based approach that can be applied by governments and public institutions. The first of these is to explicitly apply human rights values, legal standards and norms across policy, planning and practice – that is, examining how decisions and actions impact on human rights. The other principles relate to how this is achieved – ensuring accountability mechanisms to claim rights; the identification of immediate and long-term targets; effective monitoring methods; empowerment and participation of people in identifying and addressing rights issues and non-discrimination, and prioritising those most vulnerable to human rights abuses (OHCHR, 2004).

We now turn to a consideration of the extent to which the approaches to tackling child poverty in Wales reflect these key human rights principles, in contrast to the approach adopted by successive UK governments which have, over the last decade, been almost wholly premised on getting parents into work (Lister, 2008).

A human rights based approach to child poverty in Wales?

As others in this volume have noted, there is a clear divergence in the attitudes and commitment to children's human rights between successive Welsh and UK governments (see also Williams, 2007, and Clutton, 2008). The antecedents of the 'Welsh' approach to welfare are discussed in chapter 1 in this volume and elsewhere (see, for example, Butler, 2011; Drakeford, 2007). Today, in the National Assembly for Wales we see, as Butler concludes, an explicit cross-party commitment to a 'rights based agenda' and a determination to provide 'Wales relevant solutions to Wales specific problems even if this requires a break with Westminster and Whitehall' (Butler, 2011: 165). The parliamentary scrutiny function, notably of the Children and Young People Committee under the chairpersonship of Helen Mary Jones AM, helped to engender this strong cross-party consensus.

As early as 2002 the Welsh Government was commended by the UN Committee for using the UNCRC as the framework for its strategy for children and young people. In 2004, the commitment to the UNCRC was consolidated with the plenary resolution of the National Assembly for Wales adopting the UNCRC as the overarching set of principles for all of its policy on children and young people. As detailed by Butler and Drakeford in this volume, the Welsh Government used the UNCRC as an explicit source for core policy aims.

However, the apparent 'scaling back' noted above in the child poverty strategy launched by the Welsh Government in 2011 gave rise to concern that children were beginning to slip down the political agenda in Wales. One indicator is the demotion of responsibility for children within the Welsh Cabinet from a full Ministerial brief to that of a Deputy Minister in 2009, and then to being the responsibility of a Deputy Minister who also has responsibility for another major policy area, social care. While policy intentions in the draft child poverty strategy were organised around the seven core aims derived from the UNCRC (see chapters 1 and 3 of this volume), the core aims had disappeared from the final version, and the strong focus on cross-departmental working, policy integration, strategic coordination and regular monitoring of the impact of the government's policies on child poverty had lost coherence.

On the other hand, successive Welsh governments have made good progress with a number of general measures that underlie a rights-based approach and have the potential to shape more effective policies for tackling child poverty. First, an impressive range of structures and mechanisms have been established in Wales to support children's participation in governmental decision-making. These include a national children and young people's assembly (Funky Dragon), local authority youth fora, and school councils operating in the majority of schools in Wales. Secondly, prompted by the UNCRC reporting process, successive Welsh governments have taken steps to analyse their expenditure and demonstrate the proportions of the overall budget spent on children. The Welsh Assembly Government's national action plan on children's rights (2009) commits government to further improve the transparency of public expenditure as it impacts on children. Thirdly, in 2008 the Welsh Government published a report on the well-being of children in Wales which for the first time brought together data on a range of indicators to provide a state of the nation's child report. The Well-being Monitor was updated in 2011 and will be updated at regular, three-year intervals.

Perhaps the most radical and progressive of all the developments in Wales is the enactment of the Rights of Children and Young Persons (Wales) Measure 2011. We turn now to reflect on opportunities offered by the Measure and to suggest what more needs to be done at a Wales level of governance to maximise the resources and powers at Wales's disposal.

Embedding a human rights approach – what more needs to be done?

Despite the broad commitment and the several initiatives referred to above, the challenges facing the Welsh Government in meeting its commitments to eradicating child poverty by 2020 are significant. To reduce child poverty four times as fast over the next ten years as the fall over the last ten years (as the New Policy Institute's most recent analysis suggests is required) demands a far more radical and ambitious programme at both the Wales and UK levels of governance than as yet evident in their respective child poverty strategies (New Policy Institute, 2011).

The rise in the 2000s of poverty among children of parents who do some work indicates that to reduce child poverty in Wales, many more parents will have to work more hours, and this, as the New Policy Institute highlights, requires improvements in a whole range of public services including child and health care and transport (ibid.). If all the rights that children should enjoy are to be privileged, and children's best interests are to be adequately protected, it also requires, we would argue, a national debate about how parenting and caring responsibilities and employment duties can best be balanced. At the very least, the fuller employment of parents and carers in Wales requires a huge increase in affordable, accessible and quality childcare and the transformation of employment practices in both the private and the public sector, to make them far more family-friendly.

As explained by Williams in this volume, the Measure requires Welsh Ministers to have 'due regard' to the substantive provisions of the UNCRC. This duty promotes proactive behaviour by the executive. Adequate internal controls such as those recommended in the UN Committee's *General Comment No. 5* (2003) on general measures of implementation, including coordinated government, data collection, monitoring, budget impact assessments and awareness-raising, will help to ensure compliance with the duty and should assist Welsh Ministers to grasp a more holistic and joined-up understanding of children's human rights and their implementation.

The lack of a coordinated approach within successive Welsh governments continues to hinder progress on tackling child poverty. The myriad of related plans, aspirations and strategies – such as the national action plan on children's rights, the child poverty strategy, children's budgeting, the seven core aims and the Well-being Monitor – appear somehow 'disconnected', standing largely as short-term frameworks of relevance to specific branches or divisions of government and specific professional groupings, be they health workers, social workers or teachers. Given the interrelated nature of all children's rights, as well as the importance of making government structures more effective for children, this situation really needs to be addressed.

The first commencement of the Rights of Children and Young Persons (Wales) Measure in May 2012 heralds the introduction of children's rights

impact assessments on the Welsh Government's policy and budgetary proposals. Such impact assessments, if carried out effectively, should work
to encourage coordination and cooperation across government and professional 'silos', and should also work to ensure that children and young
people (and child poverty) remain visible. Continued scrutiny of Welsh
Government policy by the Children and Young People Committee in the
National Assembly for Wales, the Children's Commissioner, child-led
organisations and the non-governmental sector should provide critical
support in developing a shared understanding of how to give further effect
to the UNCRC in Wales.

Internal mechanisms for monitoring and driving progress on the child
poverty strategy across all government departments require strengthening. The Welsh Government needs to ensure that any steps it takes to
encompass a more generic approach to tackling poverty and inequality (for
example, the proposal to replace a promised 'delivery plan' for the child
poverty strategy with an 'anti-poverty' delivery plan) do not lose sight
of the child and the government's obligations under the UNCRC. Once
internal controls have been established, it is likely to be easier to utilise
external controls such as judicial review, administrative complaints, investigation by commissioners, and audit and parliamentary scrutiny processes
(Williams, 2007). Child rights impact assessments can serve to avoid that
necessity through highlighting discrimination in access to services and/or
the disproportionate impact of budget cuts on vulnerable groups.

The emphasis in section 5 of the Measure on the promotion of knowledge and understanding among members of the public (including children) of the UNCRC is particularly welcome, as it offers opportunities
to articulate the condition of children living in poverty in terms of rights
violations. Blaming and stigmatisation, and the sense of 'otherness' that
children and young people repeatedly report, should then give way to
emphasis on the legal obligations of duty bearers – most obviously, but
not uniquely, government. Despite the lack of individual redress in the
Measure, the requirement to promote awareness of the UNCRC among
children and young people is a legal requirement to which several accountability mechanisms apply (see Hoffman and Williams, chapter 12 in this
volume). Welsh governments consulted with children and young people
when preparing the child poverty strategies of 2005 and 2011, but on neither occasion published information about how they had responded to
children and young people's views, experiences or ideas. It is to be hoped
that increased awareness of the UNCRC will result in a challenge to the
idea that one-off consultation exercises are an adequate means of including

children and young people in devising and delivering strategies to give further effect, for example, to Article 27 (right to and adequate standard of living).

Conclusion

There have been progressive developments in Wales over the first decade of devolution, but more work needs to be done both inside and outside government to establish a vision for a poverty-free society based on the principles of human rights. In Wales, with its stubborn and unacceptably high levels of child poverty, we need urgently to seize on the opportunities the rights Measure provides. However, we must also understand the limits of devolved powers, especially on tax and benefit provisions. The public expenditure cuts announced by the UK coalition government in 2010 have undoubtedly dealt a severe blow to the fight against child poverty in Wales. With a government in Wales of a different ideological persuasion to the one in the UK, the welfare cuts in particular may yet prove just how little power the Welsh Government really has to affect the levels of child poverty in its midst.

References

Bradshaw, J. and Mayhew, E. (2005): *The Well-being of Children in the UK* (London: University of York, and Save the Children).

Brewer, M. and Joyce, R. (2010): *Child and Working-age Poverty 2010–2013* (London: Institute of Fiscal Studies).

Butler, I. (2011): 'Children's policy in Wales', in C. Williams (ed.), *Social Policy for Social Welfare Practice in Wales*, 2nd edition (Birmingham: BASW/Venture Press), pp. 159–84.

Clutton, S. (2008): 'Devolution and the language of children's rights in the UK', in A. Invernizzi and J. Williams (eds), *Children and Citizenship* (London: Sage), pp. 171–81.

Croke, R. and Crowley A. (eds) (2007): *Stop, Look, Listen: The Road to Realising Children's Rights in Wales* (Cardiff: Save the Children).

—— and —— (2011): 'Human rights and child poverty in the UK: time for change', in A. Invernizzi and J. Williams (eds), *The Human Rights of Children: From Visions to Implementation* (Farnham: Ashgate), pp. 263–86.

Crowley, A. (2011): 'Child poverty – a failed promise?', in C. Williams (ed.), *Social Policy for Social Welfare Practice in Wales*, 2nd edition (Birmingham: BASW/Venture Press), pp. 71–92.

—— and Vulliamy, C. (2002): *Listen Up! Children and Young People Talk About: Poverty* (Cardiff: Save the Children).

Davies, R. et al. (2011): *An Anatomy of Economic Inequality in Wales* (Cardiff: WIZERD, Cardiff University).

Department for Work and Pensions (2007): Households Below Average Income (HBAI), 1994/5 to 2005/6 (London: Department for Work and Pensions).

Drakeford, M. (2007): 'Devolution and social justice in the Welsh context', *Benefits*, 19/2, 173–80.

Egan, D. (2010): 'Educational equity and school performance in Wales', in V. Winckler (ed.), *Poverty and Social Exclusion in Wales* (Tredegar: Bevan Foundation), pp. 73–87.

Eurochild (2007): *A Child Rights Approach to Child Poverty: Discussion Paper.* Available at *http://www.eurochild.org* (accessed 16 September 2012).

Horgan, G. (2007): *The Impact of Poverty on Young Children's Experience of School* (York: Joseph Rowntree Foundation).

JRF (Joseph Rowntree Foundation) (2011): *Poverty and the 2011 Budget* (York: JRF).

Kenway, P. (2010): 'Income and wealth in Wales', in *Poverty and Social Exclusion in Wales* (Tredegar: Bevan Foundation), pp. 7–28.

Kileen, D. (2008): *Is Poverty in the UK a Denial of People's Human Rights?* (York: Joseph Rowntree Foundation).

Lister, R. (2008): 'Poverty eradication in the UK: overview of key issues, challenges and current responses', in *Human Rights and Tackling UK Poverty: Report of Roundtable Meeting*, 17 January (London: British Institute of Human Rights), pp. 9–19.

Middleton, S., Ashworth, K. and Walker, R. (1994): *Family Fortunes: Pressures on Parents and Children in the 1990s* (London: Child Poverty Action Group).

New Policy Institute (2009): *Monitoring Poverty and Social Exclusion in Wales 2009* (York: Joseph Rowntree Foundation).

—— (2011): *Monitoring Poverty and Social Exclusion in Wales 2011* (York: Joseph Rowntree Foundation).

OHCHR (Office of the High Commission on Human Rights) (2004): *Human Rights and Poverty Reduction: A Conceptual Framework* (New York: United Nations).

O'Neill, S. (2010): 'Child poverty in Wales: where there's the will, is there a way?', in V. Winckler (ed.), *Poverty and Social Exclusion in Wales* (Tredegar: Bevan Foundation), pp. 29–41.

Ridge, T. (2009): *Living with Poverty: A Review of the Literature on Children's and Families' Experiences of Poverty*, Research Number 594 (London: Department for Work and Pensions).

WG (Welsh Government) (2004): *Children and Young People: Rights to Action* (Cardiff: Welsh Assembly Government).

—— (2005): *A Fair Future for Our Children* (Cardiff: Welsh Assembly Government).

—— (2006): *Flying Start Guidance 2006–8* (Cardiff: Welsh Assembly Government).

—— (2010): *Eradicating Child Poverty in Wales: Child Poverty Indicators Progress Against the Baseline* (Cardiff: Welsh Assembly Government).

—— (2011): *Child Poverty Strategy for Wales* (Cardiff: Welsh Government).

Williams, J. (2007): 'Incorporating children's rights: the divergence in law and policy', *Legal Studies*, 17/2, 171–359.

Note

1. The block grant is the money voted annually by the UK Parliament for public expenditure in Wales.

CHAPTER 7

Housing and the independent older child

Jennie Bibbings, Simon Hoffman and Peter K. Mackie

Introduction

Housing provides shelter, and is essential for human health and personal safety and as a base for social life and participation in society (Fox, 2002; Lawrence, 2004). The contribution that good housing makes toward human well-being is recognised in the canon of international human rights instruments, most significantly in Article 11 of the International Covenant on Economic Social and Cultural Rights which guarantees adequate housing as an aspect of the right to an adequate standard of living. There is no age restriction on Article 11: children are entitled to benefit equally with adults by virtue of their status as human beings. However, the United Nations Convention on the Rights of the Child represents the ' "international standard against which to measure legislation and policies" in relation to matters which affect children' (Tobin, 2011: 68). Article 27(1) of the UNCRC recognises the right of every child to a standard of living adequate for the child's 'physical, mental, spiritual, moral and social development'. Article 27(2) places the 'primary responsibility' for securing the 'conditions of living' necessary for a child's development on the child's parents (or others responsible); Article 27(3) requires the State Party to take appropriate measures to assist parents to implement this right and, in the case of need, to provide material assistance and support programmes, particularly with regard to nutrition, clothing and housing. While State Party assistance is directed toward supporting parents, Article 27(3) is clear acknowledgment that housing is a key aspect of the right to a standard of living adequate for a child's development – irrespective of whether the child lives with their parents or carers.[1] In reality the housing needs of the majority of children will be met as a consequence of arrangements made by parents, but a minority will have separate housing needs.

This chapter discusses the position of older children aged sixteen or seventeen years who require independent housing, with a particular focus on policy and legislative responses in Wales. We begin by considering the housing experiences of older children, and how they become children in need of housing. Our understanding predominantly stems from research which has explored the different housing pathways taken by children and young people (aged sixteen to thirty years); pathways that lead to different tenure outcomes and household structures as determined by a combination of structural influences and individual actions. We discuss the housing needs of older children, including the need for support to sustain accommodation, and how these are met within the existing housing rights framework. Finally we turn to consider the Rights of Children and Young Persons (Wales) Measure 2011 and its implications for housing policy in Wales.

Housing and older children: a 'pathways' analysis

Leaving home marks a seminal point in a person's life, a step toward independence. For many children this will be a positive experience taken with the assistance and support of their families. But children leave home for a variety of reasons including maltreatment and/or familial conflict. A proportion of those in need of independent housing will be children leaving local authority care, or 'looked-after children' (Rees and Lee, 2005). Drawing on two studies of housing transitions (Ford et al., 2002; Clapham et al., 2012) we are able to identify three different pathways into independent living that are characterised by varying degrees of planning and familial support. In the first pathway, children make *planned* moves and are supported during and after transition (this will include care leavers who are supported to find accommodation). In the second pathway children face *unplanned supported* moves into independent accommodation. While many following this pathway are likely to have faced some form of life event that requires them to leave the family home unexpectedly, family support is still present. In the final pathway, children experience *unplanned, chaotic* and *unsupported* transitions into independent living, most typically into some form of homelessness. Children on this pathway frequently leave the family home as a result of maltreatment (Rees and Lee, 2005), conflict at home (ibid.), or relationship breakdown (DCLG, 2008; Mackie, 2008; Quilgars et al., 2008). In addition to those who enter an unplanned chaotic pathway from the family home, a significant proportion enter from state care or the secure estate (Rees and Lee, 2005; Mendes and Moslehuddin, 2006; Quilgars et al., 2008).

Housing needs of older children

The pathways children take into independent living result in divergent housing experiences and yet many of their housing needs are similar.

Drawing on evidence from several studies which considered the housing needs of independent older children and young people, four dominant issues are identified: the prevention of homelessness, access to suitable and affordable accommodation, access to housing-related support, and the availability of individualised crisis support.

Children who follow an unplanned and chaotic housing pathway tend to experience homelessness; hence the prevention of homelessness is a key concern. Causes of youth homelessness are well researched and frequently relate to relationship breakdown between the child and their parents (Fitzpatrick, 1999 and 2000; Mackie, 2007; Quilgars et al., 2008). Efforts to prevent homelessness must address parent-child relationships, a realisation which has resulted in a considerable increase in the provision of family mediation services (Pawson, 2007). A lack of information, advice and guidance on housing and homelessness can increase the likelihood of a young person experiencing homelessness (Mackie, 2008). Therefore, homelessness prevention must ensure that the need for relevant information, appropriate advice and suitable guidance is attended to both before a tenancy is entered into and during a tenancy. This is equally true in the case of care leavers, where the pathway planning process should reflect these imperatives in order to provide the child leaving care with sufficient preparation for independent living (Mendes and Moslehuddin, 2004; Mackie, 2008).

In each of the three pathways we have identified, children require access to suitable and affordable accommodation, yet studies have found that many are only able to afford rented accommodation in relatively undesirable areas where there are high rates of crime and antisocial behaviour, high levels of unemployment, and where they are often dislocated from major employment centres (Anderson, 1999; Mackie, 2007). A move to this type of environment increases vulnerability (Tyler, 2008) and the likelihood that the housing will fail. Currently the housing market does not meet the needs of older children: UK Government policy restricting housing benefit payable for single-room rents acts to further limit the buying power of this age group, particularly in areas where there are few properties for rent with shared rooms (Kemp and Rugg, 1998).

When children secure accommodation they almost always require some form of housing-related support (ranging from occasional financial support to advice and guidance on matters from budgeting to rights), and in some cases, often where support is absent or deficient, crisis intervention is needed. For those who make planned moves, family or local authority support increases the likelihood that housing will be sustainable. Where the move is unplanned and chaotic the need for support is arguably more significant. Despite this, research has shown that children who follow chaotic pathways into independent living frequently do so without any support or guidance, which subsequently leads to tenancy issues and eventual eviction (Mackie, 2008). There is then a very clear need for effective housing support services, particularly where children have experienced an unplanned and chaotic transition into independent living. Moreover, when housing problems do escalate and put older children at risk of homelessness, crisis support must be available. Numerous models of crisis intervention exist but all must grapple with two key issues: the need for accommodation, and the need for support. Most homelessness systems focus on meeting the immediate housing needs of homeless people, but relatively few seek to fully consider and address support issues.

Access to housing at times of crisis: an overview of key legislative measures

Having identified that some older children face particularly challenging housing pathways which often result in housing crises, we now consider the different legislative measures in place that aim to provide access to housing and support for these children. The Housing Act 1996 establishes the framework of housing rights for homeless persons in England and Wales. A child aged sixteen or seventeen years who is homeless (or threatened with homelessness) is deemed in priority need for housing (section 189). In cases of priority need, the local housing authority is under an obligation to provide emergency accommodation (section 188). The Children Act 1989 provides an alternative to the homelessness route for sixteen or seventeen-year-olds in housing need. The local social services authority is obliged to provide accommodation for any child in need who is lost, or is without parental support or whose parents are unable to provide accommodation, or whose welfare will be seriously prejudiced if accommodation is not provided (s. 20, Children Act 1989). In *R (on the application of G) v Southwark LBC* [2009] UKHL 26, it was established that while a homeless sixteen- or seventeen-year-old may be entitled to assistance from the local housing authority, where the criteria for assistance under the Children Act 1989 are met the primary responsibility is on the local social services authority to secure accommodation.

A social services authority may call upon the housing authority for assistance, or may provide housing from a range of options which include: placing the child with his or her family, relative or any other suitable person, or placing the child in a children's home (s. 23 and s. 27, Children Act 1989; ss. 10–11, Children Act 2004). Before doing so it is required to ascertain the child's wishes and feelings, and give due consideration to those wishes and feelings (s. 20 [6], Children Act 1989). The duty to accommodate triggers a much broader range of duties to looked-after children and 'eligible' and 'relevant' children under leaving care legislation (s. 23A and 23B, and Schedule 2, para. 19A, Children Act 1989). These include providing assistance to enable 'young people who have been looked after by a local authority to move [to live] independently in as stable a fashion as possible' (Explanatory Notes to Children [Leaving Care] Act 2000, para. 5). Joint working between authorities is encouraged. For sixteen- and seventeen-year-olds the objectives of joint working include providing accommodation and 'support pathways towards independent living', and the provision of a personalised support package (DCSF, 2008: 29).

Key housing legalisation in Wales
Prior to 2007 the National Assembly for Wales (NAW) had only secondary legislative powers. Housing policy therefore followed a similar pattern to England, determined within the legislative framework of the Housing Act 1996, the Homelessness Act 2002 and the Housing Act 2004. The Government of Wales Act 2006 gave the NAW the power to pass primary legislation for Wales – Assembly Measures – and established a procedure to enable the NAW to seek enhanced powers from Westminster in fields where secondary law-making competence was already devolved; these included housing and homelessness. Pursuant to these provisions, the National Assembly for Wales (Legislative Competence) (Housing and Local Government) Order 2010 ('2010 Order') conferred new powers on the NAW to pass legislation in a number of areas of housing policy. However, following the referendum vote in March 2011 in favour of primary legislative competence for NAW in all areas of devolved competence, the 2010 Order has been superseded. The NAW now has the power to make Assembly Acts on the 'subject' of housing, including homelessness (ss. 107–9 and Schedule 7, Part 1, para. 11, Government of Wales Act 2006). If the previous decade is anything to go by, it is likely that we will see significant divergence between Wales and England in several areas of housing policy (Hoffman, 2010). This is what is suggested by the NAW's use of its legislative powers prior to the 2010 Order to introduce distinctive housing policies, including those affecting young people aged sixteen and seventeen (ibid.). In 2001 the NAW introduced the Homeless Persons (Priority Need) (Wales) Order 2001 (SI 2001/607) which extended priority need status to a number of social groups, including care leavers aged eighteen to twenty-one (who had been in care at any point during their

childhood, not only when sixteen or seventeen years old as in England), and young people aged sixteen or seventeen. In 2006 the Welsh Government introduced the Homelessness (Suitability of Accommodation) (Wales) Order (SI 2006/650) which establishes minimum standards for temporary accommodation used to house young people who are homeless. The Welsh Government has announced its intention to introduce a Housing Bill during the fourth Assembly (2011–16) to address strategic priorities which include increasing the supply of available housing, and improving housing-related supported services for homeless and vulnerable individuals (WG, 2011).

The future: housing policy in Wales

The Welsh Government's strategy for housing in Wales is set out in *Improving Lives and Communities – Homes in Wales* (WG, 2010a). Unfortunately the document has little to offer young people directly, although issues such as affordability and housing standards are discussed, and are relevant to all age groups. Earlier child-specific policy statements such as *Children and Young People: Rights to Action* (WG, 2004) make reference to issues of homelessness among young people, and establish a requirement – in policy at least – that service providers should be aware of the needs of this social group. More specifically in the field of housing, recent policy statements include the Welsh Government's *Ten Year Homelessness Plan for Wales*, published in July 2009 (WG, 2009). This sets out a number of expectations regarding provision of accommodation for young people. There is an emphasis on meeting the housing needs of young people leaving home, and on helping them to prepare for independent living. This is underlined by reference to a number of priorities which are summarised below:

- homelessness planning should include young people in the preparation of children and young people's plans under section 17, Children Act 2004, and other local planning arrangements;
- there should be well-developed joint working involving education, youth, health, social care and other sectors;
- homeless young people should be assessed under both the Housing Act 1996 and the Children Act 1989 to establish what duties are owed by relevant local authorities;
- local authorities should be more proactive in meeting their corporate parenting responsibility to looked-after children, including helping them to secure accommodation and to prepare them for independent living;

- housing and related services should be accessible to young people (this may mean building a person's capacity to retain a tenancy or find their own housing solutions);
- prevention work should begin as early as possible, including education work with all young people to help them understand the risks of homelessness;
- young people should have access to housing solutions which are age-appropriate;
- every vulnerable young person should be supported by way of a pathway planning process to help them to prepare for independent living and access suitable accommodation and support;
- and where young people struggle in maintaining their housing, both housing and social services should work proactively to prevent tenancy breakdown, or to provide help finding alternative accommodation and support.

At a local level these priorities mean that the housing needs of vulnerable young people in each of the pathways we identify should feature in local planning. In September 2010 the Welsh Government issued guidance on the treatment of independent sixteen-year-olds and seventeen-year-olds in light of the Southwark judgement (WG, 2010b; see also WG, 2010c). The guidance states that where a sixteen-year-old or seventeen-year-old potentially homeless young person makes an approach to a local authority, the authority must assess whether the young person is a child in need and entitled to provision of accommodation and support under the Children Act 1989. Where a young person is excluded from home and, for example, is sofa-surfing or sleeping rough, it is very likely that they will be a child in need. The guidance also states that it is essential to establish very close contact and rapport with the young person throughout the assessment process in order to make sure their wishes and feelings are properly understood. The following basic principles form part of local authorities' approach to children and young people:

- children and young people should be supported to remain with their families wherever possible;
- account should be taken of a sixteen- or seventeen-year-old's relationship with any partner;
- and there need to be clear arrangements for integrated assessment and support with young people able to make an initial approach to either housing services or social services.

Housing and the Rights of Children and Young Persons (Wales) Measure 2011

Williams describes how the Measure will operate when fully in force (chapter 4, in this volume). The 'due regard' formula means that the listed provisions of the UNCRC will be part of the policy foreground when Welsh Ministers are thinking about exercising their functions, including when deciding on policy or legislation, or when issuing guidance to relevant authorities on the discharge of their functions. The Measure requires due regard to some 58 articles spanning diverse matters affecting children's lives, some of which will be directly relevant to housing policy, others only indirectly relevant, and others not at all relevant – the issue of relevance being something that Welsh Ministers will have to determine as part of the due regard process. The Welsh Government has already made efforts to reflect UNCRC principles in law and policy affecting children in Wales. As Williams notes, its seven core aims for children's policy are presented as explicitly linked to the values and principles of the UNCRC. Guidance has been issued requiring children and young people's plans prepared by local authorities to be structured around these aims (WG, 2010b). How these plans have been developed in practice illustrates a weakness in thinking about housing and homelessness as a self-contained policy area. Some local authorities have fallen into the mode of thinking that only certain core aims are relevant to housing and homelessness (usually core aim 6, that children should have a safe home and community; and/or, core aim 7, that children are not held back or affected by poverty). This approach fails to acknowledge the cross-cutting relevance of inadequate housing and homelessness: these issues range widely across many policy areas and demand sophisticated policy responses. Welsh Ministers will need to take a lead to correct this sort of limited policy thinking in order to ensure that the importance of housing is recognised in relation to each and all of the seven core aims.

Welsh Ministers will also need to ensure not only the seven core aims but the whole of the UNCRC's listed provisions are properly taken into account when determining housing policy, housing legislation and related guidance. Until relatively recently, with the exception of those leaving care, children received only limited attention in housing policy in Wales. For older children some progress has been made as priority is accorded to sixteen-year-olds and seventeen-year-olds who are homeless, and, as seen above, recent housing policies have highlighted specific areas of commitment. Despite this there are a number of areas in which Welsh Ministers will need to consider carefully whether due regard is being given to securing the housing rights of children, including older children. Returning to the typology of housing pathways identified earlier, those older children who follow planned or unplanned supported moves will have access to family resources and/or support services from the local authority or other agencies involved with the child. This is what is required from local authorities in Wales by existing housing policy and by children and young people's plans. There is no room for complacency, however; young people who are supported as they make the transition to independent living may require ongoing or crisis intervention support to maintain their housing. For older children who follow unplanned and chaotic housing pathways, recent guidance suggests that relevant agencies will need to take an integrated approach which addresses both housing and support needs. If the claim to link policy affecting children to the UNCRC is to be maintained, these issues will need to be addressed directly as an aspect of the proposed Housing Bill, or in accompanying secondary legislation or guidance.

Part of the Welsh Ministerial function is to make decisions about funding and prioritisation of resources. The Measure suggests that Welsh Ministers should come under close scrutiny for decisions they make in relation to funding – in particular in relation to maintaining children in the family home and in relation to housing support services at the point of transition to independent living and later. The homelessness plan notes the benefits of mediation in resolving problems that might otherwise lead to homelessness among young people. Such services may require the Welsh Government to provide financial support. Similarly, housing support services come at a cost which may need to be met in part by the Welsh Government. Where there are budgetary implications arising from the need to ensure that older children's UNCRC rights, including housing rights, are safeguarded, Welsh Ministers will have to have due regard to these rights in making funding decisions.

Another area in which the Measure is likely to provide a useful bulwark of rights is in the area of homelessness legislation. In 2009/10 Shelter Cymru, which provides a Wales-National housing advice service, saw 106 clients aged sixteen or seventeen years old. Among this client group, homelessness was by far the most prevalent problem, with 90 per cent either imminently or actually homeless, in most cases because of a breakdown in the relationship with parents. In 2009/10 Welsh local authorities found forty-three young people aged sixteen and seventeen intentionally homeless (pursuant to S191 of the Housing Act 1996, where a homeless person makes an application for housing to a local authority it must decide whether or not the applicant became homeless intentionally). These findings by the authority of intentionality on the part of the child were clustered in just over half of local authorities, some of which had determined as many as nine children intentionally homeless over the course of that year. The remaining half of local authorities, including some of Wales's most populous urban authorities, did not find any children intentionally homeless. Intentional homeless decisions have far-reaching consequences for people of any age, including those aged sixteen or seventeen, as it severely restricts available options and support, and can exacerbate a spiral of social exclusion and poverty instead of dealing with the causal issues of homelessness (Shelter Cymru, 2011). Recent research carried out with professional stakeholders working in housing in Wales confirms the negative impact of a finding of intentionality on subsequent household housing options (Mackie and Hoffman, 2011; Shelter Cymru, 2011). The statutory guidance issued by the Welsh Government has clarified that when sixteen- or seventeen-year-olds are found to be intentionally homeless, they should be immediately referred to children's social services for assessment. Nevertheless, given the punitive nature of intentional homelessness decisions, and the consequent restrictions in eligibility for housing, it is highly questionable whether it is ever appropriate to find a sixteen- or seventeen-year-old intentionally homeless.

It is a concern that a number of Welsh local authorities are prepared to make intentionality decisions against young people in Wales. Such a decision is particularly damaging for a young person whose capacity for choice in the housing market is limited. Any review of homelessness legislation in Wales – and any subsequent provision included in the proposed Housing Bill – will need to take into account how to safeguard and promote children's UNCRC rights and whether these are prejudiced if a finding of intentional homelessness remains an option against a child aged sixteen or seventeen.[2] Two factors which will need to be taken into account in this assessment are the problem of affordability, and the lack of preparedness of young people for independent living. The Welsh Government has committed to increasing the supply of affordable housing (WG, 2010a). In addition Welsh Ministers will need to consider whether due regard has been given to the interests of children in the formulation of policy on this issue, for example by asking whether social housing lettings are affordable to young people, and if sufficient priority is given to the development of social housing for letting to young people. In order to prepare young people for independent living, the Welsh Government supports Shelter Cymru's education service, which coordinates the delivery of leaving-home education to young people (and to those working with young people) across Wales. While there is a commitment to provide education on homelessness to all young people, this has not led to leaving-home education becoming part of the national curriculum in Wales, despite lobbying on this issue by Shelter Cymru and by young people themselves. Giving due regard to the listed provisions of the UNCRC may require Welsh Ministers to take a more proactive stance when discharging their statutory functions in relation to the development of the national curriculum in Wales.

Conclusion

Housing policy in Wales has taken a distinctive path, including in the way it deals with children and young people. Through the vehicle of its seven core aims, the Welsh Government has sought to incorporate UNCRC principles and values into housing services for children and young people. However, there remains a gap between policy and housing services – both accommodation and support. The practice of housing in Wales often fails to properly recognise the rights and particular needs of older children. The implications of the Measure are significant in this respect, as the development of housing policy or policies, housing legislation, guidance, action plans and other implementation strategies will need to pay attention to the right of all children to an adequate standard of living, and therefore adequate housing. As we have argued in this chapter, this will include not only the provision of affordable housing for older children, but also support services – initially to prevent homelessness, and then to deliver sustainable housing for individuals living independently.

References

Anderson, I. (1999): 'Young single people and access to housing', in J. Rugg (ed.), *Young People, Housing and Social Policy* (London: Routledge), pp. 35–49.

Clapham, D., Buckley, K., Mackie, P., Orford, S. and Thomas, I. (2012): *The Housing Scenarios Facing Young People in 2020* (York: Joseph Rowntree Foundation). Available at *http://www.jrf.org.uk/sites/files/jrf/young-people-housing-options-full_0.pdf* (accessed 16 September 2012).

DCLG (2008): *Statutory Homelessness in England: The Experiences of Families and 16–17 Year Olds; Homelessness Research Summary Number 7* (London: Department for Communities and Local Government).

DCSF (2008): *Joint Working Between Housing and Children's Services: Preventing Homelessness and Tackling its Effects on Children and Young People* (London: Department for Children, Schools and Families).

Fitzpatrick, S. (1999): *Pathways to Independence. The Experience of Young Homeless People* (Edinburgh: Scottish Homes).

—— (2000): *Young Homeless People* (Basingstoke: MacMillan Press).

Ford, J., Rugg, J. and Burrows, R. (2002): 'Conceptualising the contemporary role of housing in the transition to adult life in England', *Urban Studies*, 39, 2455–67.

Fox, L. (2002): 'The meaning of a home: a chimerical concept or a legal challenge', *Journal of Law and Society*, 29/4, 580–610.

Hoffman, S. (2010): 'Legislative competence in housing in Wales: an assessment of likely impacts', *Journal of Housing Law*, 13/3, 41–6.

Kemp, P. A. and Rugg, J. (1998): *The Single Room Rent: Its Impact on Young People* (York: Centre for Housing Policy, University of York).

Lawrence, R. L. (ed.) (2004): 'Special issue: housing, health and well-being', *Reviews on Environmental Health*, 19/3–4, 331–45.

Mackie, P. K. (2007): *Equality and Access: Research into the Housing Needs of Young People in Rhondda Cynon Taf* (Swansea: Shelter Cymru).

—— (2008): *Room for Improvement: Research into the Accommodation and Support Needs of Young People in Cardiff* (Swansea: Shelter Cymru).

Mackie, P. K. and Hoffman, S. (2011): *Homelessness Legislation in Wales: Stakeholder Perspectives on Potential Improvements* (Cardiff: Welsh Government).

Mendes, P. and Moslehuddin, B. (2004): 'Graduating from the child welfare system: a comparison of the UK and Australian leaving care debates', *International Journal of Social Welfare*, 13, 332–9.

—— and —— (2006): 'From dependence to interdependence: towards better outcomes for young people leaving state care', *Child Abuse Review*, 15, 110–26.

Pawson, H. (2007): 'Local authority homelessness prevention in England: empowering consumers or denying rights?', *Housing Studies*, 22/6, 867–83.

Quilgars, D., Johnsen, S. and Pleace, N. (2008): *Youth Homelessness in the UK: A Decade of Progress?* (York: Joseph Rowntree Foundation).

Rees, G. and Lee, J. (2005): *Still Running II: Findings From the Second National Survey of Young Runaways* (London: Children's Society).

Shelter Cymru (2011): *The Impact of Intentional Homelessness Decisions on Welsh Households' Lives* (Swansea: Shelter Cymru).

Tobin, J. (2011): 'Understanding a human rights based approach', in J. Williams and A. Invernizzi (eds), *The Human Rights of Children: From Visions to Implementation* (Ashgate Publishing: Farnham), pp. 61–98.

Tyler, K. A. (2008): 'Social network characteristics and risky sexual and drug related behaviours among homeless young adults', *Social Science Research*, 37, 673–85.

WG (Welsh Government) (2004): *Children and Young People: Rights to Action* (Cardiff: Welsh Assembly Government).

—— (2009): *Ten Year Homelessness Plan for Wales* (Cardiff: Welsh Assembly Government).

—— (2010a): *Improving Lives and Communities – Homes in Wales* (Cardiff: Welsh Assembly Government).

—— (2010b): *Children and Young People's Plans: Interim Guidance 2011–14 (Draft Guidance for Consultation)* (Cardiff: Welsh Assembly Government).

—— (2010c): *Provision of Accommodation for 16 and 17 Year Old Young People who May be Homeless* (Cardiff: Welsh Assembly Government).

—— (2011): *The Welsh Government's Legislative Programme 2011–2016* (Cardiff: Welsh Government).

Notes

1. From this point forward 'parents' is used in place of 'parents and carers' and/or 'parents and others responsible'.

2. Following submission of this chapter for publication, the Welsh Government commissioned an independent review of stakeholder opinion on homelessness legislation in Wales. The review team received evidence from the Wales Monitoring Group on the UNCRC which argued this very point. The Welsh Government White Paper on proposals for a Housing Bill, *Homes for Wales: A White Paper for Better Lives and Communities*, was published for consultation in May 2012 and included a proposal to remove intentionality for households with children. As of June 2012 the Welsh Government had not published its Housing Bill.

CHAPTER 8

Children's rights in education

Peter Hosking

The corporal punishment of children in state schools in England and Wales ended in 1987 and with it one of the more blatant abuses of children's rights within the education system. It is hard to believe that the use of corporal punishment remained legal in independent schools for a further ten years. (Banned in state schools under section 47 of the Education [No. 2] Act 1996, it remained lawful in independent schools until section 548 Education Act 1996 took effect.) If pupils in today's schools were to be subjected to such physical abuse there would be public outrage and serious consequences for the staff concerned – yet this illustrates the context in which children and young people were being educated at the time that the UNCRC came into force in 1990. In 2001 the UN Committee felt it necessary to comment: 'Children do not lose their human rights by virtue of passing through the school gates' (UN Committee *GC*, 2001).

There is no doubt that there have been major advances in securing children's rights in education since the Welsh Government's adoption of the UNCRC as its overarching framework of principle for policies on children and young people. However, it is questionable whether the UNCRC itself has always been the prime motivation for change, as there has not been a widespread awareness of it. Certainly, where it was recognised that children had rights, the UNCRC gave added impetus to change, but there remained situations that were not recognised as being issues of children's rights and no reference was made to the UNCRC.

This chapter examines some of the advances of children's rights in education – many of which are unique to Wales. The author's perspective is that of a policy officer whose role, for over ten years, has been to examine Welsh Government policy initiatives, and influence development to the benefit of children and young people.

The Care Standards Act 2000 established the Children's Commissioner for Wales and, for the first time in the UK, created an institution whose primary aim was to 'safeguard and promote the rights and welfare of children'. It is significant that 'rights' are mentioned before 'welfare'.

(The background and legal framework of the commissioner is discussed by Rees in chapter 13 of this volume.)

Being a new and unique institution in the UK both posed challenges and provided opportunities. While the search for premises and the recruitment of staff went on, the commissioner spent much of his first year travelling around Wales meeting children and young people and discovering their priorities for his work. Inevitably this entailed many visits to schools, and the consistent message was pupils' concerns about the poor state of their school toilets. The commissioner reported these messages in one of his first reports, *Lifting the Lid on the Nation's School Toilets* (Children's Commissioner for Wales, 2004). This showed that 62 per cent of children were unhappy with the state of their toilets and pupils interpreted this as the school showing a lack of respect for children, as the teachers' toilets were in a much better condition.

Although in the report this was not identified as an issue of children's rights, many of the rights enshrined in the UNCRC, such as rights to privacy and health, are clearly affected. Some children avoided drinking so that they would not have to use the toilets – the resulting dehydration could result in decreased mental capacity and so affect their learning and thus their ability to fully benefit from their right to education.

It was clearly not difficult to improve the condition of the pupils' toilets as 38 per cent of pupils reported that they were happy with their toilets. What appeared to be lacking was the will of school governing bodies to make the necessary improvements.

In September 2005 an E. coli outbreak in south Wales resulted in the tragic death of a young pupil and prompted a public inquiry conducted by Sir Roger Pennington. One of the recommendations of that inquiry was that 'Every local authority should have a programme of audits to ensure that all schools have adequate toilet and hand washing facilities' (WG, 2009: 334). This echoed the commissioner's recommendation, which had been made some five years earlier, in *Lifting the Lid*.

Since 2005 more pupils are able to say how good their toilets are and how they have been involved in renovation and decoration. However, the fact that many school toilets are still in such a poor state led the chair of the Children and Young People Committee of the National Assembly for Wales to comment: 'It is absolutely true that if many of the school lavatories that I have seen and the ones that the Commissioner reports on were in an adult workplace, the Health and Safety Executive would shut the place down' (CYPC, 2011). A summary of responses to a pupil questionnaire listed the main deficiencies:

Smelly, dirty or messy toilets: 1,030 responses (58%)
No soap for washing hands: 748 responses (42%)
People can look over/under doors: 717 responses (40%)
Doors don't lock: 716 responses (40%)
No toilet paper: 698 responses (39%)

                                                (WG, 2011a)

These responses arguably indicate a breach of several rights simultaneously in the UNCRC and there are many pressing reasons to improve pupils' toilet facilities – the health risks alone should have dictated the improvement. Nowhere, except in schools, could the problem have been ignored for so long.

One of the many questions that arise is whether pupils have felt able to voice their views and opinions about their toilets to those who are able to make the decision to improve them. What is the state of Article 12, the right of children to have their opinions considered, in the education system? Do pupils feel that they can participate in decision-making in school?

The School Councils (Wales) Regulations 2005 (SI 2005/3200 (W. 236)) came into force on 31 December 2005. These regulations required schools to establish a school council and have the first meeting of the council before 1 November 2006. Although some schools had already established councils, placing school councils on a statutory footing was a major advance in increasing children's access to their right to participate in school decision-making. In many schools it has led to an active school council and an increased feeling of 'community' within the school. However, in other schools it appears to have enabled schools simply to 'tick the box' on participation and make no other effort to actively engage with pupils or involve them in any real decision making. The Minister for Children, Education and Lifelong Learning commented in 2010:

> Although many schools in Wales now have well-established school councils, including mechanisms for communication and training, and liaison with governing bodies, we are aware that in other schools participation is patchy and tokenistic.

He also promised new guidance on participation that would:

> encourage a change of culture, where pupil participation becomes part and parcel of everything the school does, including teaching and learning. (WG, 2010a)

The Funky Dragon research published in *Our Rights, Our Story* came to a similar conclusion:

> If the initiative is to succeed then it needs to be given far more thought, by all of those involved. Too many young people are unaware of the structures in place, or feel that they are ineffective. Far too often the agenda is not in the hands of pupils. At best when school councils are achieving anything it tends to be superficial. (Funky Dragon, 2007: 84)

School council members themselves would not all agree with that assessment. A school council member recounted with pride how the council had decided on their 'Fruity Fridays' scheme – whereby the tuck shop would sell fruit instead of sweets on a Friday. In the same school there was also an eco-council through which the pupils decided that recycling paper was not enough and that the school should ensure that both sides of the paper was used first. In a video interview the commissioner was told that although there were some pupils unhappy with these decisions, the fact that they had been made by their peers, rather than their teachers, made it easier to accept them.

These are encouraging signs of a cultural change leading to pupils having a greater say in what happens in the school. A report commissioned by the Welsh Government includes many examples of real participation by children and young people (O'Kane with Dynamix Ltd, 2010). When all schools fully develop and empower their school council, pupil participation will become more widespread.

Perhaps there also needs to be a similar culture change within some schools regarding who they perceive to be the 'service user'. Until very recently it has been the parent or guardian rather than the pupil who was able to challenge decisions made in the school or local authority. It is still only parents who have the right to appeal to the local authority about school admissions. Until 2004 only parents or guardians had the right of appeal against the exclusion of their children.

There can be few decisions that affect a pupil's life chances more than the decision to permanently exclude them from school. In 2009/10 there were 185 permanent exclusions in Wales (WG, 2010b). Of these, 105 pupils had special educational needs – despite official guidance that, 'Other than in the most exceptional circumstances, schools should avoid permanently excluding pupils with statements of special educational needs' (NAW, 2004: 13.2). Although this continues the trend of a gradual reduction in the number of permanent exclusions in Wales since 2004, the Welsh Government is clear that it wants the number of exclusions to reduce even more.

The decision to permanently exclude is taken by a head teacher, and if there is an appeal, the governing body of the school will consider it. There is a further avenue of appeal to an independent panel if the governing body upholds the exclusion. But, in upholding a decision to permanently exclude, are the governors really making a decision in which 'the best interests of the child shall be a primary consideration', as per UNCRC Article 3? Do head teachers and governors really understand what alternative provision will be made available to a pupil after exclusion? Of those excluded in 2009/10, only 22 per cent were placed in another school and 18 per cent were reported as having 'no provision' (WG, 2010b: 5). It is difficult to see how a decision that results in a pupil having no educational provision can be in their best interests.

In 2004 the Welsh Government extended the right of appeal against school exclusions to pupils of secondary school age (NAW, 2004: Part 4). This same guidance required local authorities to support pupils who wished to make an appeal to 'endeavour to obtain the services of an advocate to speak on behalf of the pupil' (ibid.: para. 2.4). With such weak guidance – merely that they should 'endeavour' – few local authorities have commissioned an advocacy service for this purpose, although later statutory guidance requires local authorities to commission a universal advocacy service for all children and young people, including but not limited to those having a specific statutory entitlement to advocacy services (WG, 2011b). This should result in improvement in access to support for pupils seeking to exercise the right of appeal.

It is important that children and young people are able to challenge those in authority. The Waterhouse report into the wide scale abuse that took place in residential homes in Wales was released in February 2000. Published under the title *Lost in Care*, the report spoke of systematic abuse, a climate of violence and a culture of secrecy that had existed for more than two decades. No-one had listened either to the young people who had tried to complain or to staff who tried to blow the whistle. One of the clear messages from the report was that having an accessible and robust complaints procedure for children and young people to use was an essential element in safeguarding. In 2004 the Children's Commissioner for Wales published *Clywch: Report of the Examination of the Children's Commissioner for Wales into Allegations of Child Sexual Abuse in a School Setting*, which found that the lessons of the Waterhouse report had not been learnt and implemented in an educational setting (for further discussion, see Rees in chapter 13 of this volume). Again, pupils' complaints had not been listened to.

Until recently, complaints in school were seen to be exclusively the domain of parents since they were seen to be the 'service users'. Although it was not specifically stated that pupils could not also make a complaint, complaints procedures were often thirty-page documents written in very formal language. Many specified that the complaint must be written, sometimes by completing a form, and no support was offered to record the complaint in any other way. These procedures would deter many adults from making a complaint, let alone children and young people.

Until recently, a concern raised by a pupil would not normally have been pursued through the school complaint procedures and therefore might not have received full consideration. In 2006, guidance published by the National Assembly for Wales recognised that school policies and procedures might need to be amended to make them more accessible to pupils and that they might need more support than adults to pursue their complaint.

Most importantly, pupils need to know that they may make a complaint and how to do so. Section 29(1) of the Education Act 2002 places a statutory duty on schools to publish their complaints procedure and to include a summary of the procedure in their prospectus. Many schools publish their prospectus on their website. A recent survey conducted by the author of twenty randomly chosen schools with prospectuses on their websites shows that nine schools did not include a summary complaints procedure, six suggested that only parents could make a complaint, three did not specify whether a parent or pupil could make a complaint and only two included specific mention of receiving complaints from pupils. This would indicate that the good intentions of national guidance to afford to pupils the right to make a complaint are not well implemented throughout Wales.

Many commercial organisations encourage feedback from their customers and see this as informing their quality improvement agenda. Estyn, Her Majesty's Inspectorate for Education and Training in Wales, now inspects the extent to which pupils are enabled to participate in school decisions, and, importantly, they listen to and take account of the views of pupils during a school inspection. This is an important realisation of their rights under Article 12. Yet the question remains: how often do pupils exercise their rights of their own volition?

There is no central record of the number of pupils exercising their right to make a complaint in schools. However, a major teachers' union has reported, in conversation, that they have never been concerned in supporting a member in relation to a complaint made by a pupil. The Welsh

Government does, on the other hand, record the number of exclusion appeals made by parents and pupils to an independent panel and the author requested this unpublished information. In 2008/9 there were twenty-six appeals by parents and two by pupils. In 2009/10 there were twenty-two appeals by parents and five by pupils (information supplied to the author by the Welsh Government).

Although the number of appeals from pupils is low, it is good to see that some pupils are exercising their right in this respect. It is, of course, possible that appeals registered as being made by children have the support and encouragement of the family. Others may be made when there is no parental support. Either way, pupils will be enabled to have their voices heard when one of the most important decisions about their education is being made.

The low numbers of pupils making complaints or appeals against exclusion may indicate that pupils are not well informed and sufficiently reassured to do so. It would appear that pupils are seen as too immature to question those in authority. In 2009, pupils in England were similarly given the right to complain about their head teacher. At that time a teachers' union representative commented: 'You could end up with a situation where a parent is perfectly accepting of something and the young person still wants to complain. We should allow parents to take responsibility and not undermine their ability to take decisions. They bring a maturity you would not expect children to have' (Clark, 2009).

Teaching professionals, however, increasingly favour a rights approach in schools. When a Welsh primary school was awarded the UNICEF level 2 award for 'rights respecting schools', one assistant head commented: 'We felt that by empowering the children, giving them an improved sense of self-esteem and helping them to understand what's right for them and others, we could help enhance their confidence and improve their aspirations.' And yet a teachers' union representative commented: 'We don't want to develop a classroom culture of pupils saying, "I know my rights, you can't do this to me", because that would be a retrograde step' (Evans, 2011). This is a strange attitude coming from someone whose role is to inform union members of their rights and help them to defend them. It suggests that allowing children to exercise their rights will, in some way, undermine the authority of teachers and is indicative of a common misunderstanding of the true nature of children's rights.

This attitude is by no means uncommon and can result in children being denied their rights because they are judged to lack the capability or maturity to exercise them. The justification for this is often quoted as being that the UNCRC itself includes the caveat 'the views of the child being given due weight in accordance with the age and maturity of the child' (Article 12.1). However, 'due weight' should not be interpreted as not listening, or considering the views of a child as not being relevant.

Consider the experience of a child who is a wheelchair-user. Because of fears for her safety in busy school corridors, she was asked to come to school thirty minutes late and leave thirty minutes early. Her parents were supportive of this arrangement as they were reassured she would be safer. However, she felt she was missing out – not only on class time but the opportunity to associate with friends. After being supported in making a complaint to the school, the school made alternative arrangements that suited all. She was eight years old.[1]

The UN Committee has commented:

> By requiring that due weight be given in accordance with age and maturity, Article 12 makes it clear that age alone cannot determine the significance of a child's views. Children's levels of understanding are not uniformly linked to their biological age. Research has shown that information, experience, environment, social and cultural expectations, and levels of support all contribute to the development of a child's capacities to form a view. For this reason, the views of the child have to be assessed on a case-by-case examination. (UN Committee *GC*, 2009: para. 29)

The right of a pupil in Wales to appeal against exclusion applies only to secondary school pupils. It would clearly be wrong to suggest that no ten-year-old pupil in a primary school would be capable of appealing against exclusion, or that all pupils in a secondary school are capable. Yet age and capability are often cited as reasons to prevent pupils from exercising their rights.

In 2005 the Children's Commissioner made a proposal to the Welsh Government that children, and not just parents or guardians, should be able to appeal to the Special Educational Needs Tribunal for Wales ('the Tribunal') about their special needs provision in their statement, or to make a claim of disability discrimination in schools. Previously only parents had had the right to make an appeal or claim. The initial reaction to the proposal was mixed, with some officers supporting the proposal but with others expressing disbelief as it was clear that they felt that children with special educational needs would not be capable of making such an appeal either because of their age or their special needs. However, the basis of the proposal was that children with special needs are no more a homogenous group than any other group of children of the same age. While it is probably correct that some children would not be capable of making an appeal, other children are not only capable but, by their attendance at the Tribunal hearing, can best demonstrate their capability and potential to benefit from the provision that is being sought.

Some time later, the Education (Wales) Measure 2009 introduced the right of a child to make an appeal to the Tribunal. Later, following the passage of the Right of a Child to Make a Disability Discrimination Claim (Schools) (Wales) Order 2011 (SI 2011/1651 (W. 187)), children became able to make a claim to the Tribunal about disability discrimination in schools. The history of the development of this piece of legislation provides insight into the implementation of children's rights in Wales.

Following acceptance of the proposal by the Welsh Government, there was a long period of consultation with Tribunal user groups. These groups included special educational needs (SEN) managers from across Wales, parent partnership organisations, and parents – but, of course, no children at that time. It was clear that some Welsh Government officers were of the expectation that SEN managers would be against the proposal. This proved not to be the case and the great majority of SEN managers supported the proposal. The consensus was that they would find their work more rewarding if they were able to concentrate on the needs of children rather than the expectations of parents. They were also aware that some parents were more capable than others, and they were concerned about those pupils whose parents did not feel able to make an appeal.

These consultation sessions raised awareness of children's rights to the extent that changes were already being made to improve the participation of children throughout the SEN process. The Tribunal made changes to facilitate the inclusion of children's views in their hearings, and provided children's rights training for their members. Local authorities had always been required by the Tribunal to discover the wishes and feelings of the child, yet were sometimes prevented from doing so by parents. There was no similar duty on parents to represent the views of the child. However, regulation 20 of the Special Educational Needs Tribunal for Wales Regulations 2012 (SI 2012/322 [W. 53]) provides that in an appeal, both the parent and the local authority must state the views of the child or provide an explanation of why such views have not been obtained.

It is to the credit of the Welsh Government that, following this consultation period, it invested resources to make a child's right of appeal a reality. Two officers were appointed and a working group of interested parties was established to consider what was needed to enable children to make an appeal. It would be necessary to make changes to primary legislation but by this time the Government of Wales Act 2006 enabled the Welsh Government to apply for legislative competence in devolved areas. The first to be made was the National Assembly for Wales (Legislative Competence) (Education and Training) Order 2008 (SI 2008/1036) and this enabled the Welsh Government to make changes to SEN legislation in Wales without further application to the UK Government.

Although the legislative hurdles were removed, there remained many other concerns. Perhaps foremost of these was the potential conflict between children's rights and parents' rights. One suggestion, to avoid this potential conflict, was that children should only be able to appeal if the parent did not. Again, the suggestion was that children's rights should be subordinate to parental rights. It was also based on the assumption that parents will always act in the best interests of their children. However, this is not always the case – in many instances parents will act in their own best interests. Conflict will almost certainly arise if the child and parents do not agree on the educational provision – whether there is an appeal or not. The final decision reflected in the Education (Wales) Measure 2009 was that both children and parents were able to make concurrent appeals.

Inevitably, capability was another issue to be considered. It was argued that children who had the most severe needs would not be capable of making an appeal and that there should be a test of capability before accepting an appeal. Yet some children with profound and multiple disabilities are perfectly capable of making an appeal if given appropriate support to do so. This may mean that the Tribunal hearing would need to include, for example, signers or readers, and that the time of the hearing be extended. The Education (Wales) Measure 2009 also makes provision for the child making an appeal to have the support of a 'case friend' who may exercise the child's right to make an appeal or a claim to the Tribunal. The final decision on capability in the Education (Wales) Measure 2009 was that there should be no test of capability and that age would not be a barrier to making an appeal.

The concept that children's right of appeal or claim to the Tribunal is absolute – dependent neither on parental consent nor a test of capability or age – is what makes this Measure a ground-breaking piece of legislation. It is to be hoped that it will set a precedent for the development of children's rights in other areas. There is still much to learn before the right of appeal to the Tribunal is rolled out across Wales, and two pilot schemes, starting in the autumn of 2011, are to inform this learning process and explore the practicalities. But the Measure makes it clear that the right of appeal itself is not dependent on the outcome of the pilot schemes.

Yet some barriers to children making an appeal or claim to the Tribunal still remain. Many families making an appeal feel it necessary to engage legal representation. This is not a requirement of the Tribunal and the hearings themselves are designed to be user-friendly to those who represent themselves. However, the fact remains that many families do engage a solicitor, and if they are not eligible for legal aid, this can be costly.

In the development of the Education (Wales) Measure 2009, there were concerns expressed that parents would make a 'proxy' appeal in the name of their child as the child would be eligible for legal aid even if the parents were not. The suggestion was that this would remove the financial burden on parents. Presumably this also means that some families do not appeal because of the cost, and their child's needs may remain unmet.

In fact the fear of proxy appeals has not been realised. The Legal Services Commission has stated that eligibility to legal aid for a child making an appeal will be assessed on the family income. This seems unjust, as it means that although the child can make an appeal, the parents are still able to control whether the child can access legal support by refusing to finance it. Other support, such as a case friend, will still be available and the challenge for the Tribunal will be to ensure that its hearings are user-friendly and can be conducted without legal representation, and that this is communicated to potential appellants and claimants.

The development of children's rights in education may sometimes feel like 'two steps forward, one step back' but there is undeniably forward momentum. The Welsh Government has demonstrated its commitment to implementing the UNCRC and has produced guidance and legislation that reflects this commitment. As with much other guidance, there is sometimes a mismatch between the intentions of national government and implementation at a local level. Fortunately, there are also examples of schools exceeding the expectations of government guidance.

We have to question why, when some schools are so enthusiastic about promoting children's rights, others are so reluctant. We have come a long way from the use of corporal punishment as a means of control, but an authoritarian ethos still exists in many schools, and 'authority' does not easily equate to 'respect' for human rights. The Children's Commissioner for Wales commented in his annual report of 2004/5:

It is clear that some adults are confusing respect with fear and obedience, perhaps hankering after some bygone age when children were fearful of adults. It seems equally clear that many more adults are unwilling to think about how they might earn the respect of the young. They seem to expect automatic respect in a way that they do not from fellow adults. (Children's Commissioner for Wales, 2004/5)

Those schools that have engendered a whole-school approach to respect for the rights both of teachers and of pupils seem to feel happier places. There are measurable outcomes such as improved behaviour and attendance, and reduction in pupil-pupil bullying, as well as increased engagement in learning and improved attainment (Sebba and Robinson, 2010). It would seem that those schools that insist on maintaining the 'authority' of adults at the expense of children's rights are, quite simply, missing a trick.

References

CYPC (Children and Young People Committee), National Assembly for Wales (2011): Record of Proceedings, 15 March (Cardiff: National Assembly for Wales).

Children's Commissioner for Wales (2004): *Lifting the Lid on the Nation's School Toilets* (Swansea: Children's Commissioner for Wales).

—— (2004/5): *Annual Report 04–05* (Swansea: Children's Commissioner for Wales).

Clark, L. (2009): 'Pupils given the right to complain about their headteacher', *Mail Online*, 21 December. Available at *http://www.dailymail.co.uk/news/article-1237344/Pupils-given-right-complain-headteacher.html* (accessed 27 June 2012).

Evans, D. (2011): 'Praise for Wales' record on children's rights', *TES Connect*, 17 June.

Funky Dragon (2007): *Our Rights, Our Story* (Swansea: Funky Dragon).

NAW (National Assembly for Wales) (2004): *Guidance on Exclusion from Schools and Pupil Referral Units*, circular 01/04 (Cardiff: National Assembly for Wales).

O'Kane, K., with Dynamix Ltd (2010): *Research to Develop More Inclusive and Representative Models of Pupil Participation in Wales*, Contract No. Research 200910 (Cardiff: Welsh Assembly Government).

Sebba, J., and Robinson, C. (2010): *Evaluation of UNICEF UK's Rights Respecting Schools Awards (RRSA) Scheme: Final Report* (Brighton: Universities of Sussex and Brighton).

WG (Welsh Government) (2009): *Public Inquiry into the September 2005 Outbreak of E. Coli O157 in South Wales* (Cardiff: Welsh Assembly Government).

—— (2010a): *Proposed Statutory Guidance on Pupil Participation*, decision statement published 17 February 2010, paragraph 4 (Cardiff: Welsh Assembly Government).

—— (2010b): *Exclusions from Schools in Wales, 2009/10 (Revised), Statistics for Wales, March 2011* (Cardiff: Welsh Assembly Government).

—— (2011a): *School Toilets Good Practice Guidance for Primary and Secondary Schools in Wales, Summary of Consultation Responses*, WG 10-10560 2011 (Cardiff: Welsh Government).

—— (2011b): *Delivering Advocacy Services for Children and Young People 0–25 in Wales* (Cardiff: Welsh Government).

Note

1. Where no specific reference is given, the author is drawing on his own experience of work in the Children's Commissioner's office.

CHAPTER 9

Extended rights for children and young people in Wales? A focus on gender

Jacky Tyrie

Introduction

Gender is a major building block of social conventions and structures (Pilcher and Whelehan, 2004; Richardson and Robinson, 2008) and as such it is a potentially divisive concept that may impact on children and young people's access to their rights. In Wales, gender equality is written into law in the UK-wide Equality Act 2010, and in the Government of Wales Act 2006 (Williams, chapter 4 in this volume). Since devolution in 1999, the Welsh Government has placed a great deal of emphasis on children and young people's rights and equality (Butler and Drakeford, chapter 1 in this volume). Wales has become renowned for its progressive, forward-thinking approach in relation to the rights of children and young people (Thomas and Crowley, 2007). In theory, this forward-thinking policy rhetoric, which is so energetically embraced by the Welsh Government, combined with the Equality Act 2010 and Government of Wales legislation, means that Welsh children and young people should now benefit from increased access to their rights.

However, there is limited empirical evidence to establish whether or not these legal provisions and policy measures have afforded enhanced access to rights for all children and young people in Wales. More concerning, given the legislation that exists regarding discrimination, is the scarcity of research examining the influence that gender may have on children and young people's rights in Wales. By drawing on a study undertaken with children and young people aged eleven to sixteen in Wales (Tyrie, 2010), the influence that gender has on access to their rights by children and young people is explored here.

Rhetoric and reality: 'access' to rights is important

While academics (Case et al., 2005; Williamson, 2007; Drakeford, 2010) have extolled the virtues of the rights rhetoric, this rhetoric is meaningless without the reality of young people being able to access the rights outlined in Welsh policy (Haines et al., 2004; Fitzpatrick, chapter 5 in this volume). Indeed, there are some challenges regarding the use of policy if poorly implemented (Gran, 2010; Kaime, 2010). It is clear that the rights outlined in policy are 'intended' and worthwhile only if access to those rights is actually occurring (Williamson, 2007). There is, however, another potential barrier in making the rhetoric of policy into reality on the ground. This further barrier relates to children and young people's perspectives and perception. If young people do not feel able to access their rights, this may lead to complex problems, including issues around welfare, well-being and quality of life (Haines et al., 2004; Osmond and Morris, 2009; Bradshaw and Mayhew, 2005). It is therefore important to focus on examining young people's access to their rights, and specifically on young people's perception of their access to these rights.

Gender equality for children and young people: the policy background

The UK-wide Equality Act 2010, which replaced several earlier anti-discrimination statutes, covers many forms of discrimination including gender discrimination. It imposes duties on public bodies – including the devolved institutions – to promote equality. In addition, the devolved government in Wales is subject to the Statutory Equality Duty as well as monitoring processes (Chaney, 2002). Gender equality is therefore provided for in policy and law for all children and young people in Wales.

It is a common perception that gender equality has been achieved within British society (Esping-Anderson, 2009). However, there is evidence that gender inequalities exist in children and young people's lives (Aapola et al., 2005; Nayak and Kehily, 2008; Richardson and Robinson, 2008). While the ideals of gender equality and children's rights are well established in both policy and law (Franklin, 2002; Case et al., 2005; Williams, 2007), it is argued that they are poorly implemented (Williamson, 2007), suggesting that rhetoric and reality are discordant.

Empirical evidence – gender inequalities and children's access to rights

As discussed in Part I of this volume, the Welsh Government has a range of policies and legislative tools that protect and support children's rights. One of these is the *Extending Entitlement* policy, which focuses on universal entitlements for all young people. This flagship youth policy sets out, as far as possible, a set of rights which are free at the point of use and unconditional. Case et al. (2005) suggest that *Extending Entitlement* is a new way of thinking about support and service provision for young people. The *Extending Entitlement* policy is unusual as it clearly outlines ten specific rights for children in Wales. This specificity marks it out as different from other rights policies in the UK (Case et al., 2005). The 'ten entitlements' to which all young people in Wales should have access provides researchers with the opportunity to explore and measure young people's access to their rights in Wales. For the purposes of the research, described below are the criteria derived from the ten entitlements that were used:

1   Knowing about your rights
2   Being heard
3   Feeling good
4   Education and employment
5   Taking part/getting involved
6   Being individual
7   Easy access to services
8   Health and well-being
9   Access to information and guidance
10 Safety and security

Empirical evidence from research undertaken with young people across Wales has been examined to better understand gender inequalities in young people's experiences in accessing their rights (Tyrie, 2010). Robust mixed methodology research was undertaken between 2006 and 2008. Data was collected using an online survey of 2,043 young people and focus groups with 120 young people. Of the rights examined as part of this research, some displayed no gender inequalities. These were: knowing about your rights, being heard, having access to services, and access to information and guidance. Other rights which young people felt were not accessed equitably were: feeling good and confident, health and well-being, education, taking part/getting involved, being individual and safety and security. This chapter examines three of these: education, health and well-being, and safety and security.

Education
UNCRC Articles 28 and 29 state that children have a right to an education and that education should develop each child's personality and talents to the full. Entitlement 4 – education and employment – promises that

children and young people will be able to learn about things that interest and affect them, enjoy the job they do and get involved in the activities they enjoy including leisure, music, sport and exercise, art, hobbies and cultural activities.

Education was an area where young people in the empirical study held strong views. They felt it was relevant to their lives. The stereotype of girls achieving in education and of boys having more opportunities in school sporting activities (Vilhjalmsson and Kristjansdottir, 2003) was evident in young people's views. Educational achievement was found to be higher for girls: it was suggested this could lead to problems for boys in accessing education and also other rights later in life. In the focus groups, young people felt that females tried harder and got better marks in school. This is in line with previous research which suggests that in secondary schools females are achieving better marks than males (Hill and Tisdall, 1997). In the focus groups there was one example of a group of young people that felt that teachers in school were sexist, as they only picked girls to do responsible jobs such as taking messages, and only picked boys to do physical jobs such as lifting boxes. The young people felt quite strongly that this was sexist and not fair on the young people who did not typify the gendered judgement made by the teachers. This example would suggest that the socially constructed roles that society – in this case, teachers – give to young people can constrict what young people of different genders are allowed or supported to do, and therefore achieve. The fact that some of the young people in the focus groups discussed the treatment by teachers as reinforcing distinct gender roles could lead to some young males feeling that they are not encouraged to carry out the now-typical 'girly' traits of trying hard and being responsible.

There can be serious consequences for young people who do not feel able to achieve in education. Misbehaviour and exclusion from schools can lead to a lack of access to education or a reduction in the chances of accessing education. Lloyd (2005) states that boys accounted for 80 per cent of all exclusions in England: this would point to a section of the young male population having difficulties accessing education. Another element of education that was addressed as part of the study was learning. When discussing 'taking part in learning about things of interest', there was a gendered divide in opportunities to learn about things of interest. Boys felt that girls had more opportunities, while girls felt that boys had more. This would suggest that the perception of accessing things of interest and learning was variable based on gender, with each gender feeling that the other had advantages.

Health and well-being

UNCRC Article 24 states that children have the right to good quality health care and to clean water, nutritious food and a clean environment so that they will stay healthy. Entitlement 8 promises that children and young people will be able to lead a healthy life, both physically and emotionally.

The research revealed that males were perceived to have higher levels of health and well-being. This was in line with previous research which suggested that young females had more health difficulties than young males (Children's Commissioners in the UK, 2008). However, when the study data is examined in detail (Tyrie, 2010), a more complex picture emerges. Young people suggested that health incorporates a number of elements including diet, exercise, illness, mental health and well-being.

Generally girls were thought by young people to consider their diet more. This is supported by previous research (Byely et al., 2000), although it was suggested that this focus on diet could lead to girls thinking too much about food and weight and lead to them not eating enough. The focus by girls on image is well-documented, and evidence suggests females suffer more from eating disorders than males (Frost, 2001; Funky Dragon, 2007a). The focus group findings and past evidence suggest that this gender difference in interest about diet can have both a negative and positive ·impact on young people's health, depending on how far it is taken.

Exercise, particularly sport, was mentioned frequently by young people in the study, and previous literature suggests that sporting activities are key elements in young people's lives (Haines et al., 2004). There was evidence of a conflict of views between males and females: boys often thought that they did more sport (and occasionally the girls would agree) but girls often felt that they took part in as many sports activities, though these were of a different nature. Previous research has suggested that for boys sport and athleticism is more important as part of their gendered identity, with parents and teachers as well as children recognising that sports and athleticism are more valued in boys (Blakemore et al., 2009) and that boys participate in more sport (Funky Dragon, 2007a). It was felt by some older girls that the school system was sexist in relation to activities such as sport, as it allowed boys and girls to take part only in particular types of activities. While there was not thought to be a difference in the number of opportunities for males and females, young people suggested that they were not able to access the same activities. Past research has documented that there was a variation in the levels of sports participation between males and females, with females not enrolling or continuing with organised sports activities (Hill and Tisdall, 1997). This study suggested that young people felt that the opportunities available were not equal, and that boys had to play certain traditionally male sports, while girls were forced to play other traditionally female sports, a variation documented in other research (Richman and Shaffer, 2000; Vilhjalmsson and Kristjansdottir, 2003). In terms of being active (as a broader definition than sport), research indicates that from an early age males are more physically active than females (Coakley and White, 1992). This supports the findings of this study that boys are generally more active and take part in more sports. Although there were mixed views about gender and access to sports, young people suggested that boys had slightly more access to sports. Previous research also supports this view (Vilhjalmsson and Kristjansdottir, 2003; Blakemore et al., 2009). This would suggest that the physical health of young females may be being adversely affected by having less access to sport and exercise.

The data also revealed complex gender differences relating to mental health and well-being. Young people in the focus groups suggested that girls were more emotionally healthy as they were better at talking about any problems they had, but it was suggested that girls worry about how they look and are more self-conscious. However, the view expressed by many young people was that girls were better at being emotionally literate and therefore suffer fewer mental health issues. This is in line with previous literature which suggests that boys are more likely to experience mental health problems (Dennison and Coleman, 2000; Street, 2005) and are more likely to commit suicide than girls (Feingold, 1994; Major et al., 1999; Shaffer, 2000). However there is some conflicting research in the literature, as Shaffer (2000) found that the rate of female depression was twice as high as male depression, and Mclaughlin (2005) reports that girls were twice as likely to suffer from a depressive disorder. This previous research may support the research finding that girls worry more about body image and are more self-conscious.

The study data revealed that males had statistically higher levels of feeling good and confident about themselves. This is in line with previous research which suggests that young females reported worrying more than young males (Funky Dragon, 2007a). Bradshaw and Mayhew (2005) support these findings, suggesting that emotional health issues (for example unhappiness) are experienced more by girls. In addition, other research found that girls had higher levels of anxiety than boys (Hill and Tisdall, 1997). The study data suggested that young people felt that girls had lower levels of feeling good and confident because they worried more and were more self-conscious. This is supported by a range of research which found that in adolescence boys have higher self-esteem than girls (Dennison and

Coleman, 2000; Street, 2005) and that girls' bodies and looks are becoming increasingly high profile and often problematic (Frost, 2001).

In terms of physical health, the study data suggested that girls now smoke more than boys, a finding that is supported by research by Livingston and Room (2009). There were many references in the young people's discussions about smoking being physically bad for their health, but also suggestions that those who smoke thought they were 'cool' and more confident. This is not a universal opinion, however, as some young people suggested that, conversely, smoking could make you feel tired and less confident. In relation to alcohol use, previous literature supports the research findings which suggest that drinking is more prevalent among boys than girls (Bradshaw and Mayhew, 2005)

It is clear that gender differences in young people's perspectives about access to health were complex. Some areas, such as physical activity, were perceived as being undertaken more by males, and males were also found to smoke less. However, some evidence suggested that males suffered from more serious mental health problems, while girls appeared to be better at talking about health problems and thinking about their diet. The findings and previous literature suggest a complex and not altogether clear picture of gender and young people's health, particularly their mental health and well-being (Frost, 2001).

Safety and security

UNCRC Articles 32 to 36 state that the government should protect children from work that is dangerous or might harm their health or their education. The government should provide ways of protecting children from dangerous drugs. The government should protect children from sexual abuse. The government should make sure that children are not abducted or sold. Children should be protected from any activities that could harm their development. Entitlement 10 promises that children and young people will be able to live in a safe, secure home and community.

The data revealed that the majority of young people perceived they had high levels of access to safety and security. This is supported by research by the Children's Commissioners in the UK (2008), which revealed that most children in the UK state that they are safe from being hurt by others (Bradshaw and Mayhew, 2005). The quantitative research undertaken as part of this study found no statistically significant gender differences in young people's access to safety and security; however, the qualitative data found that girls felt less safe and secure than boys. In support of the qualitative data, research has suggested that girls are more fearful or timid of unknown situations than boys (Shaffer, 2000), and report fear more frequently than boys (Payne, 1991; Van Der Gaag, 2004). In the focus groups, some of the older participants (aged fourteen to sixteen) suggested that although girls felt less safe than boys, boys were actually more likely to come to harm and might feel less safe than they admitted. This is supported by research which found that boys from age five onwards learn to hide emotions such as fear (Children's Commissioners in the UK, 2008). In the study, young people discussed girls feeling that they could not walk home on their own. Research has suggested that the perception of risk of crime against women is not accurate for crimes that are most feared, such as attacks outside the home, when most attacks on females occur within the home (Blakemore et al., 2009; Paquette and Underwood, 1999; Seals and Young, 2003). This previous research supports the findings of the study that females feel more at risk from crime and less safe.

The research findings suggest that while young people reported no gender differences in actual safety, females felt less safe. Another possible explanation may be due to group pressures in the focus groups. It may be that boys felt less able to express any fears for their safety in the focus group situation. This hypothesis suggests that a web survey might give a more accurate view of young people's experiences, as young people would be answering in a private and individual setting and would be less likely to be influenced by peer pressure. This is supposition, however, and the results can only be used within the bounds of these possible explanations.

Moving from rhetoric to reality – the slow march forward

Previous research has explored young people's access to rights in Wales (Haines et al., 2004; Croke and Crowley, 2006 and 2007; Funky Dragon, 2007a and 2007b). Yet little research has focused specifically on gender inequalities in young people's access to their rights in Wales. Indeed, in the UK as a whole there has been little focus on gender inequalities in children and young people's access to their rights, with the exception of specific areas (Measor and Sikes, 1992; Browne, 2004; Street, 2005; Ringrose and Epstein, 2008). This suggests a gap in knowledge about gender and children's rights, and it is on this gap that this study has concentrated. It has addressed the gap by exploring gender inequalities in access to children's rights, in the focused context of young people in Wales, using the *Extending Entitlement* policy as a measure. The empirical evidence from this study suggests that overall boys had better access to their rights than girls (with the notable exception of education), but that the picture is very complex. A range of reasons were given as to why boys seemed better able to access some rights, including the following: society being sexist towards females; boys being better at saying what they want; and boys being more confident, having an active lifestyle and feeling safer than girls. The sexism that was discussed was predominantly seen in the behaviour of adults, where they had different expectations of young people based on their gender. This was a reason provided only by girls; none of the boys felt that sexism was an issue.

This large-scale piece of research was undertaken in 2008 (Tyrie, 2010) prior to the more recent legislative measures, the Rights of Children and Young Persons (Wales) Measure 2011 and the Equality Act 2010, although much of the substance of the Equality Act was in law prior to 2010. In 2008 we saw that while there was some evidence of gender equality in access to rights in areas such as accessing services, accessing information, knowing about rights and being involved in decisions, worryingly, progress was still needed in other areas such as perceptions of safety, feeling good and confident, health, exercise and education. The legislation relating to both children's rights and gender equality has placed 'due regard' duties on Welsh Ministers and other organisations (in the case of the Equality Act 2010) to take into consideration children and young people's rights. However, these laws will take some time to filter through to young people's reality. This chapter proposes that while the legal underpinning of the 2011 Measure and the Equality Act 2010 has narrowed the gap between policy rhetoric (which is very strong) and reality of children and young people's experiences (where gender inequalities still exist), more remains to be done. Progress is slow, but it must be encouraged if children and young people in Wales are to be able to access their rights equitably. Gender inequalities still exist despite common misconceptions of equality. This is not to detract from the progress made so far in achieving legal stature for equality and rights, but to emphasise the future work that is needed, both in terms of the implementation of the Rights of Children and Young Persons (Wales) Measure 2011, and in terms of broader societal changes that are needed to mainstream gender equality culturally, socially and at a household level.

References

Aapola, S., Gonick, M. and Harris, A. (2005): *Young Femininity: Girlhood, Power and Social Change* (Basingstoke: Palgrave Macmillan).

Blakemore, J. E. O., Berenbaum, S. A. and Liben, L. S. (2009): *Gender Development* (New York and London: Psychology Press).

Bradshaw, J. and Mayhew, E. (2005): *The Well-being of Children in the UK* (London: Save the Children).

Browne, N. (2004): *Gender Equity in the Early Years* (Berkshire: Open University Press).

Byely, L., Archibald, A. B., Graber, J. and Brooks-Gunn, J. (2000): 'A prospective study of familial and social influences on girls' body image and dieting', *International Journal of Eating Disorders*, 28/2, 155–64.

Case, S., Clutton, S. and Haines, K. (2005): 'Extending entitlement: a policy for Welsh children', *Wales Journal of Law and Policy*, 4, 187–230.

Chaney, P. (2002): *Women and the Post-Devolution Equality Agenda in Wales* (London: Gender Research Forum, Women and Equality Unit, Cabinet Office).

Coakley, J. and White, A. (1992): 'Making decisions: gender and sport participation among British adolescents', *Sociology of Sport Journal*, 9/1, 20–35.

Croke, R. and Crowley A. (2006): *Righting the Wrongs: The Reality of Children's Rights in Wales* (Cardiff: Save the Children).

—— (eds) (2007): *Stop, Look, Listen: The Road to Realising Children's Rights in Wales* (Cardiff: Save the Children).

Dennison, C. and Coleman J. (2000): *Young People and Gender: A Review of Research*, a report submitted to the Women's Unit (London: Cabinet Office).

Drakeford, M. (2010): 'Devolution and youth justice in Wales', *Criminology and Youth Justice*, 10/2, 137–54.

Esping-Anderson, C. (2009): *The Incomplete Revolution: Adapting to Women's New Roles* (Cambridge: Polity).

Feingold, A. (1994): 'Gender differences in personality: a meta-analysis', *Psychological Bulletin*, 116/3, 429–56.

Franklin, B. (ed.) (2002): *The New Handbook of Children's Rights: Comparative Policy and Practice* (London: Routledge).

Frost, L. (2001): *Young Women and the Body: a Feminist Sociology* (Basingstoke: Palgrave).

Funky Dragon (2007a): *Our Rights, Our Story* (Swansea: Funky Dragon).

—— (2007b): *Why Do People's Ages Go Up Not Down?* (Swansea: Funky Dragon).

Gran, B. (2010): 'Comparing children's rights: introducing the children's rights index', *International Journal of Children's Rights*, 18, 1–17.

Haines, K., Case, S., Rees, I., Isles, E. and Brown, A. (2004): *Extending Entitlement: Making it Real* (Cardiff: Welsh Assembly Government).

Hill, M. and Tisdall, K. (1997): *Children and Society* (London: Longman).

Kaime, T. (2010): ' "Vernacularising" the Convention on the Rights of the Child: rights and culture as analytic tools', *International Journal of Children's Rights*, 18, 637–53.

Livingston, M. and Room, R. (2009): 'Variations by age and sex in alcohol-related problematic behaviour per drinking volume and heavier drinking occasion', *Drug and Alcohol Dependence*, 101/3, 169–75.

Lloyd, G. (2005): *Problem Girls: Understanding and Supporting Troubled and Troublesome Girls and Young Women* (London: Routledge Falmer).

McLaughlin, C. (2005): 'Exploring the psychological landscape of "problem" girls', in G. Lloyd (ed.), *Problem Girls: Understanding and Supporting Troubled and Troublesome Girls and Young Women* (London: Routledge Falmer), pp. 49–60.

Major, B., Barr, L., Zubek, J. and Babey, S. H. (1999): 'Gender and self-esteem: a meta-analysis', in W. B. Swann, Jr., J. H. Langlois and L. A. Gilbert (eds), *Sexism and Stereotypes in Modern Society: The Gender Science of Janet Taylor Spence* (Washington, DC: American Psychological Association), pp. 223–53.

Measor, L. and Sikes, P. J. (1992): *Gender and Schools* (London: Cassell).

Nayak, A. and Kehily, M. J. (2008): *Gender, Youth and Culture: Young Masculinities and Femininities* (Hampshire: Palgrave Macmillan).

Osmond, J. and Morris, N. (2009): *What Are We Doing to Our Kids* (Cardiff: Institute for Welsh Affairs and BBC Cymru/Wales).

Paquette, J. A. and Underwood, M. K. (1999): 'Gender differences in young adolescents' experiences of peer victimization: social and physical aggression', *Merrill-Palmer Quarterly*, 45/2, 242–66.

Payne, S. (1991): *Women Health and Poverty: An Introduction* (London: Harvester Wheatsheaf).

Pilcher, J. and Whelehan, I. (2004): *50 Key Concepts in Gender Studies* (London: SAGE).

Richardson, D. and. Robinson, V. (eds) (2008): *Introducing Gender and Women's studies* (Basingstoke and New York: Palgrave Macmillan).

Richman, E. L. and Shaffer, D. R. (2000): ' "If you let me play": how might sport participation influence the self-esteem of adolescent females?', *Psychology of Women Quarterly*, 24, 189–99.

Ringrose, J. and Epstein, D. (2008): 'Gender and schooling: contemporary issues in gender equality and educational achievement', in D. Richardson and V. Robinson (eds), *Introducing Gender and Women's Studies* (Basingstoke: Palgrave Macmillan), pp. 144–57.

Seals, D. and Young, J. (2003): 'Bullying and victimization: prevalence and relationship to gender, grade level, ethnicity, self-esteem, and depression', *Adolescence*, 38, 735–47.

Shaffer, D. R. (2000): *Social and Personality Development* (Belmont: Wadsworth).

Street, C. (2005): 'Girls' mental health problems: often hidden, sometimes unrecognised?', in G. Lloyd (ed.), *Problem Girls: Understanding and Supporting Troubled and Troublesome Girls and Young Women* (London, Routledge Falmer), pp. 36–48.

Thomas, N. and Crowley, A. (2007): 'Children's rights and well-being in Wales in 2006', *Contemporary Wales*, 19, 161–79.

Tyrie, J. (2010): 'Exploring gender differences in children and young people's perceived access to their entitlements in Wales' (unpublished PhD thesis, Swansea University).

UK Children's Commissioners (2008): *UK Children's Commissioners' Report to the UN Committee on the Rights of the Child* (London, Belfast, Edinburgh and Swansea: UK Children's Commissioners).

Van der Gaag, N. (2004): *The No-Nonsense Guide to Women's Rights* (Oxford: New Internationalist).

Vilhjalmsson, R. and Kristjansdottir, G. (2003): 'Gender differences in physical activity in older children and adolescents: the central role of organized sport', *Social Science & Medicine*, 56/2, 363–74.

Williams, J. (2007): 'Incorporating children's rights: the divergence in law and policy', *Legal Studies*, 27/2, 261–87.

Williamson, H. (2007): 'Youth policy in Wales since devolution: from vision to vacuum?', *Contemporary Wales*, 19/1, 198–216.

CHAPTER 10

The rights of children and young people seeking asylum in Wales

Tracey Maegusuku-Hewett and Kathryn Tucker

Introduction

This chapter examines UK immigration policy in relation to the rights and well-being of asylum-seeking children, Welsh governance and the UNCRC. Immigration policy is non-devolved but many services that asylum-seeking children and young people receive are the responsibility of the Welsh Government, local authorities and other public bodies in Wales. Butler and Drakeford in chapter 1 of this volume identify influential strands in the emergence of children's rights in Wales, and remind us that the UNCRC was adopted as the National Assembly for Wales's bedrock of principle for policy on children and young people in 2004. The Rights of Children and Young Persons (Wales) Measure 2011 is a major further step towards integrating the UNCRC in devolved policy-making.

Of particular relevance to asylum-seeking children, UNCRC Article 22 states:

> States Parties shall take appropriate measures to ensure that a child who is seeking refugee status or who is considered a refugee in accordance with applicable international or domestic law and procedures shall, whether unaccompanied or accompanied by his or her parents or by any other person, receive appropriate protection and humanitarian assistance in the enjoyment of applicable rights set forth in the present Convention and in other international human rights or humanitarian instruments to which the said States are Parties.

However, crucially, the UK Government held a protracted reservation against this article until 2008, maintaining the stance that the reservation was 'necessary to maintain effective immigration control' (Scotland, 2004).

The impact of the reservation on children's rights and well-being has been well documented and criticised, and although Bolton (2011: 8) notes that 'the reservation only applied to matters of immigration control, such that non-immigration based welfare considerations were never subject to any reservation', it permeated the everyday lives of children confined within the immigration system. For example, health and welfare institutions misinterpreted or legitimised the reservation (intentionally or otherwise), resulting in what Crawley (2006: 3) terms the treatment of children as 'migrants first and foremost and children second'. Within this chapter we draw attention to some key vulnerabilities of asylum-seeking children which must be addressed if asylum-seeking children are to be able to enjoy the protection of Article 22 of the UNCRC. We also explore developments that have led to improvements in the treatment of asylum-seeking children, including policy and practice developments within Wales, despite retention at the UK level of powers on immigration and asylum. The chapter ends with an exploration of the potential opportunities and challenges for securing the rights of asylum-seeking children afforded by the Rights of Children and Young Persons (Wales) Measure 2011.

The UK and its obligation to refugees

The United Kingdom has a history, albeit contingent upon the social, economic and political context of the era, of providing refuge to those seeking sanctuary (Dummett, 2001; Bloch, 2002). It has ratified the United Nations Convention Relating to the Status of Refugees 1951 ('the 1951 Convention') and its 1967 protocol. This is an international rights-based instrument underpinned by fundamental principles of non-penalisation, non-discrimination, minimum standards of treatment in access to rights and non-refoulement. Within the 1951 Convention, a refugee is defined as someone who:

> has a well-founded fear of persecution for reasons of race, religion, nationality, membership of a particular social group, or political opinion; is outside the country they belong to or normally reside in; and is unable or unwilling to return home for fear of persecution. (Article 1, 1951 Convention)

The term 'refugee' is also used interchangeably or as a loose term within literature, policy and public discourse to describe people who are displaced in some way, however the 1951 Convention definition identifies those recognised as intended to benefit from the requirements of the Convention. The term 'asylum-seeker' is used within the UK to describe those who have arrived with the intention of gaining refugee status until such a time that a decision is made on that status. The difference in terminology carries implications for legal status, access to rights and citizenship in both narrow and broad senses. Those seeking asylum are subject to immigration legislation and restrictive policies which aim to monitor, confine, reduce incentive for false claims to refugee status and to remove those deemed outside the scope of the refugee definition (Mynott, 2002; Harvey, 2002; Cohen, 2002; Hayes, 2004).

More recently the UK, as an EU Member State, has engaged in the ongoing development of a Common European Asylum System (CEAS). This is intended to harmonise the reception, support and processing of asylum-seekers across the EU. Negotiation is protracted, each Member State having concerns about autonomy and national sovereignty. Nevertheless, EU directives have been drafted prescribing minimum standards on reception, support and processing. Smith (2005) provides an overview of the CEAS in relation to separated children, and concludes that to some extent children's well-being is included within the directives, for example particularly in matters of guardianship, family reunification, the opinions of the child and his or her best interests. However, in Smith's view it is remiss that 'immigration control continues to take precedence over the best interest of the child' (2005: 45).

Children's status within immigration policy

Children may arrive in the UK in the care of their families, or without the care and protection of their parents or legal guardian. The UK Government refers to these latter children as unaccompanied asylum-seeking children, or commonly utilise the acronym of 'UASCs'. However, within this chapter, unless referring to original text that uses the term 'unaccompanied' or 'UASC', we shall use the term 'separated children'. This is in fitting with the Separated Children in Europe Programme's recognition that 'separated children suffer physically, socially and psychologically as a result of being without the care and protection of their parents or previous care giver(s)' (Save the Children Alliance et al., 2009: 4). There are many reasons why children and young people may leave their home country. These include: fear of persecution due to their religion, nationality, ethnicity, political opinion or social group; parents having been killed, imprisoned or disappeared; danger of being forced to fight or become a child soldier; war or violent conflict; poverty or deprivation; or they may have been sent abroad by parents/family. Sometimes they may have witnessed or experienced traumatic events and they may be suffering the most extreme forms of loss (Machel, 1996; DeBerry and Boyden, 2001; UNHCR, 2002).

Within the UK, separated children and children in families seeking asylum are generally treated differentially in relation to their residence, support and entitlements, and asylum claim process and outcomes.

Asylum-seeking children in families

Under the Asylum and Immigration Act 1996, asylum-seeking families were no longer entitled to mainstream social housing or welfare benefits, and were prohibited from employment. For a period, children and families were supported in temporary housing by local authorities under the Children Act 1989. This situation was far from satisfactory, and with pressure from 'overburdened' local authorities mainly in the south-east of England, the government introduced a change in policy through the Nationality and Immigration Act 1999. Under this Act, destitute families are dispersed and housed across the UK. Within Wales, dispersed families began arriving from April 2001, and by the end of May 2009, a total of 2,322 asylum-seekers were residing within the four local authority dispersal areas of Newport, Wrexham, Swansea and Cardiff (Crawley and Crimes, 2009: 11). Asylum-seekers, being prohibited from employment, are dependent on the state for housing and subsistence, and these are provided by the regional asylum teams of the United Kingdom Border Agency (UKBA). As noted earlier, within Wales, political responsibility for health, social care, education, leisure and other services are the responsibility of the Welsh Government, and asylum-seeking families have the same entitlement as citizen families in their access to these (apart from higher education and social housing).

Asylum-seeking children in families are regarded as 'dependents of the main applicant' (Home Office, 2009). Some argue this status has the effect of marginalising the needs and best interests of children in decisions on refugee status, on detention and generally in the immigration system (Crawley and Lester, 2005; Cunninghan and Tomlinson, 2005; Giner, 2007). However, post-reservation (that is, after the withdrawal of the UK's reservation to Article 22, discussed above), case law and legislative developments have given the 'best interest' principle more prominence in immigration matters. These are discussed later in the chapter.

Separated children seeking asylum

Separated children are supported by the local authority where they arrive or which they approach. Consequently the numbers of separated children falling within devolved governmental responsibility are small in comparison with the larger cities of England. While exact numbers of separated children and young people residing in Wales have been variously estimated, as a rough indicator, StatsWales (2011) suggests there were 125 separated children residing in Wales within its Children in Need Census 2010. The majority reside in the larger local authorities in south Wales. However, several local authorities across Wales support small numbers of separated children and young people.

In the past, a number of research reports served to highlight disparities in support for separated children in local authority care (for example, Stone, 2000; Stanley, 2001; Ayotte and Williamson, 2001; Dennis, 2002). While there are still some concerns about the extent of provision to separated children, case law has been instrumental in improving the protection and standard of their care and support. Several judgements relating to age assessment (see below) and the Hillingdon Judgement (*R (Behre) v Hillingdon* [2003] EWHC 2075) established that local authorities should provide accommodation to separated children under section 20 of the Children Act 1989, and that such children should benefit from 'leaving care' support under the Children (Leaving Care) Act 2000. This was strengthened with *R (on the application of SO) v London Borough of Barking and Dagenham* [2010] EWCA Civ 1101, which ruled that a local authority has a general duty to provide accommodation under section 23C(4) of the Children Act 1989 to 'former relevant' separated young people to the extent that their welfare requires it. This also includes separated young people who may have been deemed 'failed asylum-seekers'. Essentially this ruling sought to prohibit local authorities from seeking to shift responsibility for accommodation of former relevant separated young people to the UKBA.

Separated children are entitled to seek refugee status in their own right. However, research has shown that separated children are less likely to be granted refugee status than adults. Reasons suggested include the adult-orientated asylum system; lack of child-specific country information; children's articulation of their experiences and narrow conceptions of childhood leading to credibility issues; disputes over a child's age; availability/quality of legal advice, and failure of claims that do not meet the 'merits test' for provision of legal aid (Finch, 2005; Crawley, 2006, 2007; Kohli, 2006; Children's Legal Centre, 2012). In Wales, it has been recognised that there is a lack of immigration legal representation in general but that this is especially pertinent for separated young people, who may be detained, or, if granted discretionary leave (usually for three years or until the age of seventeen and a half), may later be required to return to their country of origin (STC, 2008).

Pertinent issues affecting asylum-seeking children and their enjoyment of the UNCRC in Wales

Most of the vulnerabilities identified below relate to children's subjection to immigration control, and have potential to deprive children and families and separated children of the protection of Article 22 of the UNCRC, both pre- and post-reservation. We highlight these, along with a brief chronology of UK and Welsh developments that have led to potential for change.

Child trafficking

Articles 34 and 35 of the UNCRC and the Optional Protocol to the UNCRC on the sale of children, child prostitution and child pornography relate to child trafficking and exploitation. A gradual, negotiated transition in the UK's approach to these matters has been noted, from concern primarily with criminal justice to a recognition of the human rights and needs of trafficking victims (Kelley and Regan, 2000; Somerset, 2001; UNICEF, 2003; Herzfield et al., 2006). Initial reluctance to ratify the above optional protocol and the Council of Europe (2005) Convention on Action Against Trafficking in Human Beings (signed in 2007) was followed by an 'action plan on human trafficking' amended in 2007 to include strategies of enforcement and prosecution, protection measures, and increased awareness and training across education, law enforcement, and social and health service sectors. There was emphasis on collaborative working and further research to inform knowledge on the extent and characteristics of trafficking (Home Office and Scottish Executive, 2007). Research has shown that separated children are especially vulnerable to trafficking (Kappoor, 2007), and in Wales, research undertaken by Coles (2005), Save the Children (2008), and ECPAT (2009), suggests that given the clandestine nature of trafficking coupled with a lack of practitioner knowledge, trafficking may not always be identified, nor suspected cases of trafficking acted upon.

In recognition of this knowledge gap, the Welsh Government provided funding to ECPAT-UK to develop an online training resource, and since 2008 updated all-Wales child trafficking practice guidance (AWCPRG, 2011a). More strategically, following recommendations made by an all-Wales cross-party working group on the trafficking of women and children in Wales (Jones, 2010), the Minister for Social Justice and Local Government, Carl Sargeant, appointed Wales's first anti-human trafficking coordinator in March 2011.

Age assessments and age-disputed separated young people

Separated children who arrive in the UK without a parent or guardian are the responsibility of local authorities. However, many of these children who arrive may appear younger or older than their stated age and have no identification to prove their age. They may find their age disputed by the UKBA or local authority social services. It is then for the local authority to make an age assessment. There is no consistent guidance on the process of age assessment: here again case law has to some extent filled the gap, notably the Merton Judgement (*R (B) v Merton* [2003] 4 All ER 280), which established minimum requirements upon which an age assessment should be carried out. Subsequent case law has provided further direction for the practice of age assessment.[1]

Separated children who are age-disputed by the UKBA and/or a local authority are treated as adults and therefore denied the support and protection of children's services. In these circumstances they are likely to be accommodated with adults in UKBA asylum-support accommodation, or, as research has shown, age-disputed young people may be detained and removed from the UK (Crawley, 2007). Those who are in fact below the age of eighteen are thus denied the rights guaranteed to them under the UNCRC. There are no safeguards in existence to monitor the safety or protection of 'age-disputed' children/young people in this context. For these reasons the principles and practices surrounding age assessments have come under scrutiny from researchers and practitioners (for example Crawley, 2007; STC, 2008; Welsh Refugee Council, 2011). In Wales, there is now some cursory age assessment guidance for professionals to be found in *Safeguarding and Promoting the Welfare of Unaccompanied Asylum Seeking Children and Young People: All-Wales Practice Guidance* (AWCPRG, 2011b) and the UKBA is working with the Wales Strategic Migration Partnership to find a way of ensuring greater consistency relating to age assessment (WG, 2011: 3).

Detention

Perhaps the most controversial of immigration practices is the use of detention for immigration purposes. This practice was particularly relevant to and legitimised by the reservation. As noted earlier, separated children are not liable for detention but many are vulnerable to it, particularly if their age is disputed by UKBA or they have been assessed as over eighteen by children's services. Meanwhile, children in families are regarded as 'dependents of the main asylum applicant' and as such can be detained with their families prior to removal from the UK. There is insufficient room within this chapter to discuss the implications of detention on children's well-being in great detail, although a number of authors have done so elsewhere (Her Majesty's Inspectorate of Prisons, 2003; Crawley and

Lester, 2005; Nandy, 2005; Campbell et al., 2011). Detention of children is a violation of Article 37 (UNCRC), which states:

> no child should be deprived of his or her liberty . . . where detention is used, a child should be detained only as a measure of last resort and for the shortest appropriate period of time.

Section 55 of the Borders, Citizenship and Immigration Act 2009 places immigration services under a duty to afford children appropriate care and protection during asylum interviews, removal and transportation, or detention. This places safeguarding requirements for children in the immigration system on a par with other public bodies, and acknowledges the need to safeguard all children irrespective of citizenship status. Further, in May 2010, the UK Government declared an end to the detention of children for immigration purposes and committed themselves to finding an alternative to detention. In 2011 a 'family returns process' was established in an attempt to make more compassionate and humane the removal of families who have no legal right to remain in the UK.

Key elements of this new process include the creation of specialist family case owners, methods of assisted return, family conference, required return, an independent family returns panel and a 'last resort' option of pre-departure accommodation. However, there is concern that the planned alternatives fail to address fundamental issues in decision-making processes or to consider evidence of 'what works' from other countries of Europe, the USA and Canada. Essentially the proposed new system is viewed as detention under another guise (Crawley, 2010; 2011).

Welsh Ministers have expressed concerns to Westminster and the Home Office following the use of Wales's prison facilities in 2001 and 2004 for immigration detainees, including a young person (WG, 2004). While detention is a non-devolved matter, such concerns were sufficient to ensure Wales's prisons were not used more routinely. However, to date, children in families and age-disputed separated young people continue to be removed from Wales and detained elsewhere in the UK (Welsh Refugee Council, 2010; 2011). It is hoped that under the Rights of Children and Young Persons (Wales) Measure 2011, Welsh Ministers will continue to push the UK Government to respect the rights and well-being of children. Despite having no jurisdiction over non-devolved matters, the Children's Commissioner for Wales worked collaboratively with the UK's other Children's Commissioners to condemn shortcomings in safeguarding practice by the immigration services (House of Commons, 2005).

The Children's Commissioner for Wales has also provided advice and assistance to individual asylum-seeking children and their families (Children's Commissioner for Wales, 2010).

Safeguarding asylum-seeking children's 'best interests'

Article 3 of the UNCRC requires:

> In all actions concerning children, whether undertaken by public or private social welfare institutions, courts of law, administrative authorities or legislative bodies, the best interests of the child shall be a primary consideration.

The UNCRC does not further define 'best interests', and Bolton (2011) notes how UK courts are more familiar with the notion of welfare as stipulated in section 1 of the Children Act 1989. However, developments in UK case law and the European Court of Human Rights have provided precedent for the interpretation of 'best interests' in relation to asylum-seeking children. The landmark case of *ZH (Tanzania) v Secretary of State for the Home Department* [2011] UKSC 4 established that children's best interests, needs and welfare should be considered in immigration decision-making processes. The court also recognised that 'an important part of this is discovering the child's own views' (at para. 34).

This recognition of the UNCRC's approach that the voice of the child is an integral part of any best interests consideration is useful. Its application to immigration requires that the child's voice is heard in decisions made about services they receive and other decisions about their lives, their future 'home' and the kind of support they can expect to receive. In concrete terms this means, as recognised by the UN Committee in its *Concluding Observations*, that the appointment of a competent guardian – especially for a separated child – is essential to ensuring proper respect for the best interests principle (UN Committee *CO*, 2008).

Certainly in Wales, this principle is reflected in a number of reports (Hewett et al., 2005; Thomas, 2006; Croke and Crowley, 2007; STC, 2008). These make recommendations to the Welsh Government to introduce specialist advocacy or a system of guardianship. In response, the Welsh Government provided time-limited funding for a part-time child advocacy officer to provide guidance, support and advocacy to vulnerable separated children, including ensuring their statutory entitlements are met. The Welsh Government also worked with a refugee organisation to provide training to mainstream advocacy services on specific issues facing asylum-seeking children (WG, 2011). These are welcome steps, while still falling well short of a system of guardianship. By way of contrast, children and refugee charities in Scotland have begun to pilot the Scottish Guardianship Scheme specifically for separated children and young people. Evaluation of this scheme should be of interest to the Welsh Government, local authorities, public bodies, advocacy organisations and refugee children's charities.

Negotiating centralised immigration policy and devolved policy and practice

The discussion thus far has demonstrated the complexities of immigration, vulnerabilities facing asylum-seeking children and some of the challenges of ensuring children's rights amid the primacy of immigration policy. Despite this incongruence, we have highlighted the extent to which policy and practice has emerged in Wales to mediate some of the issues raised. The primacy of immigration policy is further diluted by emerging legislation, case-law precedent, and the moral gaze of wider children and human rights monitoring mechanisms and institutions such as the UN Committee and the Children's Commissioner for Wales. However, as Rees notes in chapter 13 of this volume, the Children's Commissioner for Wales has limited functions in non-devolved matters; instead, these are the long-arm responsibility of the English Children's Commissioner. Rees notes that this is recognised as being unacceptable. At the time of writing, the situation is being negotiated between the UK Government and devolved administrations.

The interpretation and extent of knowledge of immigration policies will influence the practices of service providers, and this in turn has an impact on children's enjoyment of their rights and access to services in Wales. Practitioners have mobilised to establish a range of multidisciplinary networks and joint working for the care and support of children and families and separated children, and to a great extent have pressed for developments in practice and Welsh policy. Furthermore, there is some evidence of organisations and practitioners in Wales challenging and negotiating the dichotomy between immigration and 'best interests' of the child (Dunkerley et al., 2005). On the other hand, evidence also suggests that there is a lot of work still to be undertaken, particularly with mainstream practitioners and service providers from all disciplines to raise awareness of immigration policy and its impact on asylum-seeking children's rights and well-being (STC, 2008; ECPAT, 2009; Welsh Refugee Council, 2011). It is hoped that the child trafficking and safeguarding practice guidance incorporated in the All-Wales Child Protection Procedures (AWCPRG, 2011a and 2011b respectively) will serve to inform practitioners and make a difference to the lives of children through the implementation of improved practice knowledge and consistent guidance across local authorities.

At a policy level, and in terms of non-devolved matters, asylum-seeking children should benefit from the Welsh Government's 'mainstreaming agenda'. For example, children and young people seeking asylum have been recognised as children in special circumstances within the National Services Framework for Children, Young People and Maternity Services (Welsh Government, 2005). However, the extent of this inclusion to date has not always been explicit, and neither has it been consistent across all policy areas (Hewett et al., 2005; WG, 2006; Thomas, 2006). For all Welsh children, it has been noted that there is a disparity between policy intentions and outcomes for children and young people (UN Committee *CO*, 2008). In its response, the Welsh Government committed to 'put in place systems to monitor their impact [referring to policy] and work closely with a wide range of national and local partners to support delivery of policies' (2009: 21). Meanwhile refugee-specific policy initiatives and services have also begun to emerge, although the latter tend to be contingent upon short-term funding, hindering any longer term strategy or sustainability (WG, 2006; Thomas, 2006). The Refugee Inclusion Strategy (WG, 2008) is the most prominent policy, and, due to the hard-earned efforts of child and refugee rights campaigners in Wales, coupled with supportive and receptive Ministers, includes a section on children and young people. This paved the way for the establishment of an All-Wales Refugee Children Advice and Information resource for practitioners and policy makers. Further, the Refugee Inclusion Action plan (2011) sets out a number of actions in relation to advocacy, trafficking, age assessment and child protection, albeit within the recognition that 'we are now operating in a much changed financial landscape in terms of both the funding that is available for service provision, and also the funding available to support community organisations' (WG, 2011:1).

There is limited research in Wales specifically with asylum-seeking children to ascertain their views and perceptions of how these key immigration issues and Welsh policy and service delivery impact on their lives. Earlier work undertaken (Hewett et al., 2005; Threadgold and Clifford, 2005) revealed a range of children's experiences of living in Wales, with some concerns raised by children about multiple dispersals, racism, education, housing, enduring and enforced poverty, and uncertainty and anxiety about their future. Separated children reflected on their care and support and most appear to have been accommodated under the more protection-ist section 20 of the Children Act 1989, rather than section 17. Isolation, boredom, limited access to post-16 education and anxiety about asylum determination were all stressors impacting on separated children's health and emotional well-being. More recently, the Welsh Refugee Council (2011) has engaged with separated young people resident in Wales to high-light their experiences of age assessments.

On the other hand, research with children and young people has also demonstrated resilience and enjoyment of their time in Wales, reflecting on their religion and faith, friendships and neighbourhoods, opportunities for play and leisure, and, for a great majority, school and aspirations for their future, which illustrates the bolstering effects of being able to enjoy their rights despite living in the shadow of immigration control. Some young people were of the view that specialist youth provision was invalu-able to reducing isolation, peer solidarity, maintaining cultural links and providing a platform in which to represent their needs (Hewett et al., 2005; Maegusuku-Hewett et al., 2007).

Asylum-seeking children and their rights: the way forward in Wales

This chapter has so far taken stock of salient issues facing asylum-seeking children where the political context and their status produce incongru-ence between immigration policy and children's rights and well-being. We have tried, in a whistle-stop tour, to highlight the challenges posed in the dichotomy of immigration policy and the emergence of distinctive, rights-based Welsh policy-making. In considering the way forward for Wales, it is worth reflecting on these challenges but also to take stock of developments both within and outside Wales that have led to improvements for children and young people.

As we have seen, emerging case law, changes in safeguarding legisla-tion and policy and EU harmonisation are some of the mechanisms pro-moting greater consideration of children's best interests and rights. These should be regarded as useful tools for advocacy, scrutiny and account-ability, particularly on non-devolved matters. One impact of the Rights of Children and Young Persons (Wales) Measure 2011 will be to require Welsh Ministers to interface with the UK Government over policy devel-opment and legislative proposals on non-devolved matters. In that con-text the duty to have due regard will apply to representations by Welsh Ministers about the best interests of asylum-seeking children. In particu-lar, Welsh Ministers should advocate for a child-centred asylum system, for the end to detention of children, and for UNCRC and children's best interests to be embedded in UK policy and decisions relating to asylum-seeking children.

The UNCRC confines its applicability to children under eighteen. However, in recognition of young people's vulnerability at this transitional phase of life, the UNCRC-embedded Welsh Government strategies cover ages zero to twenty-five. The provision in the Measure (section 7) that enables Welsh Ministers to extend its provisions to young people aged eighteen to twenty-five has particular resonance for asylum-seekers. For separated young people there are special issues and vulnerabilities in the transition to adulthood: we have highlighted age disputes, transition to leaving care services, access to education, asylum determination and return, and inclusion into Welsh society as a young adult. The requirement that Welsh Ministers must consult before deciding whether and how to exercise this power provides an opportunity for stakeholders to represent and advocate that the Measure should extend to separated young people, and of course to challenge the basis of less-than-favourable outcomes.

In devolved policy areas, the Measure ought to strengthen the impetus for cross-cutting policy to include asylum-seeking children more equitably. A 'children's scheme' will provide the building blocks by which Welsh Ministers must demonstrate the arrangements made to secure compliance. In devising the children's scheme, Welsh Ministers must have regard to relevant documents and must engage with key stakeholders. This may provide an opportunity for asylum-seeking children and young people, who are ordinarily silenced by their status, to have a voice. It also provides an opportunity for child welfare and refugee organisations, the Children's Commissioner and other relevant bodies to negotiate an acceptable way forward for asylum-seeking children. While there is evidence of some good practice development in Wales and of professionals mobilising to form joint working collaborations and networks, this in the main derives from professionals and providers committed to ensuring the welfare of children seeking asylum. There is much work to be undertaken with service providers and professionals across Wales to raise awareness of immigration and asylum and of the needs, experiences and rights of asylum-seeking children. Section 5 of the Measure, requiring Welsh Ministers to promote knowledge of the UNCRC and its Optional Protocol, can only help in this regard.

However the Measure does not place a due regard duty on public bodies generally. This may tend to maintain a 'gap' between policy and outcomes for children. Only when all agencies – including UKBA, children's services, support and advocacy services and the voluntary sector generally, legal representatives, Welsh Government departments, youth services, education, health and welfare – fulfil their obligations by considering wholly and without prejudice the best interests of the asylum-seeking child, will asylum-seeking children fully enjoy their rights in Wales.

Finally, there are already some good foundations in place for the realisation of asylum-seeking children's rights, and the Measure is a welcome, important and significant mechanism towards progressive improvement towards that goal.

References

AWCPRG (All-Wales Child Protection Procedures Review Group) (2011a): *All-Wales Practice Guidance for Safeguarding Children Who May Have Been Trafficked* (Cardiff: Welsh Government).

—— (2011b): *Safeguarding and Promoting the Welfare of Unaccompanied Asylum Seeking Children and Young People: All-Wales Practice Guidance* (Cardiff: Welsh Government).

Ayotte, W. and Williamson, L. (2001): *Separated Children in the UK: An Overview of the Current Situation* (London: Save the Children and the Refugee Council).

Bloch, A. (2002): *The Migration and Settlement of Refugees in Britain* (Hampshire: Macmillan Press).

Bolton, S. (2011): ' "Best interests": safeguarding and promoting the welfare of children in immigration law and practice', in L. Woodall (ed.), *Working with Refugee Children: Current Issues in Best Practice* (London: Immigration Law Practitioners' Association), pp. 1–38.

Campbell, S., Baqueriza, M. and Ingram, J. (2011): *Last Resort or First Resort: Immigration Detention of Children in the UK* (London: Bail for Immigration Detainees).

Children's Commissioner for Wales (2010): *Annual Report and Accounts 09/10* (Swansea: Children's Commissioner for Wales).

Children's Legal Centre (2012): *Seeking Support: A Guide to the Rights and Entitlements of Separated Children* (London: Children's Legal Centre).

Cohen, S. (2002): 'In and against the state of immigration controls: strategies for resistance', in S. Cohen, B. Humphries and E. Mynott (eds), *From Immigration Controls to Welfare Controls* (London: Routledge), pp. 220–34.

Coles, J. (2005): *Out of Sight, Out of Mind: Child Sexual Exploitation. A Scoping Study into Service Provision for Sexually Exploited Children in Wales* (Cardiff: Barnardo's).

Council of Europe (2005): Convention on Action Against Trafficking in Human Beings, Treaty Series No. 197 (Warsaw: Council of Europe).

Crawley, H. (2006): *Child First, Migrant Second: Ensuring that Every Child Matters* (London: ILPA).

—— (2007): *When is a Child not a Child? Asylum, Age Disputes and the Process of Age Assessment* (London: ILPA).

—— (2010): *Ending the Detention of Children: Developing an Alternative Approach to Family Returns* (Swansea: Centre for Migration Policy Research).

—— (2011): *Detention by Another Name?* (London: Migrant Rights Network).

Crawley, H. and Crimes, T. (2009): *Refugees in Wales: A Survey of Skills, Experiences and Barriers to Inclusion* (Swansea: Centre for Migration Policy Research).

Crawley, H. and Lester, T. (2005): *No Place for a Child: Children in Immigration Detention in the UK – Impacts, Alternatives and Safeguards* (London: Save the Children UK).

Croke, R. and Crowley, A. (eds) (2007): *Stop, Look, Listen: The Road to Realising Children's Rights in Wales* (Cardiff: Save the Children).

Cunningham, S. and Tomlinson, J. (2005): ' "Starve them out": does every child really matter? A commentary on Section 9 of the Asylum and Immigration (Treatment of Claimants etc.) Act 2004', *Critical Social Policy*, 25, 253–75.

DeBerry, J. and Boyden, J. (2001): 'Children in Adversity', *Forced Migration Review*, 9, 33–6.

Dennis, J. (2002): *How Refugee Children in England are Missing Out: First Findings from the Monitoring Project and the Refugee Children's Consortium* (London: The Children's Society, Save the Children and the Refugee Council).

Dummett, M. (2001): *On Immigration and Refugees*, Thinking in Action Series (London: Routledge).

Dunkerley, D., Scourfield, J., Maegusuku-Hewett, T. and Smalley, N. (2005): 'The experiences of front-line staff working with children who are seeking asylum', *Social Policy and Administration*, special issue on migration, 39/6, 640–52.

ECPAT (2009): *Bordering on Concern: Child Trafficking in Wales* (Swansea: Children's Commissioner for Wales).

Finch, N. (2005): 'Seeking asylum alone', in H. Andersson, H. Ascher, U. Bjornberg and L. Mellander (eds), *The Asylum Seeking Child in Europe* (Gothenburg: Gothenburg University), pp. 57–66.

Giner, C. (2007): 'The politics of childhood and asylum in the UK', *Children and Society*, 21/(4, 249–60.

Harvey, A. (2002): 'The 1999 immigration and asylum act and how to challenge it: a legal view', in S. Cohen, B. Humphries and E. Mynott (eds), *From Immigration Controls to Welfare Controls* (London: Routledge), pp. 187–202.

Hayes, D. (2004): 'History and context: the impact of immigration control on welfare delivery', in D. Hayes and B. Humphries (eds), *Social Work, Immigration and Asylum: Debates, Dilemmas and Ethical Issues for Social Work and Social Care Practice* (London: Jessica Kingsley), pp. 11–26.

Her Majesty's Inspectorate of Prisons (2003): *Introduction and Summary of Findings: Inspection of Five Immigration Service Custodial Establishments* (London: Home Office).

Herzfield, B., Green, S., Epstein, S. and Beddoe, C. (2006): 'Trafficking: immigration or human rights concern?', *Forced Migration Review*, 25 (May), 39–40.

Hewett, T., Smalley, N., Dunkerley, D. and Scourfield, J. (2005): *Uncertain Futures: Children Seeking Asylum in Wales* (Cardiff: Save the Children).

Home Office (2009): *Dependants on Asylum Support Applications* (London: Home Office).

Home Office and Scottish Executive (2007): *UK Action Plan on Tackling Human Trafficking* (London: Home Office).

House of Commons (2005): Select Committee on Home Affairs – *Written Evidence*, 5 December, HC775-11, memorandum submitted by the England Children's Commissioner (London: The Stationery Office).

Jones, J. (2010): *The Trafficking of Women and Children in Wales*, working paper no. 1 (Bristol: Centre for Legal Studies, University of the West of England).

Kapoor, A. (2007): *A Scoping Project on Child Trafficking in the UK* (London: CEOP/Home Office).

Kelly, L. and Regan, L. (2000): *Stopping Traffic: Exploring the Extent of, and Responses to, Trafficking in Women for Sexual Exploitation in the UK*, Police Research Series no. 125 (London: Home Office).

Kohli, R. (2006):'The sound of silence: listening to what unaccompanied asylum seeking children say and do not say', *British Journal of Social Work*, 36, 707–21.

Machel, G. (1996): *Promotion and Protection of the Rights of Children: Impact of Armed Conflict on Children* (Geneva: United Nations Department for Policy Coordination and Sustainable Development).

Maegusuku-Hewett, T., Dunkerley, D., Scourfield, J. and Smalley, N. (2007): 'Refugee children in Wales: coping and adaptation in the face of adversity', *Children and Society*, 21/4, 309–21.

Mynott, E. (2002): 'From a shambles to a new apartheid: local authorities, dispersal and the struggle to defend asylum seekers', in S. Cohen, B. Humphries and E. Mynott (eds), *From Immigration Controls to Welfare Controls* (London: Routledge), pp. 11–29.

Nandy, L. (2005): 'The impact of government policy on asylum-seeking and refugee children', *Children and Society*, 19, 410–13.

STC (Save the Children) (2008): *Agenda for Action: The Care and Protection of Asylum Seeker and Trafficked Children in Wales* (Cardiff: Save the Children).

Save the Children Alliance, UNHCR and UNICEF (2009): *The Separated Children in Europe Programme: Statement of Good Practice*, 4th edition (Geneva: Save the Children).

Scotland, Patricia [Baroness Scotland of Asthal] (2004): Hansard, HL (series 5), vol. 657, col. WA87 (2 February).

Smith, T. (2005): 'European refugee law and its impact upon children', in H. E. Andersson, H. Ascher, U. Bjonberg, M. Eastmond and L. Mellander (eds), *The Asylum Seeking Child in Europe* (Gothenburg: Centre for European Research), pp. 37–46.

Somerset, C. (2001): *What the Professionals Know: The Trafficking of Children into and through the UK for Sexual Purposes* (London: ECPAT UK).

Stanley, K. (2001): *Cold Comfort: Young Separated Refugees in England* (London: Save the Children).

StatsWales (2011): *Wales Children in Need Census 2010*, SDR19/2011 (Cardiff: Welsh Government).

Stone, R. (2000): *Children First and Foremost*, recent survey findings from local authorities presented at a Barnardo's seminar (London: Barnardo's).

Thomas, S. (2006): 'Special protection: asylum', in R. Croke and A. Crowley (eds), *Righting the Wrongs: The Reality of Children's Rights in Wales* (Cardiff: Save the Children), pp. 87–94.

Threadgold, T. and Clifford, S. (2005): *Findings from Focus Groups with Refugees: Report to the Welsh Refugee Council and the Welsh Assembly Government* (Cardiff: Welsh Assembly Government).

UNHCR (United Nations High Commission for Refugees) (2002): *Global Consultations on International Protection: Refugee Children*, 4th Meeting, 25th April. EC/GC/02/9 (Geneva: UNHCR).

UNICEF (2003): *End Child Exploitation: Stop the Traffic!* (London: UNICEF).

Welsh Refugee Council (2010): *Review of the Policy of Detaining Children*, policy position paper (Cardiff: Welsh Refugee Council).

—— (2011): *Young Lives in Limbo: The Protection of Age Disputed Young People in Wales* (Cardiff: Welsh Refugee Council).

WG (Welsh Government) (2004): Edwina Hart, statement on asylum-seekers held in Cardiff prison (9 August).

—— (2005): *National Services Framework for Children, Young People and Maternity Services in Wales* (Cardiff: Welsh Assembly Government).

—— (2006): *Refugee Inclusion Strategy: Consultation Document* (Cardiff: Welsh Assembly Government).

—— (2008): *Refugee Inclusion Strategy* (Cardiff: Welsh Assembly Government).

—— (2009): *Priorities for Wales: Taking Forward the United Nations Convention on the Rights of the Child* (Cardiff: Welsh Assembly Government).

—— (2011): *Refugee Inclusion Strategy Action Plan* (Cardiff: Welsh Government).

Note

1. *R (NA) v Croydon* [2009] EWCH 2357; *R (PM) v Hertfordshire County Council* [2010] EWHC 2056 (Admin), para. 88; *A v London Borough of Croydon, WK v Kent Borough Council* [2009] EWHC 939 (Admin); *R (on the application of Y) v The London Borough of Hillingdon* [2011] EWHC 1477 (Admin).

CHAPTER 11

The rights of Gypsy and Traveller children and young people in Wales

Trudy Aspinwall and Luke Clements

Introduction

This chapter considers the rights of Gypsy and Traveller children and young people in the Welsh context, and looks at how much steps to address the discrimination and inequalities experienced by young Gypsy Travellers have succeeded. We look at the legal and policy background, the obligations under the UNCRC on the Welsh Government, and how the rights of Gypsy and Traveller children and young people can be further realised through the opportunity presented by the passing of the Rights of Children and Young Persons (Wales) Measure 2011.

Background: a legacy of discrimination

The Welsh Government defines a Gypsy Traveller as 'a person of nomadic lifestyle regardless of their race or origin' (WG, 2009a). The term Gypsy and Traveller used generically in this chapter includes Romany Gypsies and Irish Travellers (first recognised and protected as racial groups by the Race Relations [Amendment] Act 2000), as well as traditional ethnic groups of English, Welsh or Scottish Gypsies, New Travellers, fairground families or showmen, and bargees.

The history of discrimination against 'travelling' people is a long one and persists to this day. The situation of Gypsies and Travellers in the UK and the prejudice they face has drawn criticism from a number of human rights monitoring bodies:

> Although Gypsies and Travellers are a small part of the overall population of the United Kingdom, the difficulties they face have attracted considerable, and largely negative, attention in recent years. Indeed, to judge by the levels of invective that can regularly be read in the national press, Gypsies would appear to be the last ethnic minority in

respect of which openly racist views can still be acceptably expressed. (OCHCR, 2005: 145)

The *Who Do You See?* report (EHRC, 2008) found that some of the most persistent negative attitudes and prejudice still held in Wales were against Gypsy and Traveller people, echoing an earlier report from Stonewall which found that the level of prejudice against Gypsy and Traveller people was higher than for any other group based on ethnicity, sexuality or disability (Valentine and McDonald, 2004). Gypsy and Traveller people were recently described as being 'the most disenfranchised and marginalised group in Welsh society' (WG, 2009a).

The UN Committee has repeatedly made recommendations to the UK Government to tackle the rights violations experienced daily by Gypsy and Traveller children and young people. In 2008 it highlighted the inequalities experienced in relation to socio-economic outcomes, and the fact that Gypsy and Traveller children in the UK do not enjoy the right to non-discrimination under Article 2 of the UNCRC (UN Committee *CO*, 2008: para. 25). Life expectancy for Gypsy and Traveller people is ten years below the national average; infant mortality rates are unacceptably high, and children and young people attain substantially lower educational outcomes. Adults and children alike describe the discriminatory attitudes and actions that occur in schools and where they live; on the street and from both public and private sector services – discrimination and a lack of awareness often perpetuated by biased media reporting that is rarely challenged. These negative experiences lead to further social exclusion, difficulty of access to services, and a lack of trust in those bodies which have a duty to deliver those services (Cemlyn et al., 2009; Aspinwall and Larkins, 2010). Gypsy and Traveller people are among the groups least likely to have access to or use mechanisms to seek justice and redress (Mason et al., 2009).

Legal context

Welsh Gypsy and Traveller children are born into a culture in which their health, social, educational and political opportunities are predetermined, in a manner best articulated in the language of third world caste systems. As Fitzpatrick notes in this volume, constitutional measures of themselves do nothing to address this disadvantage: their success must be measured in terms of practical outcomes.

If, as Williams (in chapter 4 of this volume) suggests, legal challenges relying on the Measure are likely to be rare, then to bring about this cultural change much will be demanded of governmental bodies and of the independent regulators – such as the Public Services Ombudsman for Wales, the Children's Commissioner for Wales and the Equalities and Human Rights Commission (EHRC) – as well as non-governmental actors. The evidence of the impact of the Human Rights Act 1998 in this respect is not positive. Research suggests that although the Act had great potential to improve the position of Gypsy and Traveller people, this was 'frustrated, or at the very least ... distorted, to conform with the pre-existing organisational norms' of the authorities that could have used it to make a difference (Clements and Morris, 2004). Even where successful legal challenges occurred there is little evidence that they resulted in positive change. The UK Government has still not complied with a 2004 judgement of the European Court of Human Rights (ECtHR) – *Connors v UK* – that the absence of security of tenure for Gypsies in England and Wales violated Article 8 of the European Convention on Human Rights (Johnson et al., 2010).

A particular difficulty in using the law to improve the position of Gypsy and Traveller people arises from the multi-layered nature of the discrimination that they experience, a phenomenon described in detail by Liégeois (1987). In the 1996 ECtHR case of *Buckley v UK* (where no violation was found), Judge Pettiti, dissenting, referred to the incremental nature of the injustices suffered by Gypsies. In his opinion, it was particularly problematic for courts to identify injustices that arose out of the 'deliberate superimposition and accumulation of administrative rules (each of which would be acceptable taken singly)' – the net effect of which was to make it 'totally impossible for a Gypsy family to make suitable arrangements for its accommodation, social life and the integration of its children at school'. Given that this is the complex multi-stranded nature of the discrimination experienced by Gypsy and Traveller people in Wales today, the question is whether other mechanisms can harness the Measure to bring about positive and practical change.

Williams (in chapter 4 of this volume) rightly highlights the powerful impact that the public sector equality duty (found in section 149 of the Equality Act 2010) has had in requiring public bodies to demonstrate that they have had 'due regard' to the aims and aspirations of the legislation. This has proved to be a weighty obligation, including not only the public body obligation (where a policy or practice may have negative impact) to consider what can be done to mitigate such impacts, but also the obligation that this analytical process must be evidenced. Many local authority policies not only fail the 'due regard test' but in fact constitute prima facie indirect discrimination based on race. An example (noted below) is the statistically significant difference in planning refusal rates for Gypsy and Traveller applicants. The Measure will bring into focus many more such irregularities, but in itself will provide no new remedial mechanism. Given that neither the Public Services Ombudsman, nor the Children's Commissioner nor the EHRC have taken action in relation to the wholly disproportionate planning refusal rates, it is difficult to see which institution will grasp the nettle when the new obligations come into being.

The rights of Gypsy and Traveller children and young people in Wales

> The stark realities laid before the Committee by a group of young people from the Gypsy-Traveller community brought home the challenges we face in making a real difference to their lives. (Chair of the Committee on Equality of Opportunity, NAW, 2003)

Despite some aspirational initiatives and expressed commitments from the government in Wales to take a Wales-wide strategic approach and improve the situation of Gypsies and Travellers, much of the progress since the National Assembly carried out its 2003 review of service provision for Gypsy and Traveller people has been characterised by slow and patchy implementation, a lack of monitoring and accountability for delivery, and a marked lack of political will at a local level to treat Gypsy and Traveller people as equal citizens.

A Road Less Travelled – A Draft Gypsy Traveller Strategy (WG, 2009a) was eventually published for consultation in 2009 and has been referred to in the national action plan on children's rights as the key, and only, mechanism to progress recommendations from the UN Committee to urgently improve the lives of Gypsy and Traveller children in Wales. Two years later the Welsh Government launched *Travelling to a Better Future: A Gypsy and Traveller Framework for Action and Delivery Plan* (WG, 2011c). Described as the first of its kind in the UK, the document sets out how the Welsh Government intends to ensure that Gypsy and Traveller communities have fair and equal access to the key priorities of accommodation, health and education.

Below we set out some key areas where we believe the rights of Gypsy and Traveller children need to be urgently addressed, and the actions that the Welsh Government should take to ensure that due regard is given to the UNCRC so that progress is achieved towards realisation of rights for this group of children and young people.

The right to non-discrimination
Wales (like the rest of the UK) fails in relation to the Article 2 UNCRC requirement that all children should enjoy their rights equally: Gypsy and Traveller children in Wales do not realise their equal rights to an adequate standard of living, to health, education and participation. As the UN Committee has noted, in the UK 'in practice certain groups of children, such as: Roma and Irish Travellers' children . . . continue to experience discrimination and social stigmatization' (UN Committee *CO*, 2008: para. 24). The government's failure to address this prejudice was identified by the Committee as a key reason as to why the problem persists. It stressed the importance of it undertaking 'awareness-raising and other preventive activities against discrimination and, if necessary, take affirmative actions for the benefit of vulnerable groups of children, such as: Roma and Irish Travellers' children' (ibid.).

While the Welsh Government has taken action to promote understanding of the UNCRC through a range of initiatives aimed at children and adults, including curriculum and training resources (WG, 2009b), it is apparent that many public bodies and individuals remain ignorant of their full obligations. In this context, the Committee recommended that the government 'strengthen its efforts' and that this include the 'reinforcement of adequate and systematic training of all professional groups working for and with children' (UN Committee *CO*, 2008: para. 21).

Monitoring children's rights – data collection
Article 4 and Article 2 of the UNCRC require the collection of data to enable the systematic monitoring of how the UNCRC is being implemented and to identify children who may need special measures to recognise and realise their rights: 'data must therefore be disaggregated to enable discrimination or potential discrimination to be identified' (UN Committee *GC*, 2003: para. 12). The Council of Europe has noted that the 'production of detailed (race) statistics has become a prime necessity for compliance with European laws' (Simon, 2007: 7), such as the EU Race Directive (2000/43/EC) which acknowledges the key role to be played by such data (preamble, para. 15). The European Court of Human Rights also accepted that statistical data would often be 'key' to establishing a rebuttable presumption that unlawful discrimination has occurred (see *DH v Czech Republic*, para. 188).

The Welsh Government acknowledges that 'Reliable data on the numbers of Gypsy Travellers in Wales is not available', that current arrangements for 'collecting data are inadequate' (WG, 2009b), and that numbers are underestimated (WG, 2011b). While difficulties, such as counting a 'transient' population, were cited, this is an unsatisfactory position – not least because the reality is that the majority of Gypsy and Traveller people no longer actually lead a fully 'nomadic' lifestyle (CRE, 2006; Niner, 2006).

While there has been some progress in collating and assessing statistics for housing needs purposes and more recently those for education, the lack of data collected by the NHS on health leaves a significant gap in knowledge in baseline data, and in the ability to monitor access to services and health outcomes (Cemlyn et al., 2009). This issue was raised by the 2003 review of service provision in Wales (NAW, 2003) and remains a concern.

Anecdotal evidence and some research suggests that Gypsy and Traveller children and young people in contact with the child protection and looked-after children services (Allen, 2012) and the youth justice system (Cemlyn et al., 2009; Mason et al., 2009) are not having their rights fully recognised, and suggests that discrimination occurs within these systems. Here, too, lack of data collection undermines effective monitoring.

The UN Committee note that measures under Article 4, including data collection on some of the most vulnerable children, are still not fully implemented across the UK. They recommend that governments should 'adopt data-collection mechanisms that allow desegregation by sex, age, origin and socio-economic status so that the situation of different groups can be followed. Data should also be collected to study the situation of specific groups such as ethnic and/or indigenous minorities' (UN Committee *GC*, 2003: para. 13).

The right to an adequate standard of living

Article 27 states that governments must recognise the right of every child to a 'standard of living adequate for the child's physical, mental, spiritual, moral and social development'. The government is expected to take appropriate measures to assist parents and others responsible for the child to implement this right, including programmes of support and housing (Article 27.3). Article 6 requires that governments take steps to ensure the right to life, to survival and development of children.

The draft Wales Child Poverty Strategy (WG, 2010a) identifies Gypsy and Traveller families as one of the 'at risk' groups most likely to be living in poverty in Wales, and the accompanying delivery plan contains a section dedicated to Gypsies and Travellers, referencing the Gypsy and Traveller National Strategy as a key mechanism for combating child poverty in the community. However the subsequently published *Child Poverty Strategy for*

Wales (WG, 2011a) disappointingly lacks any specific actions and targets to alleviate poverty for Gypsy and Traveller families.

The links between accommodation and other inequalities experienced by the community are well established (Cemlyn et al., 2009) and the lack of appropriate sites and insufficient provision has a significant detrimental impact on the lives of Gypsy and Traveller people (NAW, 2003).

The repeal in 1994 of the local authority duty to provide Gypsy and Traveller sites has, as predicted, created major problems. Families now have few options. These are: to try and secure a pitch on oversubscribed council sites; to apply for planning permission to live on their own land; to move into permanent housing; or to continue to travel and 'stop over' in places where they are vulnerable to the community hostility and constant threat of eviction which so deeply affects children and young people's emotional and physical well-being (Ureche and Franks, 2007).

In 2008 the UN Committee Special Rapporteur for the UK visited some Gypsy and Traveller sites in Wales and was so appalled by what she saw and heard that it prompted her to ask questions of the UK Government during the reporting process about its plans to improve living conditions for Gypsy and Traveller children in Wales (OHCHR, 2008).

The Welsh Government's *A Road Less Travelled – A Draft Gypsy Traveller Strategy* focused on improving the provision and planning for site accommodation, including managing unauthorised encampments; it also references the range of initiatives, planning circulars, grants and guidance that the Welsh Government has developed to assess and improve the quantity and quality of accommodation and the design and management of new sites, and to mitigate the worst effects on children and families of 'stopping over' at unauthorised sites (WG, 2009a).

The evidence, however, is that despite a clear identified need, and the guidance and support at a national level, most local authorities are reluctant to develop new public or private sites even though there is clear evidence that not investing in site-provision places a greater burden on council finances than investing in this activity (Morris and Clements, 2002). With the advent of the 'due regard' duty in the Measure, council failings in this respect may become more difficult to sustain.

Planning applications from Gypsies and Travellers seeking permission to live on or develop a site on their own land have increased, but research revealed that over 90 per cent were turned down in comparison with 20 per cent of non-traveller applications; opposition from local residents, often racist in content, was frequently found to have contributed to the decisions (CRE, 2006). Although many applications succeed on appeal, the Welsh

Government had undertaken to assess the effectiveness of their Planning Circular 30/2007 in Wales (WG, 2009a). At the time of writing there has been no publicly reported progress on this activity.

Many families now live in ordinary housing – some by choice, but many because it became so difficult to continue travelling without adverse effects on family health and well-being. Children's education in particular is a key motivation for opting for 'bricks and mortar'. But research reveals that for Gypsy and Traveller people, living in a house is associated with long-term illness, poorer health state, and anxiety; those who rarely travel have the poorest health (Parry et al., 2004). Isolation from community and family support, exposure to further discrimination from neighbours, and the additional problems associated with being housed in often socio-economically deprived areas are also experienced by house dwellers (Cemlyn et al., 2009).

The UN Committee, noting the high prevalence of child poverty in the UK, welcomed the UK commitment to end child poverty, and subsequent legislation, but stated that 'Government strategy is not sufficiently targeted at those groups of children in most severe poverty', and that 'the standard of living of Traveller children is particularly poor'. The Committee went on to recommend that in order to address some of their concerns regarding the poor standard of living for Traveller children, the government should 'reintroduce a statutory duty on local authorities to provide safe and adequate sites for Travellers' (UN Committee *CO*, 2008: para. 65d.)

The right to education

Articles 28 and 29 recognise the rights of children to education on the basis of equal opportunity, and place emphasis on this occurring in a way that shows 'respect for the child's parents, his or her own cultural identity, language and values'. In this context, the UN Committee has noted that in the UK 'significant inequalities persist with regard to school achievement of children living with their parents in economic hardship . . . and cannot fully enjoy their right to education, notably children with disabilities, children of Travellers, Roma children' (UN Committee *CO*, 2008: para. 66).

The Welsh Government's strategy *The Learning Country* made a commitment to ensuring 'an inclusive approach to education and learning that is responsive to individual educational needs, including those of Gypsy and Traveller pupils, and which supports all children and young people to reach their full potential'. (WG, 2001: 8). This commitment is supported by the provision of grants and matched funding to support Traveller education, and by the specific guidance in *Moving Forward – Gypsy Traveller Education* (WG, 2008); the commitment is also supported by initiatives to help specialist education staff and develop culturally relevant curricula for Gypsy and Traveller pupils.

In Wales, however, Gypsy and Traveller children are the lowest-achieving ethnic group in terms of formal educational outcomes (WG, 2011b). The familiar, well-documented issues and barriers (Estyn, 2005, and Jones et al., 2006) remain a problem, including bullying, teaching styles and a curriculum content which does not take account of the particular needs or culture of Gypsy and Traveller pupils. Consequently some parents still choose not to send their children to school, seeing formal education as irrelevant to the needs of the community but also potentially damaging both individually and culturally.

For many years dedicated Traveller Education Services (TES) in some Welsh authorities have provided key specialist support, teaching, and trust-building and links between schools and Gypsy and Traveller families, and have had substantial success in improving educational outcomes, aspirations and employment opportunities. However Estyn (2011) highlights just how much progress still needs to be achieved by schools and education authorities as a whole, noting lack of progression of their previous recommendations; parental attitudes remaining mistrustful and negative towards schools; pupils still reporting bullying and discrimination in education and generally not participating in decisions about school life or being included on school councils; and few schools offering a curriculum that actively promotes Gypsy and Traveller culture.

The same Estyn report notes that while dedicated provision has resulted in excellent outcomes, there is not enough drive to integrate and include Gypsy and Traveller pupils in mainstream schooling, leading to concerns about 'segregation' in some areas. This finding was echoed by the UN Committee, which, in 2008, stressed that more needed to be done to promote the rights of Gypsy and Traveller children to an inclusive education; and more needed to be done to tackle bullying, and to ensure full participation in school life and in learning for all marginalised groups.

The right to health
The UNCRC requires that governments ensure 'the enjoyment of the highest attainable standard of health and rehabilitation of health . . . and to ensure that no child is deprived of his or her right of access to such health care services' (Article 24). There are a number of initiatives in Wales that address this duty, including a framework of national standards based on the

UNCRC, within which 'Travellers' children' and children from minority ethnic groups are identified as being in 'special circumstances' (WG, 2005a). In addition, recently published standards (WG, 2010b) reiterate the obligation of health services under equalities legislation to address the needs of individuals, reduce health inequalities, challenge discrimination and uphold the rights of children in accordance with the UNCRC. Concerns about the impact of roadside living are acknowledged, and local authorities are asked to adopt a 'policy of toleration' and develop formal procedures including a health assessment prior to any decisions being made about evictions or attempts to move Gypsies and Travellers (WG, 2005c).

The health of Gypsy and Traveller children and young people is considered to be among the worst of all groups of ethnic minority children in the UK (WG, 2005b). The link between health and accommodation and living conditions is clear, and those families living on sites, especially unauthorised encampments, are particularly at risk of health problems relating to poor environmental conditions. Families experience practical difficulties in accessing preventative and primary health care services, and the lack of access to safe playing areas (an issue regularly raised by young people themselves) contributes toward a higher accident rate for children (Niner, 2006).

The key barrier to accessing health services appears to be discriminatory practice and attitudes of some professionals. Families still report difficulties in registering with GPs and dentists, refusal of some health professionals or services to go out to sites, and a lack of understanding and awareness of cultural issues. Reports (for example NAW, 2003: 58) have highlighted the need to ensure more formal mechanisms that prevent people being denied access to primary care, including 'incentives' and in the long term 'more coercive means' for GPs and other primary health care providers. Specialist health staff and dedicated projects have been effective in targeted areas (Wrexham LHB, 2008) but this good practice is far from consistent across Wales.

The shortcomings outlined here are recognised by the UN Committee, which recommends that the 'inequalities in access to health services are addressed through a coordinated approach across all government departments and greater coordination between health policies and those aimed at reducing income inequality and poverty' (UN Committee *CO*, 2008: para. 55).

Participation
The 'voice of the child' under Article 12 is an underpinning principle of the UNCRC, giving children the right to freely express their views in all

matters that affect them, and for these views to be given due weight in accordance with their age and maturity. The Welsh Government sets out a clear vision to progress the rights in Article 12 for Gypsy and Traveller children and young people in Wales (WG, 2009a). However, the views of Gypsy and Traveller children rarely shape services despite the efforts Wales has put into promoting, developing and legislating for participation (Crowley, chapter 15 in this volume). Those examples of positive consultation practice, especially at a national level, can be rendered ineffective by the long delays in implementing changes, which often leads to consultation 'fatigue' and lack of faith in the process, as children and young people give their views repeatedly on the same issues and see little change or feedback. This is exemplified by the delay in producing and implementing the national strategy.

Mainstream consultation mechanisms have struggled to include Gypsy and Traveller people. They are not often represented on school councils and youth fora, and are marginalised in decision-making where they live, or in contributing to site design and day-to-day management decisions that affect them. The levels of discrimination they face on a daily basis understandably lead young people, like their parents, to have little faith in those participatory structures that do exist in local communities (STC, 2009).

Largely as a result of the work done by specialist agencies, the Welsh Government has for some time commendably acknowledged the need to focus additional resources on developing the participation of Gypsy and Traveller children, and has supported a number of initiatives such as the *Travelling Ahead* DVD (2006), the Varde Venture and the Gypsy, Roma and Traveller History Month in Wales.

A scoping exercise commissioned by the Welsh Government on the engagement of Gypsy and Traveller children and young people to inform government strategy made a number of recommendations. This included, in the first instance, identifying the need to work directly with children and young people to develop their confidence and skills alongside their peers, with the aim of progressing to regional or national participation structures; these in turn could act as a platform for young Gypsy and Traveller people and make an impact on tackling discrimination and shaping policy at a national level (STC, 2009). The Welsh Government then funded a three-year post (2009–12) with Save the Children's Travelling Ahead project to develop this work.

The local Gypsy and Traveller youth fora around Wales that resulted have self-selected some inspiring projects to work on, including raising awareness and combating racism. A variety of imaginative formats and media are used, including creating community play spaces, changing parental attitudes on the value of secondary education, a participation in democracy project and a forum to influence local policy-making.

Through young people choosing to tackle discrimination in their schools and communities, educate their peers and parents, and raise awareness themselves about the difficulties they face, they may succeed where rafts of policy recommendations have failed. The first Wales-wide gathering of these youth fora took place in late 2011.

These developments build on the 2008 UN Committee recommendations that the government should promote respect for the views of children in practice and through legislation in all areas of their lives, should support fora for children's participation, such as Funky Dragon, and should continue to collaborate with NGOs to increase opportunities for children's meaningful participation, including in the media (UN Committee *CO*, 2008: para. 33). There remains an urgent need to ensure support and sustainability for the groundbreaking work these Welsh young people are doing, and the impact it could have on their own communities as well as more widely.

What opportunities does the Measure offer to further the rights of Gypsy and Traveller children and young people?

Williams in chapter 4 of this volume details the legal implications and the scope of the Rights of Children and Young Persons (Wales) Measure. These include a consideration of the timetable for implementation; the duty to prepare a 'children's scheme'; the duty to have due regard; and the nature of the 'progressive realisation' obligation.

The broad due regard duty is intended (among other things) to raise the knowledge and awareness of politicians and officials alike, and should contribute to a better understanding across government of the rights of Gypsy and Traveller children and young people. Such an improved understanding should also result from the process of preparing the children's scheme. Gypsy and Traveller children and young people in particular should be involved and consulted on both the interpretation of 'due regard' and in the content of the children's scheme, and the wealth of material that children and young people have already contributed to government and NGO consultations and reports must be reflected in the scheme's contents.

'Due regard' in this context should embrace consideration of all the issues highlighted above in terms of the requirements of the UNCRC. Policy development, law-making, direct Welsh Government service provision (where applicable) and Welsh Government oversight or direction of service provision by others should be affected by this. Examples, far from exhaustive, are as follows:

Due regard to the general measures of implementation
In practice this will require regular child rights impact assessments, improved budget analysis and equality impact assessments to determine the proportion of spending and the impact of policies and any cuts in services on the ability of Gypsy and Traveller children and young people to access their rights. Associated with this, one would expect the strengthening of targets, monitoring of outcomes and implementation of existing legislation, policies and strategies in health, education, participation and poverty eradication to address the inequalities and rights violations experienced by Gypsy and Traveller children and young people. The national action plan on children's rights (WG, 2009b) should act as an overarching framework to increase scrutiny and accountability, and the framework for action and delivery plan (WG, 2011c) should include clear rights-based indicators and outcomes, emphasising the effect of the Rights of Children and Young Persons (Wales) Measure 2011 on the legality of any exercise of Welsh Ministers' functions. Systematically collected disaggregated data, as noted above and elsewhere in this volume, is essential.

Due regard to the 'general principles' of the UNCRC
Implementing the Measure provides an opportunity to embed the general principles of the UNCRC into existing and forthcoming strategies and guidance, and to monitor and hold to account public services and their decision-making processes to respect the rights to best interests, non-discrimination, to life, survival and development and respect for the views and experiences of Gypsy and Traveller children and young people. The issues highlighted here require affirmative action to tackle discrimination and negative media portrayal, and working with independent monitoring bodies to address discrimination effectively, including with 'disciplinary, administrative and if necessary penal sanctions' (UN Committee *CO*, 2008: para. 25). The same is true of promotion of participation, where responsibility needs to be shared by all agencies, backed up by monitoring and improvement mechanisms.

Standard of living
The National Assembly for Wales has legislative capacity to implement the UN Committee's recommendation to reintroduce a statutory duty on local

authorities to provide safe and adequate sites for Gypsies and Travellers. This is a concrete step which would represent the kind of progressive law reform intended to be stimulated by the Measure.

Conclusion

We have seen how the situation for Gypsy and Traveller families and their children in Wales continues to require urgent attention, as this is probably the most 'at risk' group of children in terms of their lack of enjoyment of their rights and the inequalities they experience.

Efforts at a national level in Wales are hampered by delays and a lack of scrutiny and accountability, and at a local level by a lack of political or institutional will to stand up for the human rights of Gypsies and Travellers. The Rights Measure provides the opportunity and indeed requires that Welsh Ministers address the rights violations experienced by Gypsy and Traveller children and their families.

References

Allen, D. (2012): 'Gypsies, Travellers and social policy: marginality and insignificance: a case study of Gypsy and Traveller children in care', in J. Richardson and A. Ryder, *Gypsies and Travellers: Accommodation, Empowerment and Inclusion in British Society* (Bristol: Policy Press), pp. 83–100.

Aspinwall, T. and Larkins, C. (2010): *Travellers and Gypsies: Generations for the Future: A Report of the Consultations with Children and Young People on the Welsh Assembly Government's Draft Gypsy Traveller Strategy* (Cardiff: Ear 2 the Ground and Save the Children).

Cemlyn, S., Greenfields, M., Burnett, S., Matthews, Z. and Whitwell, C. (2009): *Inequalities Experienced by Gypsy and Traveller Communities: A Review* (Manchester: Equality and Human Rights Commission).

Clements, L. and Morris, R. (2004): 'The Millennium blip: local authority responses to the Human Rights Act 1998', in S. Halliday and P. Schmidt (eds), *Human Rights Brought Home: Socio-Legal Studies of Human Rights in the National Context* (Oxford: Hart Publishing), pp. 209–29.

CRE (Commission for Racial Equality) (2006): *Common Ground: Equality, Good Race Relations and Sites for Gypsies and Irish Travellers: Report of a CRE Inquiry in England and Wales* (London: CRE).

EHRC (Equality and Human Rights Commission) (2008): *Who Do You See? Living Together in Wales* (Cardiff: Equality and Human Rights Commission).

Estyn (2005): *The Education of Gypsy Traveller Learners: A survey of provision made by schools and local authorities to meet the needs of Gypsy Traveller learners* (Cardiff: Estyn).

—— (2011): *The Education of Gypsy Traveller Pupils: An Update on Provision in Secondary Schools* (Cardiff: Estyn).

Johnson, C., Ryder, R. and Willers, M. (2010): 'Gypsies and Travellers in the United Kingdom and security of tenure', *Roma Rights: Journal of the European Roma Rights Centre*, 1 (*Implementation of Judgments*), 45–9. Available at *http://www.errc.org/cms/upload/file/roma-rights-1-2010-implementation-of-judgments.pdf* (accessed 1 July 2012).

Jones, G., Powell, R. and Reakes, S. (2006): *Research into the Education of Gypsy Traveller Children in Wales* (Slough: National Foundation for Educational Research).

Liégeois, J-P. (1987): *Gypsies and Travellers* (Strasbourg: Council of Europe).

Mason, P., Hughes, N., Hek, R., Spalek, B. and Ward, N. (2009): *Access to Justice: A Review of Existing Evidence of the Experiences of Minority Groups Based on Ethnicity, Identity and Sexuality*, Ministry of Justice Research Series 7/09 (Birmingham: Institute of Applied Social Studies, University of Birmingham and Allan Norman Celtic Knot).

Morris, R. and Clements, L. (2002): *At What Cost? The Economics of Gypsy and Traveller Encampments* (Bristol: Policy Press).

National Assembly for Wales (2003): Committee on Equality of Opportunity, *Review of service Provision for Gypsy Travellers – Report* EOC(2) 01–03 (Cardiff: National Assembly for Wales).

Niner, P. (2006): *Accommodation Needs of Gypsy-Travellers in Wales* (Cardiff: Welsh Assembly Government).

OHCHR (Office of the High Commissioner for Human Rights) (2005): *Gil-Robles: A Report on Visit to the United Kingdom 2004*, Comm DH (2005) 6 (Strasbourg: Council of Europe).

—— (2008): 'Committee on Rights of Child considers report of the United Kingdom of Great Britain and Northern Ireland', press release 24 September. Available at *http://www.ohchr.org/EN/NewsEvents/Pages/DisplayNews.aspx?NewsID=8869&LangID=E* (accessed 2 July 2012).

Parry, G., Van Cleemput, P., Peters, J., Moore, J., Walters, S., Thomas, K. and Cooper, C. (2004): *The Health Status of Gypsies and Travellers in England* (Sheffield: University of Sheffield).

Simon, P. (2007): *'Ethnic' Statistics and Data Protection in the Council of Europe Countries* (Strasbourg: Council of Europe).

STC (Save the Children) (2009): *Getting Involved: A Report into Engaging with Young Gypsy Travellers in Wales* (Cardiff: Save the Children).

Travelling Ahead (2006): DVD. See *http://www.travellingahead.org.uk.*

Ureche, H. and Franks, M. (2007): *This is Who We Are: A Study of the Views and Identities of Roma, Gypsy and Traveller Young People in England* (London: The Children's Society).

Valentine, G. and McDonald, I. (2004): *Understanding Prejudice: Attitudes Towards Minorities* (London: Stonewall).

WG (Welsh Government) (2001): *The Learning Country: A Paving Document* (Cardiff: Welsh Assembly Government).

—— (2005a): *National Service Framework for Children, Young People and Maternity Services in Wales* (Cardiff: Welsh Assembly Government).

—— (2005b): *Health Assert Programme Wales: Review of the Literature on the Health Beliefs, Health Status and Use of Services in Gypsy Traveller Population and of Appropriate Health Care Interventions* (Cardiff: Welsh Assembly Government).

—— (2005c): *Guidance on Managing Unauthorised Camping: Circular 4/2005* (Cardiff: Welsh Assembly Government).

—— (2008): *Moving Forward – Gypsy Traveller Education: Circular 003/2008* (Cardiff: Welsh Assembly Government).

—— (2009a): *A Road Less Travelled – A Draft Gypsy Traveller Strategy: Consultation Document* (Cardiff: Welsh Assembly Government).

—— (2009b): *Getting it Right 2009: United Nations Convention on the Rights of the Child. A 5-year rolling Action Plan for Wales setting out key priorities and actions to be undertaken by the Welsh Assembly Government in response to the Concluding Observations of the UN Committee on the Rights of the Child 2008* (Cardiff: Welsh Assembly Government).

—— (2010a): *Child Poverty Strategy for Wales and Delivery Plan – Consultation Document* (Cardiff: Welsh Assembly Government).

—— (2010b): *Doing Well, Doing Better: Standards for Health Service in Wales* (Cardiff: Welsh Assembly Government).

—— (2011a): *Child Poverty Strategy for Wales* (Cardiff: Welsh Government).

—— (2011b): *Children and Young People's Well-being Monitor for Wales* (Cardiff: Welsh Government).

—— (2011c): *Travelling to a Better Future. A Gypsy and Traveller Framework for Action and Delivery Plan* (Cardiff: Welsh Government).

Wrexham Local Health Board (2008): *Coronary Heart Disease and Gypsies and Travellers: Redressing the Balance Project* (Welsh Assembly Government Project Reference IIH/2001/012). See *http://wales.gov.uk/topics/health/improvement/communities/fund/inequalitiesnorth1/balanceproject/?lang=en* (accessed 16 September 2012).

PART III

Ensuring it works: accountability and participation

CHAPTER 12

Accountability

Simon Hoffman and Jane Williams

Introduction

'Rights without remedies are of symbolic importance, no more.' Thus wrote Professor Michael Freeman (2010: 18) in an article informed by over forty years of research and advocacy for the human rights of children. In chapter 5 of this volume Fitzpatrick makes the same point from a moral perspective. Fitzpatrick points to the necessity of recognising that moral obligation precedes rights, so that rights can be seen as demands for fulfilment of obligation. Freeman's concern is to move children's rights from rhetoric to 'fora for action', so that they become an 'advocacy tool, a tool for change, a weapon to use in the battle to secure recognition' (ibid.). For both writers, participation of rights-bearers is crucial, and this requires, as an essential component, accessible remedies. For persons under eighteen, classed as not (or not fully) legally competent, there are additional barriers to those social and economic barriers that apply to many persons who are most in need of assertion of their rights. For children's rights to have more than 'symbolic importance' there must be effective mechanisms of accountability for the-day-to-day decisions that impact on the distribution of accessibility to rights. Put another way, those making the decisions must be called to account if they fail to recognise and fulfil the obligations precedent to those rights.

This chapter is concerned with accountability for the discharge in Wales of obligations to respect and protect the human rights of children and young people, in a context of multi-layered structures of governance and in light of the Rights of Children and Young Persons (Wales) Measure 2011. Consideration of accountability of Welsh Ministers for compliance with their 'due regard' duty under the Measure raises a number of important questions. How will we know that Welsh Ministers have complied with this duty? What can we do if they fail? And, reflecting both Freeman and Fitzpatrick's concern, will children and young people be participants in the processes for holding the Welsh Ministers to account? If the answers to these questions are 'we won't', 'not much' and 'probably not', then the new law will be no more than of symbolic importance.

We argue here that such a bleak appraisal would be misconceived. The Measure establishes a number of potentially powerful levers to help monitor and challenge Welsh Ministers' compliance. We also argue that the Measure's provisions confer new potency on existing mechanisms of accountability, including by facilitating the participation of children and young people. This potential will not, however, be realised without effort on the part of key actors within and external to the machine of Welsh government to effect significant changes in practice.

We first briefly explore the notion of accountability, then how multi-level governance (of which Welsh devolved government is one level) impacts on governmental accountability and in turn on the exercise of citizenship, including children's citizenship. We consider how the Measure plays in pre-existing routes to accountability within judicial, administrative and political mechanisms. Finally we suggest that, although much depends on practices that may develop, the Measure offers significant improvements in accountability of Welsh Government, and some new opportunities for redress, albeit stopping short of providing for individual claims of rights violations.

Accountability

At a most basic level, accountability is about holding a duty bearer to account for the discharge of a duty. This apparently straightforward idea is complicated by the fact that duties arise in different contexts and from different concepts, and generate different structures and processes for accountability. Legal duties may arise from agreement reflecting the private choices of legally competent individuals: these may be enforceable before a court as a contract or trust. Irrespective of individual choice, law imposes duties and remedies for breach: for example, the common-law duty of care in negligence, or the duty owed by an occupier to visitors, or an employer to employees. The Human Rights Act 1998 imposes a duty on public authorities to act in compliance with rights under the ECHR, and provides for an individual legal claim where a violation is alleged. Where there is a legal duty the usual structure for accountability is the judicial system, embracing local through national and supra-national courts. At the same time, public duties may be enforced through political and administrative as well judicial structures. The institutional architecture of public accountability encompasses elections, bureaucracy, judicial review, tribunals and complaints procedures, enquiries, parliamentary scrutiny, ombudspersons, the media and markets. (For further discussion about the nature of public accountability see Dowdle, 2006.) The rules administered within these structures are the result not of one but several layers of law-making and governance, from the local to the international.

Multi-level governance and citizenship

Devolution is envisioned as a means of increasing political accountability (see the 1997 White Papers on devolution to Scotland and Wales, *Scotland's Parliament*, Cm. 3658, and *A Voice for Wales*, Cm. 3718). Paradoxically, it also contributes to a fragmentation of public accountability which is inherent in multi-level governance, as responsibilities are distributed among different levels of government, a phenomenon which Dowdle (2006) portrays as a crisis in accountability. For our purposes, the formal levels of governance are: the UK Government which is competent for non-devolved (Wales) or 'reserved' (Scotland and Northern Ireland) matters; the devolved administrations; local authorities; and community or parish. Each of these generates institutional responsibility and associated structures for accountability: the UK electoral system; the jurisdictional 'unit' of England and Wales; regional elections to devolved parliaments; local government elections; community elections (including those for community-based representative bodies such as local health boards); statutory bodies with oversight responsibilities; statutory tribunals; complaints procedures; and investigatory processes. Beyond the UK, the European Union and the Council of Europe contribute additional levels of governance as well as distinct accountability structures via elections to the European Parliament, references from UK domestic courts to the European Court of Justice (for EU law), and petitions to the European Court of Human Rights (for the ECHR). Beyond Europe, institutions and structures contributing to accountability include bodies established by international treaty obligations such as the UN Committee and the State Party reporting mechanism established under the UNCRC.

Citizens – the 'governed' – wishing to hold governmental duty bearers to account thus need to engage with several different levels of governance. Different rules and underlying notions govern such interactions at the different levels, determining the obligations imposed on duty bearers and the rights of individuals in relation to the duty bearers. Each has its own political culture and overall purpose and function. This complex picture demands a broad view of citizenship encompassing a guarantee of rights, a right to participate as members of a community (or communities), and equality – recognition of equal dignity and worth – which in turn links with respect for and protection of human rights (Lister, 2008). Across the several layers of governance, different (sometimes linked) institutions, each with their own procedures, carry formal obligations to ensure respect and protection for human rights. A construction of children as citizens in these processes presents a number of challenges. As Lister observes: 'some of the building blocks of citizenship are more compatible with childhood than others' (2008: 10). For that reason the development of effective government structures for children, including structures for accountability, is a crucial part of developing a practice as well as a status of children's citizenship and, as an essential component of that, access to their human rights.

Extending the rules of engagement

Children face a number of challenges in establishing their claim to citizenship rights (Clutton, 2008). Access to social welfare entitlements is often mediated via the family; access to key aspects of the political system (notably voting) is denied, and access to fundamental freedoms is often withheld or restricted on the ground of assumed lack of developmental capacity or vulnerability (exemplified in the setting of education, as discussed in chapter 8 of this volume by Hosking, and exemplified elsewhere as discussed by Cantwell, 2011). Recognition of children's citizenship requires acceptance – at all levels of governance – that children have rights in the domains in which policy and law-making take place. This in turn requires structures for accountability to be appropriate to enable decisions and actions in these domains to be monitored and challenged. The complexity of multi-level governance, together with the multiplicity of citizenship rights across several policy and legal domains, creates a need for careful attention to processes and rules to safeguard and promote rights, and to increase the accountability of duty bearers. It has been noted that legal challenges under the Human Rights Act 1998, with its mechanisms designed to protect all people, including children, while scoring some notable successes for children's rights have often tended to focus in practice on the rights of parents and other adults involved (Fortin, 2006).

The Rights of Children and Young Persons (Wales) Measure 2011 'gives further effect' to the UNCRC in Wales, and in so doing introduces some new rules of engagement between the Welsh Government and children and young people. The Measure applies at one level within the strata of governance impacting on children's rights in Wales. It does not overlook other levels but adds to law already in place at international, European, UK and devolved levels: the UNCRC, the ECHR, equalities legislation, and sector-specific legislation. At the time of the enactment of the Measure the effects of this wider patchwork of legal rules included that:

- reference in Welsh Government strategy documents and guidance to the UNCRC as a source of informal rules and policies could be taken into account by a court on judicial review, if relevant to a question of the rationality or fairness of a governmental decision or its intended effect;
- the UNCRC was already an international obligation to which, as a matter of international law, the Welsh Ministers, as a manifestation of the State Party to the UNCRC, must have regard;
- the European Court of Human Rights in interpreting the ECHR had referred to the text of the UNCRC in reaching its decisions in cases concerning children;
- such decisions of the European Court of Human Rights had to be considered by the UK courts where relevant (this being a requirement of section 2 of the Human Rights Act 1998);
- the UK courts had already for some years been referring directly to aspects of the UNCRC when deciding cases that came before them (see Williams, 2007: n.1);
- 'protection of the rights of the child' had become one of the stated objectives of the European Union (Article 3[3] of the Treaty on European Union);
- the UNCRC had come to be regarded as a fundamental rights instrument to which the EU must adhere and as such a point of reference when the European Court of Justice decides questions of the legality of EU decision-making (Case C-540/03, *Parliament v Council* [2006] ECR I-5769);
- and the Children's Commissioner for Wales was already obliged to take into account the UNCRC when carrying out the functions of that office (Regulation 22 of the Children's Commissioner for Wales Regulations 2001).

The Measure extends these rules by importing new considerations into their application to questions of legality of Welsh Government decisions. By imposing the due regard duty on Welsh Ministers, the Measure provides further grist to the mill of a legal challenge to a decision if it can be argued to have been made without due regard to a requirement of the UNCRC. Any examination by the Children's Commissioner of the exercise of functions by the Welsh Government will take in the question of compliance with the due regard duty (as well as being conducted in accordance with the commissioner's own duty with regard to the Convention). The Measure potentially strengthens arguments based on the UNCRC's requirements in complaints, audit and review processes, such as those of the Public Service Ombudsman for Wales, Auditor General for Wales, local complaints and appeals. It also provides statutory underpinning for parliamentary scrutiny by the National Assembly for Wales. By requiring Welsh Ministers to act to improve knowledge and awareness of the UNCRC among the public, including children and young people, by insisting on 'involvement' of stakeholder organisations and individuals in the development of the children's scheme, and by institutionalising formal review of compliance with the due regard duty by the National Assembly, the Measure provides a channel in which the requirements of the UNCRC can flow in all these processes.

We turn now to consider in more detail these judicial, administrative and political mechanisms of accountability, identifying how the Measure may go some way towards meeting the need for remedies. This is followed by a section in which we address the further concern raised by both Freeman and Fitzpatrick: the need for *accessible* remedies.

Judicial accountability and municipal law

The Measure operates within what has been described as 'public officer's law' (Williams, chapter 4 in this volume and Williams, 2012), engaging with decision-making processes within the Welsh Government: the matters taken into account, the weight attached to different factors and the balance struck between competing – or even complementary – interests. The Measure does not establish any mechanism by which an individual as victim may bring a claim for damages, alleging a violation of a requirement of the UNCRC by a Welsh Minister. This contrasts with the approach taken under the Human Rights Act 1998, whereby a 'victim' may bring a claim against a public authority alleging violation of any of the ECHR rights imported in to the Human Rights Act. In that sense, there is no increase in accountability via the courts. However, Welsh Ministers' duty to have due regard is a public law duty, the exercise of which is amenable to challenge by way of judicial review in the Administrative Court. Put another way, by analogy with the public sector equality duty under the Equality Act 2010, Ministers' failure to have due regard invites a legal challenge by way of judicial review (see Williams, chapter 4 in this volume). From May 2012, when the Measure comes partly into effect, and from May 2014 when it will be fully in effect, children and others with sufficient interest will be able to look to the judiciary to hold the Welsh Ministers to account for compliance with the Measure. The question whether in practice due regard has been had to the requirements of the UNCRC becomes a criterion of the legality of Welsh Ministers' actions.

The Measure draws down into the law of Wales the specified require-ments of the UNCRC, setting them out in a Schedule. Judges deciding cases within Wales may thus come to adjudicate on the meaning of the text as part of the decision whether due regard has been had to it. In this way, through judicial supervision of Welsh Ministers in the discharge of their functions, accountability for compliance with the UNCRC in Wales is enhanced at two levels: first, because the courts will be able to rule on whether Welsh Ministers have achieved the correct balance between obligations imposed by the UNCRC and other priorities, and secondly, because as an adjunct of this process, new and developed understandings of the different provisions of the UNCRC are likely to emerge which will delineate Welsh Ministers' conduct.

That said, it is anticipated that challenges in the courts will not be com-mon even where failure in discharge of the duty can be identified. Many practical barriers, not least cost, stand in the way of mounting an applica-tion for judicial review. One or two such challenges might well be useful in terms of consolidating understanding of the effect of the duty to have due regard on the conduct of official business in the Welsh Government. But in practice other mechanisms are likely to have more currency, simply because they are cheaper and more accessible to those with an interest in compliance.

Administrative accountability

The office of the Children's Commissioner for Wales provides the most obvious administrative mechanism of accountability for governmental action under the Measure. Rees (chapter 3 in this volume) notes that the functions of the Children's Commissioner for Wales are, at the time of writ-ing, under review and could be the subject of new legislation before 2015. He explains the commissioner's current powers and duties, and suggests how these might be enhanced to enable more and better use of the office as a mechanism for holding Welsh Government to account for its obligations under the Measure. However, as he also notes, the commissioner's existing powers offer considerable potential even without those desirable changes. Any 'function review', 'arrangements review' or 'examination' (borrowing Rees's terms) and any individual case work which engages with the exer-cise of Welsh Ministerial functions will embrace the way in which the due regard duty has been fulfilled. Furthermore, the Measure itself contains new 'functions' of Welsh Ministers: not only the due regard duty but also the duty to ensure public knowledge of the UNCRC, the duty to produce a children's scheme, and the duty to review it from time to time, plus a power to propose remedial legislation. All or any of these could be the subject of a 'functions review' by the commissioner.

In addition, the Welsh Ministers are obliged to ensure the 'involvement' of the commissioner in the preparation of the children's scheme (as well as children and young people and others the Welsh Ministers consider appropriate, which could include, for example, the Equality and Human Rights Commission, the Public Service Ombudsman and local government). Rees considers this role 'extremely important' and 'an excellent opportunity to directly influence policy development at the highest level' (ibid.). Indeed it is, but like so many aspects of the Measure its potency depends on how it is implemented in practice. In the first draft scheme, issued for consultation in November 2011 (WG, 2011), there was little information about how this obligation had been given effect. There needs to evolve a practice of 'involvement' of the Children's Commissioner and others which is transparent and different from the traditional approach of consultation only after a draft is developed.

This requires a step change in traditional approaches to policy development – policy here being the substantive content of the children's scheme. Examining accountability in a different context, Harrington and Turem (2006) consider the potential of negotiated rulemaking as a solution to problems of accountability. The design with which they are concerned has a statutory footing in the Negotiated Rulemaking Act 1996 (5 USC 561 *et. seq.*), aimed at bestowing greater legitimacy on and reducing litigation in relation to rule-making by federal agencies in the United States. While not suggesting that a similar legislative framework is either necessary or desirable for Wales, the Measure can be seen as building upon the 'inclusive exercise of functions' provisions in the statutory base for Welsh devolution from the outset, now in sections 72 to 79 of the Government of Wales Act 2006. A practice of negotiated rulemaking would be consistent with those provisions. The Measure, by requiring that the Welsh Ministers ensure the 'involvement' of the Children's Commissioner for Wales, and of children and young people and others in the preparation of the draft scheme, clearly implies that some such practice should develop as part of the exercise of the Ministerial function of designing a children's scheme. In short, the Measure invites outsiders in to the process of implementing this particular 'public officer's law'. Its full potential in this regard remains to be proved: if it happens, such a practice might be expected to take some time to evolve, but if it does not happen, a question may arise about the legality of the process of preparing the children's scheme.

Another important aspect of administrative accountability is the use of complaints procedures. The draft children's scheme places this first in a list of options that can be used if 'children or their representatives think that the Welsh Ministers have not had due regard to the UNCRC' (WG, 2011: 7). Increased knowledge and understanding of the UNCRC, which ought to result from Welsh Ministerial compliance with section 4 of the Measure, can be expected to lead to an increase in references to the UNCRC in complaints. Monitoring of references to the requirements of the UNCRC in such complaints and in responses to complaints would be a useful tool for estimating the impact of both the due regard and the awareness-raising duties in the Measure.

The Equality and Human Rights Commission (EHRC) plays an important role in promoting and protecting human rights in the UK, acting as an advocate for equality and human rights. The Equality Act 2010 gives the EHRC extensive legal powers to enforce equality laws. The EHRC can exercise its functions in relation to 'human rights', including rights under the UNCRC (section 7 of the Equality Act 2010), and the EHRC is able to use its powers to offer advice and to support the promotion of children's human rights in planning and commissioning services for children and young people in Wales. As an official human rights body, the EHRC has a key role in engaging with the United Nations human rights system. One of the EHRC's roles is to submit evidence and reports to the various international human rights committees, relating to the situation in Britain. Under the Equality Act 2010, children and young people can be regarded as a 'community' defined by age. The EHRC could make representations and challenge measures (including legislative measures) that have a particularly adverse effect on children and young people. Controversially, children are excluded from protection of specific non-discrimination provisions in the Equality Act, for example in the provision of services and exercise of public functions (section 28 of the Equality Act). But where these exemptions do not apply, the EHRC's powers – which include launching inquiries and formal investigations and, where appropriate, taking cases to judicial review under the Human Rights Act 1998 – are applicable to alleged violations of the human rights of children and young people, and could embrace questions of compliance with Welsh Ministers' duties under the Measure.

The Public Services Ombudsman is yet another mechanism by which government may be held to account in Wales. The ombudsman's role is to investigate complaints made by members of the public alleging maladministration or service failure on the part of a public body in Wales, including the Welsh Government. The ombudsman can investigate complaints and make recommendations for redress. Public authorities' failures to comply with the duty under section 6 of the Human Rights Act 1998 have become a familiar aspect of the ombudsman's consideration of complaints. Most of the complaints in the ombudsman's casebook (published quarterly and accessible at the website of the Public Services Ombudsman for Wales) concern the exercise of local authorities' functions, unsurprisingly, since most decisions on individual eligibility and entitlement to services are made at local authority level. However, the ombudsman's powers extend to review of the exercise of functions by the Welsh Ministers. This would, post-Measure, include the functions of paying due regard to the require-ments of the UNCRC, preparing the children's scheme and raising aware-ness of the UNCRC in Wales. Furthermore, since the functions of Welsh Ministers include making decisions about and giving directions and guid-ance to local authorities, the ombudsman's consideration of administrative practice in local authorities ought, over time, to include questions about whether the local authorities have responded in ways that help implement the UNCRC.

Parliamentary accountability
Under the Measure, Welsh Ministers are required to lay both the draft children's scheme and the final scheme before the National Assembly for Wales, and must do the same when the scheme is remade or revised. This gives the National Assembly the opportunity to debate the scheme and to challenge the Welsh Ministers on its content. Such challenges could be on any matter relevant to the UNCRC but also on the issue of whether rec-ommendations made by the UN Committee in its *Concluding Observations* on periodic UK State Party reports are properly taken into account when the scheme is made or revised.

Parliamentary scrutiny is further enhanced by a provision that the scheme may include a requirement for a regular report on compliance and by the requirement of a mandatory quinquennial report on how the Welsh Ministers have complied with the due regard duty. This (or these) reports must be laid before the National Assembly for Wales, once again giving opportunity for public debate.

Several matters will be key to the effectiveness of parliamentary scru-tiny. The first of these is the extent to which the Children and Young People Committee of the National Assembly for Wales is able to engage in rigorous scrutiny of Welsh Ministers' implementation of the Measure. This commit-tee, together with the Assembly's Legislation Committee No. 5, played a part in advocating for the duty of due regard to impact across all exercises of functions by Welsh Ministers (see Sullivan and Jones, and Aspinwall and Croke, chapters 2 and 3 in this volume). The Children and Young People Committee's legacy report from the 2007–11 Assembly (highlights this 'unusual step' (CYPC, 2011: para. 129) of scrutinising pre-legislative proposals, and notes calls for future committees to scrutinise implementation of the Measure (para. 181). It further notes a regrettable perception that Wales is 'policy rich but implementation poor' (para. 179), and the consequent benefit of the committee returning to issues that had previously been the subject of its recommendations to investigate progress in implementation. The Children and Young People Committee in the 2011–15 Assembly opened an inquiry into the implementation of another Assembly Measure (Learning and Skills (Wales) Measure 2009), and can be expected to take similar steps in relation to implementation of the rights Measure.

The second matter that will be key to the effectiveness of parliamentary scrutiny is the extent to which Assembly scrutiny, especially through the Children and Young People Committee, is able to continue to draw in expertise from external groups, and to engage, directly or indirectly, with children and young people themselves. The Children and Young People Committee has an excellent record on this (see its 2011 *Legacy Report*, above). Coupled with the committee's direct questioning of Ministers and civil servants, this feature gives the committee potency as a forum of both parliamentary accountability and advocacy for specific and systemic change, and as a space in which participation as an aspect of citizenship can be practised.

The third matter is the relationship that the National Assembly for Wales is able to develop with the process of the UNCRC itself. The Measure directs Welsh Ministers to take account of the reports, recommendations and opinions of the UN Committee: parliamentary scrutiny of implementation of the Measure thus encompasses how this is done and to what effect. The Welsh Government worked hard and was supported by the UNCRC Monitoring Group in developing good relations with the UN Committee during the third and fourth reporting periods (Aspinwall and Croke, chapter 3 in this volume). There is no reason why the 'dynamic' of the UNCRC should not embrace also the parliamentary function of the state: indeed this is actively encouraged by the UN Committee itself (Doek, 2011). The adoption by the UN General Council, at the end of 2011, of an Optional Protocol on individual complaints to the UNCRC, is an important additional tool, the potential of which will begin to be proved during the early years of implementation of the Measure.

Accessibility

The totality of the potential of the Measure through these various structures for accountability justifies hope of remedies in some cases, as well as systemic improvement in realisation of the requirements of the UNCRC. But how accessible will these processes and remedies be?

For any of the mechanisms discussed above to be utilised, there must first be a trigger of knowledge, and then a capacity to act. A potential challenger needs knowledge that a function has been exercised, combined with sufficient knowledge to be able to conceptualise what has been done as a failure to comply with a duty imposed by the Measure. In turn, this requires understanding of the way the Measure works and understanding of the requirements of the UNCRC pertinent to the particular exercise of a function. In addition, the would-be challenger needs to know what mechanisms of accountability are available, to be equipped to make an informed choice as to which to pursue, and have the resource in time and expertise, not to mention money, to pursue it. A person who possesses or has access to this knowledge, understanding, judgement and resource can set out along one or other road to a remedy.

Freeman is right to point out that 'remedies themselves require the injection of resources' (2010: 18). In times of austerity, pleas for public funds to be made available to help challenge governmental action, some of which will itself be attributed to the imperative to reduce public expenditure, are no doubt optimistic. Advocacy and representation, for example, require significant resources. However, we should not forget, as Freeman also points out, that 'resources' here does not mean simply cash injected from government funds. Rights themselves are a resource, a language for persuasion and negotiation of priorities. Successful outcomes to such persuasion and negotiation include different use of existing resources, as well as allocation of additional money. The Measure should have the effect of ensuring such negotiation and persuasion within Welsh Government, but this can also occur as a result of activism in a range of civic organisations. As Freeman observes, remedies also require 'a commitment on behalf of all of us that we view rights with respect, that we want them to have an input into the lives of all people, and not just the lives of the powerful and the privileged' (2010: 18). In order to succeed in practice, the Measure needs civic participation – the exercise of participative citizenship.

Thus, in practice, effective use of any of the accountability mechanisms discussed here will rely heavily on the ability of external stakeholders to maintain vigilance and a good level of coordination through informal networks. As we have noted, external stakeholders (the Children's Commissioner for Wales, other organisations, and, crucially, children and young people themselves) should be 'involved' in aspects of implementation by the Welsh Government. It is just as important that these stakeholders and others interested in progress in realisation of human rights for children and young people maintain sufficient independence from the Welsh Government to be ready to challenge it using one or more of the several mechanisms for accountability discussed here.

Conclusion

Both the Welsh Government and the National Assembly for Wales broke new ground when passing the Measure. Now these still young institutions face the challenge of implementation, in which continued innovation and energy is needed not least to secure optimal effectiveness of use of resources in the widest sense. Persuasion and participation, involving a dynamic relationship between governmental and non-governmental organisations, are much to be preferred over the taking up of adversarial positions. However, as we have sought to demonstrate here, the Measure does provide new opportunities to move rights from 'rhetoric to fora for action' (Freeman, 2010: 18) and to use them as tools to ensure that those making decisions can be called to account if they fail to recognise the obligations precedent to those rights.

References

Clutton, S. (2008): 'Devolution and the language of children's rights in the UK', in A. Invernizzi and J. Williams (eds), *Children and Citizenship* (London: Sage), pp. 171–81.

CYPC (Children and Young People Committee), National Assembly for Wales (2011): *Legacy Report*, 29 March (Cardiff: National Assembly for Wales).

Doek, J. (2011): 'The CRC: dynamics and directions', in A. Invernizzi and J. Williams (eds), *The Human Rights of Children: From Visions to Implementation* (Farnham: Ashgate), pp. 99–116.

Dowdle, M. W. (2006): 'Public accountability: conceptual, historical, and epistemic mappings', in M. W. Dowdle (ed.), *Public Accountability: Designs, Dilemma and Experiences* (New York: Cambridge University Press), pp. 1–29.

Fortin, J. (2006): 'Accommodating children's rights in a post Human Rights Act Era', *Modern Law Review*, 69, 299–326.

Freeman, Michael (2010): 'The human rights of children', *Current Legal Problems*, 63, 1–44.

Harrington, C. B. and Turem, Z. U. (2006): 'Accounting for accountability in neoliberal regulatory regimes', in Michael W. Dowdle (ed.), *Public Accountability: Designs, Dilemmas and Experiences* (New York: Cambridge University Press), pp. 195–219.

Lister, R. (2008): 'Unpacking children's citizenship', in A. Invernizzi and J. Williams (eds), *Children and Citizenship* (London: Sage), pp. 9–19.

WG (Welsh Government) (2011): *Draft Children's Scheme*, consultation document 13321 7 (November) (Cardiff: Welsh Government).

Williams, J. (2007): 'Incorporating children's rights: the divergence in law and policy', *Legal Studies*, 27, 261–87.

—— (2012): 'General legislative measures of implementation: individual claims, "public officer's law" and a case study on the UNCRC in Wales', *International Journal of Children's Rights*, 20, 224–40.

CHAPTER 13

'Holding government to account': the role of the Children's Commissioner for Wales

Osian Rees

Introduction

The Rights of Children and Young Persons (Wales) Measure 2011 was introduced a decade after the establishment of the Children's Commissioner for Wales, and can in many ways be viewed as a natural continuation of the idealism and political commitment to children's rights in Wales which led to the creation of the commissioner's office. In this respect, it is no surprise that Wales is the first country within the UK to take steps to incorporate the UNCRC. Devolution has, from the outset, been synonymous with children's rights in Wales, and the commissioner has played a central role in this respect.

Bearing in mind this context, this chapter has a number of linked objectives. It will explain the commissioner's powers and functions, and consider some of the ways in which the office has worked to help promote and safeguard children's rights in Wales. It will also examine the potential impact of the Measure on the commissioner, explaining how the commissioner has an important role in facilitating its effective implementation, both by what the current commissioner, Keith Towler, terms 'holding government to account' (NAW, 2010a: para. 168), and by being a key part of what has been termed the 'interpretive community' (Tobin, 2010).

It must be acknowledged from the outset, however, that both the commissioner's legal framework and the Measure have some shortcomings. The commissioner's powers and functions are outdated, and in some respects fail to meet the internationally recognised standards for national human rights institutions (NHRIs) for children. The Measure, meanwhile, does not amount to full incorporation of the UNCRC. While the latter is unlikely to change in the foreseeable future, the Welsh Government has finally recognised the need to reform the commissioner's powers and functions, and in setting out the five-year legislative programme in July

2011, the First Minister stated the intention of introducing a Children and Young Persons (Wales) Bill to 'expand the role' of the commissioner so as to 'build on' the Measure (NAW, 2011). This is to be welcomed. Indeed, experience elsewhere suggests that even full incorporation of the UNCRC may not necessarily in itself lead to practical developments (STC, 2011a: 7). Instead, the crucial factor is effective implementation. Accordingly, the chapter will consider how the commissioner's legal framework could be improved, thereby enhancing the commissioner's current role, and providing the office with the strongest possible mechanisms to help ensure that Welsh Ministers take their duties under the Measure seriously.

Measures of implementation: NHRIs for children and the UNCRC

NHRIs for children are not a new idea. The first such institution, the Children's Ombudsman for Norway, was established as far back as 1981. However, over recent years they have proliferated, and have become common in countries across the world (for an overview see Hamilton, 2010). This is a direct result of the UNCRC, particularly Article 4, which places a duty on States Parties to 'undertake all appropriate legislative, administrative, and other measures for the implementation of the rights recognized in the present Convention'. NHRIs for children are widely perceived to be an important means of fulfilling this duty.

The UN Committee acknowledges the importance of NHRIs for children in the light of Article 4, and issued a *General Comment* in 2002 calling on States Parties to establish such institutions, and to review the status and effectiveness of institutions already in place (UN Committee *GC*, 2002). In doing so, they set out detailed standards relating to the powers and functions of NHRIs, and the activities they are expected to undertake. These are wide-ranging in nature and include, for example, conducting inquiries, reviewing the adequacy of law and practice relating to children's rights, ensuring that children's views are heard in line with Article 12, and making independent contributions to the UNCRC's reporting process. In addition, NHRIs for children are expected to have the power to try to remedy breaches of children's rights by dealing with individual cases (for further discussion see Rees, 2010a). The extent to which the Children's Commissioner for Wales complies with these standards is considered below.

It should be noted that there is also a more general set of international standards for NHRIs termed the 'Paris Principles' (UNCHR, 1992). These do not go as far as the UN Committee's standards in some respects, in that they do not insist, for example, that NHRIs should be able to deal with individual cases, nor do they relate specifically to NHRIs for children. They are, nonetheless, a useful point of reference as they represent the bare minimum in terms of what should be expected from the commissioner's legal framework.

The Children's Commissioner for Wales: background and legal framework

The commissioner was established in 2000, soon after the creation of the National Assembly for Wales, and was the first office of its type within the UK. At the time, the Assembly did not have the competence to legislate in this manner, but a high level of cross-party political support, combined with the publication of the Waterhouse report (Waterhouse, 2000) meant that Parliament was willing to legislate on the matter on behalf of the Assembly (for further discussion see Rees, 2010b). The commissioner's powers and functions were initially set out under the Care Standards Act 2000. These were limited in scope, applying only to children receiving 'regulated children's services' in Wales. Soon after, however, the commissioner's powers and functions were broadened under the Children's Commissioner for Wales Act 2001, which amends the provisions of the Care Standards Act 2000. Further provisions were made by the Assembly in the Children's Commissioner for Wales Regulations 2001.

Under the legislation as it currently stands, the commissioner has an overarching aim of promoting and safeguarding the rights and welfare of children in Wales, and has a range of powers to facilitate this. These include a general power to review the exercise of the functions of devolved bodies so as to consider the extent to which the rights and welfare of children are taken into account (function reviews); a specific power, coupled with an ability to compel the provision of information, to review the adequacy of complaint, whistleblowing and advocacy procedures of certain public authorities in Wales (arrangement reviews); a power to provide advice and assistance to individual children; and a power to undertake inquiries (termed examinations), where a matter is exceptionally serious, provided that the matter in question raises a question of principle which has a more general application or relevance to the rights or welfare of relevant children than in the particular case concerned. In undertaking examinations, the commissioner has powers equivalent to those of the High Court, so may, for example, compel witnesses to give evidence. Following an amendment made under the Children Act 2004, the commissioner has the power to enter any premises, other than a private dwelling, for the purposes of interviewing any child accommodated or cared for there. Along with these powers, the commissioner may consider, and make representations to the Assembly about, any matter affecting children's rights in Wales. It should be noted that the commissioner does not have the power to compel any body to provide any form of redress, nor to issue any binding recommendations. Instead the main sanction in this respect is to publicise noncompliance. While this clearly limits the commissioner's effectiveness, the same is true for the vast majority of NHRIs for children, emphasising that their role is seen as being to invoke a moral authority in order to influence public bodies, and to seek to persuade them to improve their practices in relation to children's rights.

Coupled with these powers, the commissioner also has a number of duties. These include raising awareness among children as to how they may contact the office, as well as seeking the views of children when developing a work programme. The commissioner must also produce an annual report, which should include a review of issues relating to the rights and welfare of children in Wales. Crucially, the commissioner must 'have regard' to the UNCRC while exercising all his functions. This provision is set out under the 2001 regulations, and suggests that the Assembly was committed to the UNCRC, and viewed the commissioner as an important mechanism for facilitating its implementation.

As the Welsh Government has acknowledged, the commissioner's powers and functions are in need of reform. The commissioner's office shares this view, as does the Wales UNCRC Monitoring Group (STC, 2011b: 14). Indeed, there is a similar feeling with regard to the other children's commissioners in the UK (STC, 2011c: 60), in particular the Children's Commissioner for England, which has been subject to criticism for its limited powers, lack of independence and narrow mandate from the outset (see, for example, Williams, 2005). The English commissioner was subject to a detailed independent review carried out by John Dunford in 2010, which made a number of recommendations for reform (Dunford, 2010). The UK Government has accepted the recommendations in principle, and in July 2011, the Department for Education launched a consultation on how to put them into effect (Department for Education, 2011).

Calls for reform in Wales are not new. In 2007 a review was undertaken by the author on behalf of the then commissioner (CCfW, 2007a). It identified a number of weaknesses in the legislation and made a total of sixteen recommendations for reform. Some of the recommendations related to specific problems that the office was experiencing at the time, but many remain of relevance today, particularly insofar as meeting the standards set out by the UN Committee and the Paris Principles is concerned. Key recommendations in this respect include consolidating the legislation under one instrument; clarifying the commissioner's role in undertaking examinations, and abolishing the distinction between arrangement reviews and function reviews, so as to simplify the legislation and to strengthen the commissioner's powers insofar as function reviews are concerned.

It is also recommended that the commissioner should have the power to bring, intervene in or assist in legal proceedings, in the same way as the Northern Ireland Commissioner for Children and Young People. This would meet the requirements set out by the UN Committee (UN Committee *GC*, 2002: 14), and would serve to bolster the commissioner's authority. In addition, it is recommended that the commissioner should be provided with a research function, and should be placed under a duty to develop effective links with NGOs.

Perhaps the most significant problem with the current framework is that the commissioner's functions do not extend to non-devolved matters. Instead, and in a similar manner to Scotland and Northern Ireland, the English commissioner has responsibility for such matters. The effect of this is that the Children's Commissioner for Wales could not, for example, carry out an examination into matters relating to youth justice or asylum and immigration. This goes against the basic requirement set out in the Paris Principles that 'a national institution shall be given as broad a mandate as possible' (UNCHR, 1992: Principle A.2). The experiences of the commissioner suggest that the limitation has not proven as problematic in practice as might be expected. In addition, it is likely that the legislative competence of the Assembly will increase over time, and there have been calls for matters such as youth justice to be devolved (Morgan, 2009). Nonetheless, it is widely recognised that the position is not acceptable, and the review into the Children's Commissioner for England recommended that: 'The children's commissioners in devolved administrations should in principle be responsible for all relevant matters in respect of children and young people who normally reside in their countries' (Dunford, 2010: 42). In response, the UK Government states:

> We accept the principle behind this recommendation, although we are still working out the most practical way to proceed. There is not an obvious legislative solution, as each of the four Children's Commissioners has a slightly different set of functions and powers. It is for Parliament in Westminster to legislate on non-devolved matters rather than the devolved administrations, and any transfer of powers could impact on the terms of the devolution settlements. Discussions

are continuing with the devolved administrations to identify a work-able solution. (Department for Education, 2011: para. 9.2)

Despite being long overdue, this is a welcome development. Due to the complexities highlighted, it is unclear how it would work in practice, but the best solution, and the one advocated by the four commissioners in the UK (UK Children's Commissioners, 2008: 8), would be for each commissioner to be able to exercise the full range of powers and functions in respect of all matters affecting children in their respective countries, irrespective of whether the matter is devolved or non-devolved. Another potential solution, though less desirable, would be for the powers of the English commissioner to be delegated to the other commissioners regarding non-devolved matters affecting children in each of their respective countries. This would involve a high level of cooperation between the four UK commissioners, though, as is stated in the review of the English commissioner, a greater level of cooperation would be desirable in any event so that the commissioners can maximise their impact across the UK and share best practice; they have been criticised for not working together sufficiently closely in this respect (Dunford, 2010: 41–2).

A final area where reform would be desirable in order to comply with the international standards is the manner in which the commissioner's budget is determined. Although the budget, which is currently £1.83 million, has not been increased since 2007/8, it compares relatively favourably to the budgets of the other children's commissioners in the UK and elsewhere (Dunford, 2010: 53). The main problem is that the commissioner is funded by the Welsh Government rather than by the Assembly. As the Wales UNCRC Monitoring Group points out, this 'severely undermines its independence' (STC, 2011b: 13). Accordingly, the current arrangements should be amended so as to ensure that there are greater safeguards in place.

Promoting and safeguarding children's rights in Wales: the commissioner in practice

Despite having faced some difficulties, most notably the tragic death of the first commissioner, Peter Clarke, the commissioner's office has carried out a wide-ranging work programme over the past decade, and has made a positive impact, both in terms of assisting individual children, and in seeking to ensure that children's rights are taken into account in law and policy in Wales.

In terms of individual projects, two arrangement reviews have been carried out, the first into local authority social services departments

(CCfW, 2003), and the second into education departments (CCfW, 2005). In 2011, an arrangement review was announced into the provision of independent professional advocacy for looked-after children and young people, care leavers and children in need. The final report was published in March 2012 (CCfW, 2012).

In addition, research has been carried out relating to the condition of school toilets (CCfW, 2004a), disabled children's access to play facilities in local authorities in Wales (CCfW, 2008), unofficial school exclusions (CCfW, 2007b), and a scoping exercise on child and adolescent mental health services (CCfW, 2007c). The office has also commissioned research into children trafficked in Wales (CCfW, 2009a), and into problems faced by young carers (CCfW, 2009b). In July 2011 a detailed report was launched examining the experiences of young people leaving care (CCfW, 2011a). It reveals considerable problems with the level of support provided, and makes twenty-nine recommendations, predominantly to local authorities, but also to local health boards, independent reviewing officers, the Care and Social Services Inspectorate Wales and the Welsh Ministers. The report, which is accompanied by a resource providing advice and information for young people preparing to leave care (CCfW, 2011b) is a fitting way to mark ten years of the commissioner's office, particularly given the factors that led to its establishment.

From the outset, dealing with individual cases as part of the advice and assistance function has been central to the role of the office, to the extent that in 2009/10 475 cases were brought to the attention of the office. The majority of these involved education or social services, though a wide range of other issues also arose, including child protection, family law, immigration and youth justice (CCfW, 2010: 19). Whereas some cases are passed on by the office to other organisations, many are fully investigated, often leading to outcomes which would not have otherwise occurred. Significantly, these outcomes often go beyond providing a remedy for the individual child concerned. Despite this, however, dealing with individual cases has proven to be a contentious aspect of the commissioner's role, due to the tension between allocating resources to assisting individual children and working in a more proactive capacity to bring about longer-term systemic changes (for further discussion, see Rees, 2010a).

This is a particular issue that arises from the commissioner's power to undertake examinations. The commissioner has only carried out one examination to date, which resulted in the *Clywch* report published in 2004 (CCfW, 2004b). The examination stemmed from allegations of sexual abuse carried out by a secondary school drama teacher, and resulted in a substantial report accompanied by recommendations as to how to prevent such abuse from taking place in the future. The factors that led to the examination were exceptionally serious, and the recommendations stemming from the report have been largely implemented. Nonetheless, it was an extremely costly and time-consuming process, and it may be suggested that examinations should, if deemed necessary, be funded separately.

As well as specific projects, the commissioner carries out more general policy work, including following up issues from reviews and responding to consultations. There is also a wider level of engagement. Towler, for example, currently sits on the review panel for the Family Justice Review, with the aim of providing a Welsh perspective and representing children's interests. He is also a member of the Welsh safeguarding children forum. As would be expected, Towler and his staff also travel across Wales to attend and participate in various events, and to generally meet with children and young people. There are offices both in Swansea and Colwyn Bay, which lessens concerns of the commissioner being too south Wales centred.

A final point to note is that the UNCRC has been an important part of the commissioner's work. All the commissioner's reports are set out in the context of the UNCRC, and the review of issues affecting children and young people in Wales in the annual reports are set out in the context of the Welsh Government's 'core aims' for children and young people which relate to the UNCRC. The commissioner also co-authored a joint report by the four UK children's commissioners to the UN Committee as part of the reporting process (UK Children's Commissioners, 2008).

On the basis of this overview it is fair to say that, as stated above, the commissioner has made a positive impact. Despite this, perhaps some things could have been done differently. There have been issues relating to children and young people's awareness of the commissioner, and despite a good working relationship with the Welsh Government, the commissioner's recommendations have not always been put into full effect – school toilets being an obvious example. What is also clear, however, is that any criticism of the commissioner, or indeed of any NHRI for children, will necessarily be subjective, due to the breadth of the mandate of such institutions, and the conflicting demands and expectations that are placed upon them. Nonetheless, as the Welsh Government is seeking to reform the commissioner's powers and functions, perhaps some reflection is needed on the work of the office, and indeed, what it is expected to achieve. In this sense, now may be an appropriate time to carry out a detailed review of the commissioner in a similar manner to the review of the Children's Commissioner for England.

The Rights of Children and Young Persons (Wales) Measure 2011: a role for the commissioner?

As has already been stated, the 2011 Measure does have some shortcomings. Whereas it is an important development, it nonetheless represents a compromise between non-incorporation and full incorporation in the same way as the incorporation, for example, of the European Convention on Human Rights under the Human Rights Act 1998. It applies only to the Welsh Ministers, and the duty to have due regard has been designed to be as non-justiciable as possible. In this respect it does not meet the requirements of the UN Committee, which states in a *General Comment* relating to general measures of implementation issued in 2005 that:

> incorporation should mean that the provisions of the Convention can be directly invoked before the courts and applied by national authorities and that the Convention will prevail where there is a conflict with domestic legislation or common practice. (UN Committee *GC*, 2005: para. 20)

This does not mean that the Measure is insignificant. What it does mean, however, is that its success will revolve around the steps that are taken to ensure its implementation. Given that the courts are unlikely to have a significant role, and given that the children and young people whom the Measure is designed to protect have no say at the ballot box, it is crucial that there is a means for the Welsh Ministers to be held to account. It goes without saying that the obvious contender for this role is the commissioner, and that the office represents an important, if not the most important, mechanism for ensuring accountability. This highlights the role of the commissioner as a 'measure of implementation' of the UNCRC, particularly in the light of the factors set out under paragraph 19 of *General Comment No. 2* (UN Committee *GC*, 2002), including: reviewing the adequacy and effectiveness of law and practice relating to the protection of children's rights; promoting harmonisation of national legislation, regulations and practices with the UNCRC; ensuring that national economic policy-makers take children's rights into account, and monitoring ways in which the government is meeting its obligations to make the principles and provisions of the UNCRC known under Article 42.

There are challenges facing both the commissioner and the Welsh Government in this respect. The commissioner needs to respond appropriately, thereby maximising the influence of the office as a catalyst for change, and the Government needs to ensure that the commissioner's legal powers and budget enable the office to work to its optimum capacity. Accordingly it is necessary to consider what the commissioner should be expected to do, and what legal reforms are necessary, above and beyond the general points that have already been set out.

The commissioner has an extremely important part to play in developing the children's scheme. This is envisaged in the Measure, as the commissioner is to be 'involved in the preparation of the draft' under section 3(4). This, it should be noted, resulted from an amendment during the passage of the Measure, as it was initially envisaged that the commissioner should only be 'consulted'. It is suggested that the commissioner should embark on a programme of research as soon as possible to consider what the scheme should entail. It is an excellent opportunity to directly influence policy development at the highest level.

The commissioner should also have the function of providing advice and guidance to the Welsh Ministers on implementation. This could include advice on specific questions, or general training. To go a step further, there should be an obligation on the Welsh Ministers to consult with the commissioner when making any new policies or legislation, so that the commissioner can comment on whether the Ministers have had due regard to the UNCRC. One way of facilitating this task would for the commissioner to develop an independent child impact assessment tool that could be utilised by the office.

Following on from this, and with the caveat that it should in no way detract from the obligations of the Welsh Ministers, a monitoring role for the commissioner is essential in ensuring that the Measure is properly implemented. Under section 4 of the Measure, the Welsh Ministers are obliged to publish a report setting out how they have complied with their duty to have due regard to the UNCRC. This must be done on a five-yearly basis, or a period of such other length as may be specified in the children's scheme. A report every five years is inadequate. It equates to more than a term of office for Assembly Members and could lead to a lack of commitment. The commissioner should press for a more frequent reporting structure in the scheme. This could be annual, particularly given that the UN Committee states in *General Comment No. 5* that it 'commends States parties which have introduced annual publication of comprehensive reports on the state of children's rights throughout their jurisdiction' (UN Committee *GC*, 2005, para. 49). As has already been stated above, the commissioner currently has the function of providing a review of issues affecting children's rights in Wales as part of the office's annual report. Were the Welsh Ministers to publish an annual report on their progress, the commissioner would have a good context for responding. Monitoring in this respect should include consideration of the effectiveness of the Welsh Ministers in promoting knowledge and understanding of the UNCRC as required by section 5 of the Measure.

A final issue to consider is the potential role of the commissioner in providing redress to children where the Welsh Ministers have failed to have due regard to the UNCRC. During the passage of the Measure, the Conservative AMs tabled an amendment which provided that a child who is aggrieved by an alleged failure of Welsh Ministers to have regard to requirements referred to in section 1(1) (or a representative of that child) may refer that matter to the commissioner, and that the commissioner may investigate such a matter and make representations to Welsh Ministers regarding the result of that investigation. In addition, the proposed amendment provided that:

> the Children's Commissioner for Wales may also make more general representations to Welsh Ministers regarding the operation of this Measure, which may include recommendations for a more formal system of redress. (NAW, 2010b: 11)

This was rejected by the Welsh Government (NAW, 2010c), which stated that the commissioner's power to carry out function reviews was already sufficient in this respect. To an extent, this is correct. However, as emphasised above, there is currently a disparity between the commissioner's power to undertake function reviews and arrangement reviews, in that the commissioner only has the power to compel the provision of information if a matter relates to complaints, whistleblowing or advocacy provisions. In this sense the most obvious solution, as has already been suggested, would be to rationalise the review powers so as to abolish the current disparity. Nonetheless, it may be desirable to include separate provisions relating to the Measure when the commissioner's powers are reformed, which could include a duty on the Welsh Ministers to provide a response to any recommendations made by the commissioner.

Insofar as introducing a 'more formal system of redress' is concerned, this would go beyond the normal scope of an NHRI for children. However, the power to insist on a response could be coupled with a power to bring legal proceedings. This has already been suggested above as part of the general reforms that are needed. The effect of this would be that if the Welsh Ministers failed to make an appropriate response and to rectify an issue, then the commissioner could bring proceedings against them.

Conclusion

The Rights of Children and Young Persons (Wales) Measure 2011 is an important development, and this chapter has sought to argue that although responsibility for its implementation ultimately lies with the Welsh Ministers, the commissioner has an important role to play. Despite its limitations, the commissioner was supportive of the Measure during its passage. This is understandable, as the commissioner took the view that a limited Measure was preferable to no Measure at all. However, now that the Measure has been passed, it is suggested that the commissioner should campaign for fuller incorporation at the Welsh level. In particular, the duty to have due regard to the UNCRC should be extended to all public bodies in Wales. This would strengthen the commissioner's role considerably, particularly given that the majority of individual cases brought to the commissioner's attention relate to delivery by service providers. Indeed, if the UNCRC were to be fully incorporated, the role of the commissioner could further develop, making the office more similar to the Equality and Human Rights Commission, which has a stronger set of legal powers, including the power to bring legal proceedings in relation to the equality legislation. In particular, and as was suggested in the 2007 review (CCfW, 2007a: para. 25), the commissioner could have the power to compel a body that has acted unlawfully to produce an 'action plan' for the purpose of avoiding repetition or continuation of the act, coupled with the power to bring legal proceedings if the plan is inadequate or is not properly implemented.

As with the establishment of the commissioner, the 2011 Measure is a first for Wales, and represents a remarkable achievement. There is nonetheless still room for improvement. In the long term, full incorporation of the UNCRC is needed. In the short term, however, it is vital that the commissioner is properly equipped to hold the Welsh Ministers to account.

References

CCfW (Children's Commissioner for Wales) (2003): *Telling Concerns: Report of the Children's Commissioner for Wales' Review of the Operation of Complaints and Representations and Whistleblowing Procedures and Arrangements for the Provision of Children's Advocacy Services* (Swansea: Children's Commissioner for Wales).

—— (2004a): *Lifting the Lid on the Nation's School Toilets* (Swansea: Children's Commissioner for Wales).

—— (2004b): *Clywch: Report of the Examination of the Children's Commissioner for Wales into Allegations of Child Sexual Abuse in a School Setting* (Swansea: Children's Commissioner for Wales).

—— (2005): *Children Don't Complain . . . The Children's Commissioner for Wales' Review of the Operation of Complaints and Representations and Whistleblowing Procedures, and Arrangements for the Provision of Advocacy Services in Local Education Authorities in Wales* (Swansea: Children's Commissioner for Wales).

—— (2007a): *Response to the National Assembly for Wales Consultation on the Proposed Vulnerable Children and Child Poverty Legislative Competence Order 2007* (Swansea: Children's Commissioner for Wales).

—— (2007b): *Report Following Investigation into Unofficial School Exclusions* (Swansea: Children's Commissioner for Wales).

—— (2007c): *Somebody Else's Business? Report of a Scoping Exercise of Child and Adolescent Mental Health Services in Wales in 2007* (Swansea: Children's Commissioner for Wales).

—— (2008): *A Happy Talent: Disabled Children and Young People's Access to Play in Wales 2007: A Review of Local Authority Strategies* (Swansea: Children's Commissioner for Wales).

—— (2009a): *Bordering on Concern: Child Trafficking in Wales* (Swansea: Children's Commissioner for Wales).

—— (2009b): *Full of Care – Young Carers in Wales 2009* (Swansea: Children's Commissioner for Wales).

—— (2010): *Annual Report and Accounts* (Swansea: Children's Commissioner for Wales).

—— (2011a): *Lost After Care* (Swansea: Children's Commissioner for Wales).

—— (2011b): *My Planner* (Swansea: Children's Commissioner for Wales).

—— (2012): *Missing Voices* (Swansea: Children's Commissioner for Wales).

Department for Education (2011): *Establishing a New Office of the Children's Commissioner for England (OCCE): Consultation on Legislative Proposals* (London: Department for Education).

Dunford, J. (2010): *Review of the Office of the Children's Commissioner (England)* (London: Department for Education).

Hamilton, C. (2010): 'Children's rights and the role of the UN Committee on the Rights of the Child: underlying structures for states in implementing the Convention on the Rights of the Child', *International Family Law Journal* (March), 31–50.

Morgan, R. (2009): *Report to the Welsh Assembly Government on the Question of Devolution of Youth Justice Responsibilities* (Cardiff: National Assembly for Wales).

NAW (National Assembly for Wales) (2010a): Legislation Committee No. 5, Record of Proceedings, 8 July (Cardiff: National Assembly for Wales).

—— (2010b): Proposed Rights of Children and Young Persons (Wales) Measure. Marshalled List of Amendments. Available at *http://www. assemblywales.org/rcyp_ml_stage2_221110.pdf* (accessed 10 July 2011).

—— (2010c): Legislation Committee No. 5, Record of Proceedings, 25 November (Cardiff: National Assembly for Wales).

—— (2011): Record of Proceedings, 12 July (Cardiff: National Assembly for Wales).

Rees, O. (2010a): 'Dealing with individual cases: an essential role for National Human Rights Institutions for children', *International Journal of Children's Rights*, 18, 417–36.

—— (2010b): 'Devolution and the Children's Commissioner for Wales', *Contemporary Wales*, 23, 52–70.

STC (Save the Children) (2011a): *Governance Fit for Children: To What Extent Have the General Measures of Implementation of the UNCRC been Realised in Five European Countries (Executive Summary)* (Stockholm: Save the Children).

—— (2011b): *Policy Briefing: Reporting Progress on the General Measures of Implementation of the Convention on the Rights of the Child in Wales* (Cardiff: Save the Children).

—— (2011c): *Governance Fit for Children: To What Extent Have the General Measures of Implementation of the CRC been Realised in the UK* (London: Save the Children).

Tobin, J. (2010): 'Seeking to persuade: a constructive approach to Human Rights Treaty interpretation', *Harvard Human Rights Review*, 23, 1–50.

UK Children's Commissioners (2008): *UK Children's Commissioners' Report to the UN Committee on the Rights of the Child* (London, Belfast, Edinburgh and Swansea: UK Children's Commissioners).

UNCHR (United Nations Commission on Human Rights) (1992): Resolution 1992/54 (3 March 1992), *Official Records of the Economic and Social Council, 1992, Supp. No. 2, E/1992/22* (Geneva: United Nations).

Waterhouse, R. (2000): *Lost in Care: Report of the Tribunal of Inquiry into the Abuse of Children in Care in the Former County Council Areas of Gwynedd and Clwyd since 1974* (London: The Stationery Office).

Williams, J. (2005): 'Effective government structures for children?: the UK's four children's commissioners', *Child and Family Law Quarterly*, 17, 37–63.

CHAPTER 14

Funky Dragon's Children as Researchers project: a new way of enabling participation

Funky Dragon

Children as researchers

This chapter outlines a project run by Funky Dragon called 'Children as Researchers'. The project aspired to offer another process of enabling participation of children under the age of eleven at local and national level. It involved eight groups of children from around Wales and each group was supported to produce its own local action research projects; each group was made up of between six and ten children aged between six and eleven. They were trained in the traditional social research process and were then supported to direct their own research projects. Each group identified a topic, decided how to research this topic, conducted research, analysed its data and relayed its findings via recommendations and reports.

As part of this project all the children travelled to Cardiff for Funky Dragon's first children's conference, where the groups presented their projects in the National Assembly for Wales. During the conference, the groups met with Welsh Ministers where they discussed their findings and recommendations and received feedback on their work.

This chapter outlines the theory of research as a mechanism for participation and how Funky Dragon accomplished this project. It is hoped that it will not only inspire others to facilitate this method of participation within their own organisations but also that it will offer insight into the capabilities of this age group.

Funky Dragon

Funky Dragon is the Children and Young People's Assembly for Wales and is peer led. Our aim is to give children and young people from birth to twenty-five the opportunity to get their voices heard on issues that affect them. The opportunity to participate and be listened to is a fundamental right under the UNCRC. Funky Dragon tries to represent as wide a range of children and young people as possible and work with decision-makers to achieve change.

Funky Dragon's main tasks are to make sure that the views of children and young people are heard, particularly by the Welsh Government, and to support participation in decision-making at national level.

The main way this is achieved is through Funky Dragon's Grand Council. The Grand Council is made up of one hundred young people from around Wales. Each local authority has a young person's forum or council and each forum elects four representatives to be part of the Grand Council: one representative from the statutory sector, one from the voluntary sector, one from school councils and one as an equality representative who represents young people in their authority with additional needs or issues. The remaining twelve spaces are co-options which are empty spaces from around Wales. These spaces are for young people who are part of organisations that feel they are not being represented through the forum or at national level, for example young farmers.

The Grand Council meets four times a year, and meets with Ministers annually to discuss the issues and concerns of the young people they represent.

Child-led UNCRC reporting

November 2007 saw the launch of *Our Rights, Our Story* and *Why Do People's Ages Go Up Not Down?* reports that were submitted to the UN Committee outlining how children and young people in Wales are able to access their rights as stated in the UNCRC. The reports included the views of over 14,000 children and young people in Wales. A steering group made up from the Grand Council coordinated the report, and three members of this steering group delivered the *Our Rights, Our Story* report to the UN Committee in formal and informal hearings in Geneva. The Welsh Government has responded to all sixty-one recommendations made by children and young people. Further to this, members of Funky Dragon have met with members of the Cabinet committee on children and young people at the Welsh Government to discuss their issues and recommendations.

Both the children and youth team continue to work on coordinating the next report to be submitted to the UN when the fifth UK State Party report is presented in 2013.

The children's team

The children's team joined Funky Dragon in March 2007. Two workers were recruited after funding was secured from the Welsh Government to produce a report to submit to the UN Committee on how children under the age of eleven are able to understand and access their rights as stated in the UNCRC. Submitted to the UN in November 2007, the report included the views of over 2,500 children from around Wales and was called *Why Do People's Ages Go Up Not Down?*

Further funding was secured for another year in 2008, and with the report submitted to the UN Committee, the children's team wanted to create a project where children were able to voice their opinions at a local and national level, instigated and led by the children themselves. This resulted in the Children as Researchers project (CARs).

So why research?

So why was the research process chosen as a mechanism for enabling participation? There were three main reasons. First, Funky Dragon staff had gained experience and knowledge of the research process through their work supporting *Why Do Children's Ages Go Up Not Down?* Secondly, the research process gave children the freedom and scope to develop their ideas in their own way and to be fully informed. Thirdly, and most importantly, it gave children the opportunity to not only access information on the issues that affect them but also empowered children to create their own knowledge (Kellett, 2005a). We are all aware that children can learn and teach, but this process enabled children to create knowledge.

Work done to date in empowering children as researchers

Work in the field of empowering children as researchers has been small. Where work has been conducted, it is usually confined to older children – that is, young people over the age of eleven. This is also the case with toolkits and good practice guides (for example Kirby, 2004; Worrall and Naylor, 2004).

Other work has focused on child-centred research, where research is conducted with children as participants rather than completely hand-ing over the reins to children to direct their own work. Similarly, most resources focus on how to include children as participants, and the ethical dimensions that working with children brings (Farrell, 2005).

Mary Kellett at the Children's Research Centre at the Open University has, however, addressed these issues and conducted projects where chil-dren were trained as researchers and produced their own projects. Up until the Funky Dragon project, this was the only working example of the under eleven age group where the process of empowering children as researchers can be seen at each step. Resultant reports are published electronically by the Children's Research Centre.

Kellett's approach responds to some adults' belief that children are not competent or able to acquire the skills needed to take ownership of their own research projects. Kellett (in Kellett et al., 2004) asserts that children *are* competent and that these competencies are different from those of adults, rather than less competent. Kellett reminds us that most adults would not be able to produce a research project without sufficient knowledge or training. Regardless of age, a researcher is someone who has acquired the requisite skills.

The aim of the CARs project was to enable children with limited adult intervention to highlight the issues that matter to them. It gave children the opportunity not only to access information on the issues that affect them but also to empower children to create their own knowledge (Kellett, 2005b). It enabled children to highlight their issues and research them within their own paradigms of understanding; this created a body of work and ways of understanding that adults could not replicate.

The children's projects

Do you care about your environment?
This group was made up of seven girls from Rhondda Cynon Taff aged between seven and ten years old. Their project focused on both environmental questions and anti-social behaviours in their local area. The children met with Jane Hutt, then Minister for Children, Education, Lifelong Learning and Skills. The group had prepared three questions to ask the Minister: 'Is anything being done to improve play facilities in local areas?'; 'Is your local area good or bad?'; and 'Do you feel safe when there are teenagers in the street?'

The Minister informed the group that there was a plan for improving play facilities and a group to monitor its progress in each local authority. The Minister also told the children that she did feel safe in her local area and understood that teenagers just want to enjoy themselves and not intimidate others. The Minister did, however, understand that not everyone felt this way.

How can we make [our local area] a safer place?
The group was made up of eight children aged between seven and ten years old, half boys and half girls. The group called their project 'How can we make [our local area] a safer place?' and focused on anti-social behaviour in their area.

The children met with Brian Gibbons, then Minister for Social Justice and Local Government, at the conference in Cardiff. The group had three questions to ask him based on their project: 'Do you think Newport is a safe place?'; 'Can we have more police in [our local area]?'; and 'What's being done to stop drug and alcohol problems in Newport?'

The Minister agreed that teenagers drinking on the street made people, including other teenagers, feel unsafe. He also advised the children to invite their local police officers to one of their school council meetings to discuss their issues with them. With regard to drug and alcohol problems, the Minister discussed with the children educational and awareness-raising activities as well as the police authorities' obligation to make sure no-one is drinking on the streets.

The problem with pollution

Eight children from year six took part in the project. There were four girls and four boys, all of whom were part of the school council. Their project focused on attitudes towards the environment as well as looking at recycling facilities offered by Swansea council.

The group had a meeting with the Minister for children, Jane Hutt, to discuss the findings. The children also had a list of questions to ask the Minister: 'Do you compost at home?'; 'Why is it important to recycle?'; 'What do you plan on doing with landfill sites when they become too full?'; 'Is it true that people's homes are being knocked down to make room for landfill sites?'; and 'Do you think that people should be fined if they don't do any recycling?'

The Minister was standing in for Jane Davidson, Minister for Environment, Sustainability and Housing, which meant the answers had to be pre-prepared, resulting in less of a conversation. The children were pleased with the answers received from the Minister. She explained about the importance of recycling and why it was better to have people recycling voluntarily than to force people to do it.

Revive our parks

The group was made up of eight children aged between six and eleven and there were three boys and five girls. Their project, 'Revive our parks', focused on their local parks and what could be done to improve their condition and access to them. The group met with Jane Hutt – Minister for Children, Education, Lifelong Learning and Skills – at the conference in Cardiff. The group had questions to ask based on their project: 'Could someone check our parks regularly to make sure they are clean and safe?';

'How can we get more toys for our parks?'; and 'What money is available locally for parks?'

The Minister agreed that these were important question and explained that the local council is responsible for local parks. The Minister explained to the children that there are a number of grants available but the local council should provide good play parks and the children should not be responsible for raising extra money. The Minister agreed to take it up with the local authority and also to inform their local Assembly Members.

Untidy places in our village
This group was made up of children from two schools in Holyhead. The group was brought together by Llais Ni – Anglesey's youth forum. They met with Jane Hutt, and the following questions were discussed with the Minister: 'Can you help us clean up the station in Holyhead?'; 'Is it possible to upgrade the train station to make it look like the bridge and the port?'; and 'Can you help us get more shops in Holyhead – it's very empty at the moment?'

The group were told that changes were afoot, and she encouraged them to get involved in future regeneration projects.

Rubbish in the village?
This group comprised nine pupils from age nine to eleven who were the class representatives for the school's Eco Council (part of the Eco-schools project) and their school council. There were four boys and five girls. In Cardiff, they had the opportunity to question social justice Minister Brian Gibbons, asking: 'Twenty-six per cent of children in our survey said that our village isn't a safe place. What is the Assembly doing to make Wales a safer place?'; 'We don't think that there are enough bins in Wales – is money available to buy more?'; and 'How many people get a fine for dropping litter in Wales?'

The group arranged for Sarah from the local community council, and Shane from the Keep Wales Tidy project Tidy Towns to see them. They arranged their photos and graphs into a presentation and the group were lent some litter pickers to coordinate a tidy up day. The group wanted to do the first litter pick together before the Cardiff conference, but unfortunately on both attempts by the Funky Dragon facilitator snow was covering the rubbish. It was conducted after the conference.

Anti-social behaviour in our area
This group looked at what anti-social behaviour actually means, how much went on in their local area and what the main anti-social activities were.

They also took the opportunity to ask questions of social justice Minister Brian Gibbons: 'In your opinion how would you describe anti-social behaviour?'; 'What do you think is the worst sort of anti-social behaviour?'; 'How is your party going to try to stop anti-social behaviour in areas like ours?'; and 'How can we help to stop anti-social behaviour?'

The group decided that it wanted to show everyone what it had found out by making a drama: this evolved into making a video. The group split into two groups – one wrote the script and props list, while the other worked on a PowerPoint presentation which included photos, a video of the Communities First visit, and a list of 'Top Ten Reasons for ASBOs'; these included riding a bike on the pavement, dropping litter in the street, stealing from shops and joy riding.

How often do the police pass through our village?
The group was made up of ten children aged between nine and eleven – six boys and four girls. The group looked at crimes that had happened in the area, and who they could have affected. The group had an opportunity to speak with Brian Gibbons. They asked why so few Welsh-speaking police officers had been recruited by North Wales Police, whether the Minister could ensure that all jobs associated with the decision to build a jail in Caernarfon went to local people, whether the Minister thought there were enough police stations in Wales, and in each case also informed the Minister of local concerns about these issues.

Members of the group found that actually their village was extremely safe and that the worries people had were unfounded. The statistics showed minimal amounts of crime and frequency. The group created a presentation featuring their results and photos; they showed it to PC Paul Tunnah and PCSO Alaw Roberts from North Wales Police who visited the school. The officers stayed for the morning and showed them all their equipment, and the class all got their fingerprints taken as well as learning about the arrest process.

A full report of the project, *Children as Researchers*, is available to download from the Funky Dragon website. It shows the work the children did and copies of their presentations made at the Assembly.

Children as Researchers conference – Cardiff 2009
The conference was a mid-week overnight stay at the Urdd centre in Cardiff Bay in February 2009. It was decided before the project began that there would be a national event where the children could voice their issues with Ministers, but the event was by no means the aim of the project.

Rather the aims of the conference were to provide the opportunity for all the children involved to meet each other, present and discuss their projects, to meet with Ministers, and receive feedback on their work and issues, and for Funky Dragon to show the children some appreciation for the hard work and commitment they had shown.

In total, sixty-two children who were involved in the project attended the conference: only two children were unable to attend. The conference opened with speeches in Siambr Hywel, which is the old chamber in Tŷ Hywel, Cardiff Bay, that was previously used by National Assembly Members before the Senedd was built. Speakers were Jane Hutt, the Minister for Children, Education, Lifelong Learning and Skills; Keith Towler, the Children's Commissioner for Wales; and Darren Bird, chief executive of Funky Dragon.

The morning involved each group presenting their projects to the rest of the children. It was important the children saw what other groups had chosen as a research topic and how they had interpreted the project differently in different parts of Wales. The children then split into workshops with the Welsh Minister responsible for their area of research: Jane Hutt and Brian Gibbons. Jane Davidson, Minister for the environment, was unable to attend and so Jane Hutt agreed to speak with those groups as well as the groups that covered areas within her portfolio. Each workshop lasted around thirty minutes and each group had prepared questions to ask their Minister. A craft room was also available for children who were not in a workshop.

The workshops were kept short, lasting half an hour to limit any negative effects, such as the children feeling intimidated or getting bored. The children did not do their formal PowerPoint presentations to Ministers but gave an introduction to their project and main findings before asking the Minister their questions. It was thought that the time with the Minister would be better spent asking questions and receiving feedback.

After the workshops, the children returned to Siambr Hywel and ended with closing speeches by Darren Bird and Keith Towler, the latter making an impromptu speech, having changed his schedule in order to stay throughout the day. The children left with a Funky Dragon statuette and a certificate for their involvement in the project.

Impact

The children

Assessing the impact of participatory activities on individuals is a particularly troublesome and difficult task. It was hoped prior to this project's commencement that not only would the children learn research skills but also develop soft skills and confidence. The following quotes are from the children who took part, and were made during the evaluation of the project. They have been outlined here to illustrate the effect being part of the project had:

'I have really enjoyed the whole Funky Dragon experience.'

'It was great coming to Cardiff; I made new friends!'

'Having a day off school and having fun with my friends.' (Best thing?)

'Let kids from high school be part of it as well.' (What would you change?)

'The amount of days, please increase them.' (What would you change?)

'That we are gonna help people, instead of them making complaints we're like making the complaints for them.' (What have you learnt?)

'Simple, simple stuff that can be changed but nobody changes them.' (What do you think about other projects you saw in Cardiff?)

'Now we know there's a bigger chance that our parks will be improved and it's down to us.' (Why do you feel proud?)

'Its better for future generations of kids when they come in.' (What will your project change?)

'It was a really good experience; it was good for the Minister to hear our points of view.'

'I'm proud that Tudweiliog is a safe place. . . [the project] may have changed people's feelings towards the police.'

During the evaluation of being part of this project some children said they felt 'special', 'different' and 'talkative' after going through the process. The children also said that they learnt how to stand up and talk in front of other people, and about what other people think, and understood better how things can change.

Local level
From the beginning of this project it was decided that the children taking part would be given the chance to present their work to Welsh Ministers.

However, it transpired that the real influence was at a local level. The importance of partnership working ensured the children's projects received the best platform to affect change locally. Adults who worked with Funky Dragon varied, depending on the topic and change wanted, but included council workers, police officers, local councillors and Communities First teams. Their cooperation strengthened the children's work in terms of both sharing information and ensuring dissemination at a local level and to the relevant bodies.

Another benefit of this way of working was that adults were giving their projects credibility and so in turn the projects were taken seriously by others. Key partnerships were made and in most cases they met the children and helped them with their work. Some adults were unable to meet the children face to face, and so information was also sent out to local organisations. These organisations were identified and selected collectively by the children, Funky Dragon staff and other adults. The work itself received a good response from these adults. For example representative of a local housing association stated: 'As a landlord, one of our main aims is to tackle anti-social behaviour and create safer communities. We think that the work carried out is very important and if possible could we use the statistics in future meetings to highlight problems?'

This level of impact at the local level was not anticipated at the start of this project. The work had excellent local support and it was this partnership working that provided the impact the children wanted.

National level

The Welsh Ministers also reflected the credibility of the children's work. The conference event may provoke criticisms such as 'too often children are expected to fit into adult ways of participating' (Prout, 2003: 20). Some of the children did become nervous about meeting the Welsh Ministers, but to deal with this, Funky Dragon ran sessions about the National Assembly for Wales and the Welsh Minister they would be meeting with. By the time the children came to speak with the Ministers they knew their topic thoroughly and had no problems speaking with Ministers. In fact, as one boy aged ten reported, 'Phoebe actually asked him a question based on what he said'. The children were more than able to converse with Ministers and discuss their issues.

Ensuring the children felt comfortable and confident was of the utmost importance. However, future projects should ensure adults are equally comfortable conversing with children, particularly if adults' work does not involve direct work with children. There has to be a balance between appropriating processes for children and appropriating them for adults. The sessions were informal and the children were in control of their meeting. This also ensured the Ministers responded well and could be equally comfortable conversing with children.

The children enjoyed their time in Cardiff and one girl aged eleven would advise other children: 'don't be scared of the Minister, they're just normal people'. This aspect of the project worked well and gave the children an aim, a definite outcome and an opportunity to get their voices heard by the Minister responsible for their topic.

Summary

Funky Dragon, as the Children and Young People's Assembly for Wales, is the system in Wales to allow regular, inclusive and consistent participation, through its Grand Council, in the business of the National Assembly for Wales. However, this is for the over-eleven age group, and the progress of participation by children under this age is still developing (Leverett, 2008). Systems need to be put in place to allow children under the age of eleven to participate on a local and national level regularly and in a way that is fair and inclusive. The point of conducting this project was to show that children could be trained as researchers and make recommendations on a national level. This project demonstrated that children are more than capable of working at a national level and that the next step in enabling children's participation needs to be taken in order to truly show the constructive and positive effect children can have. This point is reiterated by Mary Kellett, who has worked in the field of children as researchers for many years:

> genuine participation cannot happen without some power sharing and . . . this will only occur when we move beyond consultation and joint decision making to a position where children are empowered to take the lead on some of the issues which directly affect their lives. Children undertaking their own research about matters which concern them is a significant step in this direction. (Kellett, 2005a: para. 5)

The children who took part in the project also realised how important it was for them to be involved in decision-making on issues that concerned them. As one child commented:

> We have to have their say, if we don't have their say we don't know what's wrong round here and they won't have a say'. (Boy aged nine)

This understanding that children not only have a right to have their say, but have a necessity to say it, or else others won't know what issues are affecting them, demonstrates the importance of children as researchers, and shows the impact that their research can have at the local and national level.

References

Farrell, A. (ed.) (2005): *Ethical Research with Children* (Open University Press: Berkshire).

Kellett, M (2005a): *Children as Active Researchers: A New Research Paradigm for the 21st Century?*, ESRC National Centre for Research Methods Review Paper 003. Available at *http://oro.open.ac.uk/7539/1/ MethodsReviewPaperNCRM-003.pdf* (accessed 1 July 2012).

—— (2005b): *How to Develop Children as Researchers: A Step by Step Guide to the Research Process* (London: Sage).

Kellet, M, Forest, R. (age 10), Dent, N. (age 10) and Ward S. (age 10) (2004): 'Just teach us the skills please, we'll do the rest: empowering ten-year-olds as active researchers', *Children and Society*, 18/5, 329–43.

Kirby P. (2004): *A Guide to Actively Involving Young People in Research: For Researchers, Research Commissioners, and Managers* (Hampshire: Involve).

Leverett, S. (2008): 'Children's participation', in M. Foley. and S. Leverett (eds), *Connecting with Children Developing Working Relationships* (Bristol: Policy Press), pp. 161–203.

Prout, A. (2003): 'Participation, policy and the changing conditions of childhood', in C. Hallett and A. Prout (eds), *Hearing the Voices of Children: Social Policy for a New Century* (London: Routledge Falmer), pp. 11–25.

Worrall, N. and Naylor, A. (2004): *Students as Researchers: How Does Being a Student Researcher Affect Learning?* (London: National Teacher Research Panel, Department for Education and Skills).

CHAPTER 15

Children's participation in Wales

Anne Crowley

Introduction

This chapter reviews the development of policy to support children's participation in decision-making in Wales, assessing the extent to which the provisions measure up to the obligations contained within the UNCRC and provide for effective accountability mechanisms. The chapter concludes with an outline of what the author believes is needed by way of government support to ensure compliance with Article 12 in light of the implementation of the Rights of Children and Young Persons (Wales) Measure 2011.

In many ways the attention given to children's participation by the first National Assembly for Wales (1999–2003) proved to be the gateway through which broader understandings of children's rights and government obligations in respect of the UNCRC were developed both within and outside government. Other contributions to this volume have noted how the institutions of devolution in Wales from their very beginnings privileged children and children's rights, but in those early days understandings of the concept of children's rights in Wales (and indeed across the UK) were very much rooted in the concept of children having a say or a 'voice' and participating in decisions that affected them. The idea that children's rights also encompassed a child's right to survival and development, to protection, and to the provision of health care and education, among others, was yet to be fully understood. So too was the complete range of government's obligations under the UNCRC, including, for example, a children's budget, a national plan for implementation, regular state of the nation reports on children and other general measures of implementation.

Children's participation is a broad concept which a chapter of this size cannot hope to unravel in its entirety, The analysis presented here explores children's participation in Wales as a mechanism by which children can hold government to account for fulfilling its obligations to uphold children's rights (as set out in the UNCRC). Hoffman and Williams in chapter 12 of this volume provide for a more in-depth exploration of the concept of accountability, what it means in the context of the UNCRC, and the accountability mechanisms introduced under the Rights of Children and Young Persons (Wales) Measure 2010.

Ironically, the UNCRC itself does not include the term 'participation'. Cantwell's argument (2011) that sometimes we try to obtain too much from the UNCRC at the expense of securing everything possible on the basis of its actual requirements, is persuasive. The inflation of children's participation rights, Cantwell continues, serves to water down the accountability aspect of *human* rights (his emphasis). As this chapter examines children's participation as a mechanism for accountability under the UNCRC, it seems only correct that we should refer back to the legal text and stick closely to its intentions.

Children's participation and the UNCRC

'Participation' is an ill-defined concept, with understandings ranging from 'taking part' to full citizenship (Thomas, 2007). Models have been developed to assist understanding of different types, levels and degrees of civic participation for children – using the metaphors, variously, of a ladder (Hart, 1992), a circle (Treseder, 1997) and a series of pathways (Shier, 2001). For the purposes of this chapter, the more legalistic definition in the UNCRC is adopted. This definition, expanded upon in the UN Committee's *General Comment No. 12*, equates participation with the right of the child to be heard (UN Committee *GC*, 2009).

Article 12 of the UNCRC sets out the obligations of the State on realising a child's right to be heard as follows:

> 1. States Parties shall assure to the child who is capable of forming his or her views the right to express those views freely in all matters affecting the child, the views of the child being given due weight in accordance with the age and maturity of the child.
>
> 2. For this purpose the child shall in particular be provided the opportunity to be heard in any judicial and administrative proceedings affecting the child, either directly, or through a representative body, in a manner consistent with the procedural rules of national law.

The first paragraph of the article guarantees that all children have the right to express their views freely. The only qualification is that the child is capable of forming a view. As it is now understood that even very young babies are capable of expressing a view in their own way (Alderson et al., 2005), this really does mean *all* children. The second element of paragraph 1, that children's views are given 'due weight' *in accordance with their age and maturity* (my emphasis) is, some commentators suggest, often neglected and widely misunderstood (see, for example, Lundy, 2007; Council of Europe, 2008). Paragraph 2 of Article 12 specifies the right of the child to be heard in judicial and administrative proceedings, including decisions affecting family placement, care and adoption; immigration, criminal or child protection proceedings, and education tribunals.

The right to be heard applies to every child without discrimination on any grounds such as age, race, gender, disability, socio-economic circumstances or any other status. The *General Comment* makes it clear that States Parties are required to make particular efforts to enable children with fewer opportunities (including those who are vulnerable) to be heard (UN Committee *GC*, 2009).

If children are entitled to express their views freely, space and time for this must be created by the relevant duty bearers, be they governments, parents or schools. Children are entitled to express their views on 'all matters that affect them' – matters that affect them as individuals (such as medical treatment or a court order on custody) and matters that affect them collectively as children (such as education policy, transport, budget expenditure, urban planning and poverty reduction). The *General Comment* expands on the matters children should be enabled to participate in, suggesting that they include the family, the school and healthcare, and matters determined in civil court proceedings, juvenile justice systems and child protection proceedings, as well as in local communities and in local and national government policy making (UN Committee *GC*, 2009).

Article 12 is instrumental to achieving all of the other rights in the UNCRC, and forms one of the four general principles of the UNCRC alongside non-discrimination (Article 2), the right to life and development (Article 6), the right to protection (Article 19) and the primary consideration of the best interests of the child (Article 3). As such, in the interpretation and implementation of all the other rights of children within the UNCRC, Article 12 must also be considered.

It is also important to understand Article 12 in the context of other key provisions in the UNCRC which work to support children's entitlement to engage actively in decisions that affect them. Article 13 (the right to freedom of expression) and Article 17 (the right to information) are important in connection with a child's right to be heard. Age-appropriate information and advice has been described as a prerequisite to effective realisation of Article 12 (UN Committee *GC*, 2009: para. 80). The connection of Article 12 to Article 5 (evolving capacities of the child and appropriate direction and guidance from parents) is of special relevance, since it is crucial that the guidance given by parents takes account of the evolving capacities of the child to exercise his or her rights (Lansdown, 2010).

A child's right to be heard – understanding the obligations of States Parties

Lundy (2007) is one of a growing number of academics and commentators who are becoming increasingly uneasy with the discourse on 'children's voices', their 'right to be heard' and, in education circles, 'pupil's voice' (see also Mannion, 2010). Lundy argues that the use of such terms misrepresents the meaning behind Article 12 of the UNCRC. For her, cosy conservative readings of the UNCRC mean that sometimes the right of the child to be heard is seen as a gift where 'what matters' can be constrained by adults. She advocates a new model for conceptualising Article 12 which 'attempts to capture more fully the true extent of the UK's legal obligations to children' (2007: 931). Lundy separates out the two elements of Article 12: (i) the right to express a view, and (ii) the right to have that view given due weight. Successful implementation of Article 12, she advocates, requires States Parties to consider their obligations in respect of four separate factors: space, voice, audience and influence, as follows:

- space: opportunities provided for children to express their views
- voice: children must be facilitated to express their views
- audience: opportunities for children's views to be listened to
- influence: how children's views have been acted upon.

Lundy's concepts of 'voice' and 'space' correspond to structures and mechanisms and opportunities for children to express their views. Article 12 of the UNCRC requires States Parties to 'assure' these opportunities, suggesting a positive obligation to take proactive steps to encourage and support children to express their views – that is, to invite and encourage children to actively provide input, 'rather than simply acting as a recipient of views if children happen to provide them' (2007: 934).

As previously noted, Article 12 then requires children's views to be given due weight (subject to the age and maturity of the child), which brings into play Lundy's concepts of 'audience' and 'influence'. Implicit within the notion of views being given due weight, she argues, is 'the fact that children have a right to have their views listened to (not just heard) by those involved in decision-making processes' (2007: 936). Lundy goes on to suggest that children should have a 'right of audience', which she defines as 'a guaranteed opportunity to communicate views to an identifiable individual or body with responsibility to listen' (2007: 937). 'Influence', in Lundy's analysis, is about change and what the 'due' of 'due weight' actually is. As others have also noted, the giving of 'due weight' to a child's wishes or views in the decision-making process is firmly in the hands of adults who may decide that children are not sufficiently mature (for example, Tisdall and Bell, 2006).

The challenge here is to find ways of ensuring that adults not only listen to children but also take children's views seriously. Lundy (2007) suggests that while influence cannot be guaranteed, one safeguard is to ensure that children are told how their views are taken into account. The importance of feedback is also emphasised in the UN Committee's *General Comment No. 12* which states: 'Children are also entitled to be provided with clear feedback on how their participation has influenced any outcomes' (UN Committee *GC*, 2009: 30).

Lundy's conceptualisation of Article 12 as involving voice, space, audience and influence suggests that as well as *protecting* the right of the child to be heard with legislation (including the removal of any legal barriers), the State Party is also obliged to *create spaces* for children to be heard. The UNCRC also places obligations on States Parties to *promote* the right of the child to be heard. The promotion of the child's right to be heard, as the *General Comment* makes clear, involves the training of all professionals working with and for children on Article 12 and its application, and providing information in an age-appropriate manner, as well as informing children of their rights and providing advocacy support to assist children in claiming their right to be heard, or challenging rights violations (UN Committee *GC*, 2009). The next section provides a brief examination of key policy developments in Wales and assesses the extent to which Welsh governments since 1999 have met these core obligations.

Giving effect to Article 12 in Wales (1999–2011)

Prior to the Government of Wales Act 1998 and the establishment of the National Assembly for Wales, policy as it affected children and indeed adults was determined in Westminster and Whitehall, and mediated by the Secretary of State for Wales who was a member of the Cabinet. In the period leading up to 1999, political support for children's civil rights and for the child's right to be heard had been gaining momentum in the UK (Butler and Drakeford, 2005).

One of the first tasks for the first, newly elected National Assembly for Wales was to respond to the recommendations of an inquiry into the abuse of children in public care in Wales (Waterhouse Report, 2000). This report illustrated starkly the abuse of children's rights and how vulnerable children who were living away from home in residential care had not been listened to and how adults had failed to protect them. The Assembly's response to Waterhouse included the establishment of the UK's first children's commissioner or ombudsperson. This was seen as a signal of the importance that the new Assembly in Wales was going to give to Wales's children (see Rees in chapter 13 of this volume).

Advocacy services for children

The Waterhouse report also prompted some expansion of advocacy services, not least to ensure effective support for hearing complaints and representations direct from children. Following a further report, this time on the safeguards for children and young people treated and cared for the NHS in Wales (Carlile Review Report, 2002), the Welsh Government announced a review of advocacy arrangements for children and young people.

The review was informed by a study of advocacy services undertaken by Cardiff University (Pithouse et al., 2005). The research identified the following: children and young people were generally unaware of their right to make representation; few children actually made a complaint; some had poor experiences of making a complaint; and many were left confused about the process and the outcome. On the other hand, those who had access to an advocate valued the emotional and practical support. However, access and quality of services across Wales varied widely and difficulties were compounded by short-term contract arrangements and poor monitoring.

The Children's Commissioner's *Clywch* inquiry reported on the handling of allegations of abuse of children and young people in a school in south Wales (Children's Commissioner for Wales, 2004), and led to widespread procedural changes to try to ensure that, in the future, schools, governing bodies and local authorities listened to pupils and properly investigated any allegations of child abuse made against teaching and non-teaching staff. The changes introduced by the Welsh Government in response to the *Clywch* report included, for the first time, guidance to school governing bodies on the right of pupils to complain (WG, 2006).

The Welsh Government's review of advocacy services eventually led to the announcement in 2008 of proposals for a new service framework for the provision of advocacy services for children in Wales (Hutt and Thomas, 2008). The proposals included a new national advocacy and advice service, and the regional commissioning of integrated specialist advocacy services covering education, health and social care services. This announcement by the Minister for Children, Education and Lifelong Learning and Skills made it clear that the Welsh Government saw the provision of comprehensive advocacy support as fulfilling part of the state's obligations to children and their right to be heard:

> The Welsh Government has a long-standing commitment to provide universal access to effective advocacy services for all children and young people in Wales. The right of children and young people to be heard directly on matters that affect them is a key component of our approach to developing policy that is firmly grounded in the UNCRC. It is particularly important that children and young people have every opportunity to seek redress when things go wrong and that service providers learn from the experience of service users in order to truly become citizen focussed. (Hutt and Thomas, 2008: 1)

The National Advocacy and Advice Service – known as 'Meic' (an abbreviation of *meicroffon*, the Welsh word for microphone) – was launched in May 2010, but at the time of writing, new regulations and guidance on the provision of integrated local services have still to be issued following a further period of consultation (WG, 2011b). Progress towards securing universal access to effective advocacy services for all children, as the Children and Young People Committee of the National Assembly has documented, has been very slow (CYPC, 2010).

However, government obligations under Article 12 are not just about ensuring support for children to make complaints or get redress for rights violations. Article 12, as noted above, requires States Parties to take steps to protect and to promote the child's right to be heard, to create spaces for children to express their views, and for those views to be listened to and to be taken seriously by decision-makers.

Creating spaces for children's participation in Wales
The first Welsh Government made a strong commitment to listening to children and valuing their contributions. Its first strategic plan for Wales, *A Better Wales*, contained a commitment to the principle that every young person in Wales had the right to be consulted, to participate in decision-making and be heard on all matters concerning them or having an impact on their lives (WG, 2000). Within two years of *A Better Wales*, the Welsh Government had funded Llais Ifanc/Young Voice, a national assembly of children and young people, which subsequently became known as Funky Dragon (see Funky Dragon, chapter 14 in this volume). Young people from

Funky Dragon work to influence the Welsh Government's policy-making in a variety of ways. Not only do young people regularly respond to government consultations, they also sit and debate their issues and concerns directly with Ministers and officials.

In 2005 Funky Dragon began a process of engaging children and young people across Wales in the periodic review by the UN Committee. It canvassed the views of over 14,500 young people in Wales and submitted a report to the UN Committee with recommendations covering areas such as health, education, the environment and play. In July 2008, members of Funky Dragon presented their *Our Rights, Our Story* report to the UN Committee to great acclaim both at home and abroad. Funky Dragon subsequently had the opportunity to present its key recommendations to the Welsh Government's Cabinet committee on children and young people, and the UN Committee invited Funky Dragon back to meet with it and advise it on how it should be listening to children.

In order to stimulate developments across Wales the Welsh Government took what it called a strategic approach to developing children's participation. It funded an All-Wales Children and Young People's Participation Unit to be steered by a multi-sector participation consortium to develop policy and practice on participation, and to create opportunities for children and young people's participation across Wales. An internal participation project was established to support children's involvement in policy-making at the heart of government and to support the establishment of school councils across Wales.

Young people were involved in developing a number of the Welsh Government's policies, for example *Extending Entitlement*, the Welsh Assembly's strategy for supporting young people, and the *National Service Framework for Children, Young People and Maternity Services in Wales,* which established standards for health, social care, education, housing and leisure services. A young person-friendly version of the draft national service framework was developed to assist young people to give their views (WG, 2004a). Successive Welsh governments have subsequently produced other key consultation documents in child-friendly formats.

Protecting the right of the child to be heard
While in many ways the provision of funding and other resources as well as the passing of laws and the issuing of guidance can be seen as steps taken by governments to protect children's rights, here the focus is specifically on the key legislative and administrative measures governments in Wales have put in place since 1999. Post-devolution legislation for Wales has reflected

the commitment of successive Welsh governments to the right of the child to be heard, both in administrative and judicial procedures and in the planning of public services. There is insufficient space here to detail all of the relevant Welsh legislation, but some key measures have been selected to illustrate the range and chronology.

The guidance and regulations accompanying the Children Act 2004 identify children and young people's participation as an underlying principle and theme for local co-operation between agencies to deliver stronger and more effective partnerships (WG, 2004b). In the same year, a statutory requirement for all primary, secondary and special schools in Wales to have a school council was introduced. Encouraging support for children and young people's participation at a local authority level, the Welsh Government funded the local authority-led strategic partnerships to establish youth fora which still exist in the vast majority of areas. In 2007 supplementary guidance was issued asking the partnerships to produce and implement local participation strategies (WG, 2007a). The same year, the Welsh Government endorsed a set of national standards for children and young people's participation in decision making (WG, 2007b), which emphasises first principles of inclusion, choice, information, benefits, reflection and feedback.

More recently the Education (Wales) Measure 2009 introduces a statutory right for children and young people to make special educational needs appeals to the Special Educational Needs Tribunal for Wales (see Hosking, chapter 8 in this volume). However, provision in the Children and Families (Wales) Measure 2010, placing a requirement on local authorities to 'make such arrangements as it considers suitable to promote and facilitate participation by children in decisions of the authority which might affect them' (section 12), has not, at the time of writing, been implemented.

Promoting the right of the child to be heard

As noted, the UN Committee's *General Comment No. 12* sees States Parties' obligations in respect of promoting the right of the child to be heard as including the following: the training of all professionals working with and for children; providing information to children in an age-appropriate manner; informing children of their rights, and taking steps to encourage and support parents to respect children's views on matters that affect them.

This is perhaps where successive Welsh governments have made the least progress. There have been some patchy efforts to distribute leaflets to young people, and more recently funding was provided to Children in Wales to provide training on children's rights, including their right to be heard, for professionals across Wales who are working directly with children and young people. Work undertaken by the Participation Unit (funded by the Welsh Government and the European Structural Fund) to develop a set of national standards and embed these in inspection frameworks, and to establish a kite marking scheme with teams of Young Inspectors (STC, 2010), has also helped to spread the word. There has been no specific encouragement or support given to parents to respect children's views, although previous Welsh governments have done much to support positive parenting and to speak out against the physical punishment of children in the home (see, for example, Morgan, 2003).

Meeting obligations – a critique
The provision and investment made by successive Welsh governments towards realising the right of the child to be heard and to be involved in policy-making must be viewed positively, and for many years Wales was seen as leading the way in this field (Thomas and Crowley, 2007). However, children's non-governmental organisations have long argued that more needed to be done by government to ensure the sustainability of measures taken to support children's participation in Wales (Crowley and Skeels, 2010). National and local structures, such as youth and children's fora, were seen as too dependent on short-term funding streams. In the wake of the public expenditure cuts that started to bite in 2011, anecdotal reports suggest that structures and mechanisms for supporting children's participation across Wales are under threat, as local authorities prioritise the resourcing of their statutory functions.

The lack of an overarching strategy for developing and supporting children and young people's participation has also been criticised, along with the lack of action to inform children about their right to be heard and have their views taken seriously. While children undoubtedly have many more opportunities than they had before devolution for civic participation through youth fora and school councils, engaging children under the age of eleven in decision-making, and embracing obligations to promote children's participation in the family, remain key issues for the future. Government obligations in respect of promoting the right of the child to be heard have not been approached systematically, with low levels of awareness among children in Wales highlighted in the last reporting round by Funky Dragon (Funky Dragon, 2007), and elsewhere (Thomas and Crowley, 2010), and picked up as a cause for concern in the UN Committee's *Concluding Observations* (UN Committee CO, 2008). Action with regard to this obligation remains an urgent priority.

The extent to which vulnerable children such as those in public care, in custody, homeless or living in poverty are supported to participate in administrative and judicial procedures as specified in paragraph 2 of Article 12 is not being routinely assessed through inspections or regulatory frameworks. We just do not know whether this is happening or not, nor, on occasion, even where the accountability lies.

It must also be recognised that despite plenty of expenditure and activity on the part of the government to support children in expressing their views, there is little evidence as yet to indicate that children's views are being listened to and given 'due weight'. Wales is strong on Lundy's 'voice' and 'space' but arguably weaker on 'audience' and 'influence'. Research that was commissioned by the Welsh Government into the benefits of children and young people's participation struggled to find examples of where children's views had brought about a recorded change in policy or practice (Kendall, 2010).

Despite significant efforts to embed the participation of children into policy development within the Welsh Government machine, much of this activity has taken the form of one-off consultation exercises rather than the 'intense exchange between children and adults on the development of policies, programmes and measures in all relevant contexts of children's lives' envisaged by the UN Committee (UN Committee GC, 2009: 7). Children were consulted, for example, on the Welsh Government's Child Poverty Strategy (WG, 2011a), but there is no published record of how their views were considered and given 'due weight', and no understanding of what influence children's views have had on the final policy product.

Pressure on Welsh Ministers and officials to be seen to be involving children in decision-making is likely to increase after the part commencement of the Rights of Children and Young Persons (Wales) Measure 2011 from 1 May 2012. The threat of even more tokenism must not be discounted, but the Measure also provides a real opportunity for further progress on realising the right of the child to be heard, by its privileging of children's participation as a key mechanism of accountability. The next section of this chapter considers these opportunities and outlines what will be needed by way of government support to ensure compliance with Article 12 in light of the implementation of the Rights of Children and Young Persons (Wales) Measure 2011.

Looking forward: the Rights of Children and Young Persons (Wales) Measure 2011 – what needs to be done?

This review of policy developments in Wales since 1999 has revealed strong political commitment and a great deal of activity and investment, especially in creating spaces for children to express their views collectively, but less progress on protecting and promoting the right of the child to be heard. With the exception of schools, children's participation is not yet required of *all* public bodies, and the Welsh Government has not yet invested in public education campaigns to promote the right of the child to be heard, nor embedded children's rights into the training of professionals working directly with children. Neither has it taken steps to include sensitisation towards respecting and encouraging a child's right to be heard in the parenting programmes that it supports. The Rights of Children and Young Persons (Wales) Measure 2011 provides an opportunity to ensure that, in Wales, progress on the States Parties' obligations to create spaces is sustained, and government obligations in respect of promoting and protecting the right of the child to be heard are delivered. The priorities for government in respect of the latter obligations are set out below.

Promoting children's rights to be heard
In order to promote knowledge and increase understanding among the public (including children) of the UNCRC, and specifically children's right to participate in decisions affecting their lives, the Welsh Government needs firstly to provide children with information appropriate to their age and circumstances on their right to participate, the opportunities available to them to do so, and where they can get support to take advantage of those opportunities. Secondly, it needs to put in place a systematic and ongoing programme of training for professionals working with and for children. Training on children's participation needs to be embedded into professional training – both the initial qualifying training and in continuous professional development programmes. Thirdly, the Welsh Government needs to promote the child's right to be heard and respect for children's opinions within the family – with parents and carers – through public education (for example, booklets to new parents) as well as through parenting programmes and public service delivery. Fourthly, the Welsh Government needs to support children and their organisations to participate in the monitoring of the implementation of Article 12 and other relevant articles of the UNCRC.

Protecting children's right to be heard
In order to ensure adequate protection of the right of the child to be heard, the Welsh Government needs to take stock of current provision and undertake an assessment of the extent to which children and young people's opinions are heard and taken seriously in existing legislation, policies and

practices (including judicial and administrative procedures), and provide the greatest possible legal protection for the right of the child to be heard and taken seriously. On the basis of this review, the Welsh Government needs to reconsider any barriers based on age limits, either in law or in practice, which restrict the child's right to be heard in all matters affecting her or him. All children have the right to express a view, at whatever age, and this should be reflected in legislation, in administrative and judicial procedures, and in practice. In line with children's evolving capacities, the amount of weight given to a child's views will then be in accordance with her or his age and maturity.

A priority for the Welsh Government should be to devise a national strategy on realising the right of the child to be heard, located within a broader national strategy for implementing children and young people's rights. Finally, by way of its obligations to protect the right of the child to be heard, the Welsh Government needs to ensure that in these financially austere times it does not dilute its commitment to children's participation, that it protects relevant budgets, and that it allocates adequate financial resources to support children and young people's participation in decision-making affecting their lives.

With regard to 'creating spaces', the Welsh Governments needs to continue to create and sustain spaces for children's participation. This should include supporting children's participation at a very local and infor-mal level – in the family; in the cities, towns, villages and hamlets where children live; in the schools and colleges they attend; and in the clubs and spaces they frequent.

Conclusion

By way of conclusion, it is important to note the role children will be expected to play in holding the Welsh Government to account for the effective implementation of the Rights of Children and Young Persons (Wales) Measure 2011. The Measure specifically requires Welsh Ministers to support the participation of children in the development of the chil-dren's scheme that it is required to publish by May 2012. When the Welsh Government is 'involving' children in the drawing-up of the scheme, it must be a process of 'deliberative engagement' (see Williams, chapter 4 in this volume), not just a tick box or one-off exercise as we have seen enacted in relation to the preparation of the child poverty and other Welsh Government flagship strategies.

Effective implementation of the Measure requires the Welsh Government to set up appropriate internal mechanisms for monitoring implementation – and monitoring in particular the extent to which Welsh Ministers are paying due regard to children's right to be heard and to have their views taken seriously. The brief review of policy developments with regard to children's participation set out in this chapter reminds us that the realisation of the fundamental right to 'participate' requires 'long term political, social, institutional and cultural structures changes' (Tobin, 2011: 89). It is important that the Welsh Government conducts regular reviews (involving children) to assess progress and identify strengths on which to build and challenges to address. While, as Tobin (2011) reminds us, the obligation of States with respect to civil and political rights is immediate rather than progressive and subject to available resources (as with economic, social and cultural rights), nonetheless in reality, moving to a situation where there is full respect for children as active citizens has to be a journey, and those within and without government have a responsibility to make sure that in Wales we continue to head in the right direction and continue to make progress.

In terms of the accountability of those responsible for fulfilling the right of the child to be heard, the implementation of the due regard duty requires monitoring by and collaboration with those outside government as well. As the Children and Young People's Assembly for Wales, Funky Dragon has a key role to play in holding Welsh Ministers to account on this and other rights – especially when, through new government actions to promote children's rights (including their right to participate), we have a newly empowered and knowledgeable population of young rights-holders who want to make sure that the state fulfils its duties. Currently Funky Dragon is core-funded by the Welsh Government, and unlike the Children's Commissioner has no statute to protect its existence in the event that future governments might not want to hear its messages. It is important, therefore, that the Welsh Government finds legislative opportunity to put the children and young people's assembly onto a statutory footing.

Finally, we should note that while this chapter concentrates on the right of the child to be heard in Wales, the Welsh Government cannot be accountable for the realisation of all children's rights: there are other duty-bearers and other governments that have responsibilities. The Welsh Government has little power over or responsibility for immigration, tax and benefits, policing or the administration of justice in Wales, and work also needs to be done to strengthen accountability mechanisms with the UK Government in order to ensure it, too, delivers on the obligations it has to the children of Wales.

References

Alderson, P., Hawthorne, J. and Killen, M. (2005): 'The participation rights of premature babies', *International Journal of Children's Rights*, 13/1–2, 31–50.

Butler, I. and Drakeford, M. (2005): *Scandal, Social Policy and Social Welfare*, 2nd edn (Basingstoke: Palgrave Macmillan).

Cantwell, N. (2011): 'Are children's rights still human?', in A. Invernizzi and J. Williams (eds), *The Human Rights of Children: From Visions to Implementation* (Farnham: Ashgate), pp. 37–60.

Carlile Review Report (2002): *The Review of Safeguards for Children and Young People Treated and Cared for by the NHS in Wales: Too Serious a Thing* (Cardiff: National Assembly for Wales).

Children's Commissioner for Wales (2004): *Clywch: Report of the Examination of the Children's Commissioner for Wales into Allegations of Child Sexual Abuse in a School Setting* (Swansea: Children's Commissioner for Wales).

Council of Europe (2008): *Promoting the Participation of Children in Decisions Affecting Them: Explanatory Memorandum. Report to the Social, Health and Family Affairs Committee*, Doc. 11615 2 June 2008 (Strasbourg: Parliamentary Assembly of the Council of Europe).

Crowley, A. and Skeels, A. (2010): 'Getting the measure of children and young people's participation: an exploration of practice in Wales', in B. Percy-Smith and N. Thomas (eds), *Handbook of Children and Young People's Participation* (London: Routledge), pp. 184–92.

CYPC (Children and Young People Committee), National Assembly for Wales (2010): *Further Review of Developments in the Provision of Advocacy Services to Children and Young People in Wales* (Cardiff: National Assembly for Wales).

Funky Dragon (2007): *Our Rights, Our Story* (Swansea: Funky Dragon).

Hart, R. (1992): *Children's Participation: From Tokenism to Citizenship*, Innocenti Essay No. 4 (Florence: UNICEF International Child Development Centre).

Hutt, J. and Thomas, G. (2008): *New Service Framework for the Future Provision of Advocacy Services for Children in Wales*, written statement 13 March (Cardiff: Welsh Assembly Government).

Kendall, S. (2010): *Children and Young People's Participation in Wales*, Research Report No. 051/2010 (Cardiff: Welsh Assembly Government).

Lansdown, G. (2010): 'Children's right to participation', in K. O'Neill (ed.), *Speaking Out, Being Heard. Experiences of Child Participation and Accountability to Children from Around the World* (London: Save the Children), pp. 2–17.

Lundy, L. (2007): 'Voice is not enough: conceptualising Article 12 of the United Nations Convention on the Rights of the Child', *British Educational Research Journal*, 33/6, 927–42.

Mannion, G. (2010): 'After participation: the socio-spatial performance of intergenerational becoming', in B. Percy-Smith and N. Thomas (eds), *Handbook of Children and Young People's Participation* (London: Routledge), pp. 330–42.

Morgan, R. (2003): *Statement on the Welsh Assembly Government's Response to the Annual Report of the Children's Commissioner for Wales* (Cardiff: National Assembly for Wales).

Pithouse, A., Crowley, A., Parry, O., Payne, H., Dalrymple, J. (2005): *A Study of Advocacy Services for Children and Young People in Wales: A Key Messages Report* (Cardiff: Welsh Assembly Government).

STC (Save the Children) (2010): *Making the Connections Final Report* (Cardiff: Save the Children).

Shier, H. (2001): 'Pathways to participation: openings, opportunities and obligations', *Children and Society*, 15, 107–17.

Thomas, N. (2007): 'Towards a theory of children's participation', *International Journal of Children's Rights*, 15, 199–218.

Thomas, N. and Crowley, A. (2007): 'Children's rights and well-being in Wales', *Contemporary Wales*, 19/1, 161–79.

—— (2010): 'Evaluating the Children's Commissioner for Wales: report of a participatory research study', *International Journal of Children's Rights*, 18/1, 19–52.

Tisdall, E. K. M. and Bell, R. (2006): 'Included in governance? Children's participation in "public" decision-making', in E. K. M. Tisdall, J. M. Davis, M. Hill and A. Prout (eds), *Children, Young People and Social Inclusion: Participation for What?* (Bristol: Policy Press), pp. 105–20.

Tobin, J. (2011): 'Understanding a human rights based approach to matters involving children: conceptual foundations and strategic considerations', in A. Invernizzi and J. Williams (eds), *The Human Rights of Children: From Visions to Implementation* (Farnham: Ashgate), pp. 61–98.

Treseder, P. (1997): *Empowering Children and Young People Training Manual: Promoting Involvement in Decision-making* (London: Save the Children and the Child Rights Development Unit).

Waterhouse Report (2000): *Lost in Care: Report of the Tribunal of Inquiry into the Abuse of Children in Care in the Former County Council Areas of Gwynedd and Clwyd since 1974* (London: The Stationery Office).

WG (Welsh Government) (2000): *A Better Wales* (Cardiff: Welsh Assembly Government).

—— (2004a): *National Service Framework for Children, Young People and Maternity Services in Wales: Young People's Consultation Document* (Cardiff: Welsh Assembly Government).

—— (2004b): *Stronger Partnerships for Better Outcomes, Guidance on Local Co-operation under the Children Act 2004* (Cardiff: Welsh Assembly Government).

—— (2006): *Guidance for School Governing Bodies on Procedures for Complaints Involving Pupils* (Cardiff: Welsh Assembly Government).

—— (2007a): *Local Participation Strategies 0–25* (Cardiff: Welsh Assembly Government).

—— (2007b): *National Standards for Children and Young People's Participation* (Cardiff: Welsh Assembly Government).

—— (2011a): *Child Poverty Strategy for Wales* (Cardiff: Welsh Government).

—— (2011b): *Delivering Advocacy Services for Children and Young People 0–25 in Wales (Consultation)* (Cardiff: Welsh Government).

Index